A DIFFERING VIEW OF CUBA'S HISTORY

An American Family's Journey
from 16th Century Spanish Colonialism
To Modernity (1509-1960)

PART I. THE VIOLENT COUNTRY

PART II. MODERNITY

By Charles A. Santos-Buch, MD

Cover Photo: The peaceful, but still ominous, site of the deadliest naval battle in the Caribbean which took place on July 3, 1898, outside the entrance of the Bay of Santiago de Cuba. Photo by Antonio G. Valle-Friend, 2015, Image taken from the ramparts of "El Morro," the 17th century fortress.

PUBLISHED BY TRIMARK PRESS, INC., DEERFIELD BEACH, FLORIDA.

LIBRARY OF CONGRESS CATALOGING-IN-PUBLICATION DATA

A DIFFERING VIEW OF CUBA'S HISTORY
BY CHARLES A. SANTOS-BUCH, M.D.

P. CM.

ISBN: PAPERBACK - 978-1-943401-71-0
HARDCOVER- 978-1-943401-72-7
LIBRARY OF CONGRESS CONTROL NUMBER: PENDING
D-20
10 9 8 7 6 5 4 3 2 1
FIRST EDITION
PRINTED AND BOUND IN THE UNITED STATES OF AMERICA

A PUBLICATION OF TRIMARK PRESS, INC.
368 SOUTH MILITARY TRAIL
DEERFIELD BEACH, FL 33442
800.889.0693

WWW.TRIMARKPRESS.COM

DEDICATION

This book is dedicated to the memory of
Doña Adolfina Cossío y de Céspedes of La Caridad de
Macaca, Cuba, my grandmother, whose strength of
character, based on intrinsic principles of liberty,
individual rights and love of our ancient family,
inspired our family's members through thick and thin.

Table of Contents

Two Experienced Criollo Generals And Their Successful Cuban Liberation Army Units.

◊ The Critical Battle of El Viso/Caney Is Won By Mambi And American Soldiers Under General Garcia And General Ludlow, Who Wipe out An Entire Elite Spanish Regiment.

◊ Spain's Atlantic Squadron Is Destroyed By The American Atlantic Fleet At The Entrance Of Santiago de Cuba's Bay.

◊ How A New Constitutional Republic Was Born In America Under General Leonard Wood's Supervision (1902).

◊ The Cultural, Political, And Economic Impact Of A Massive Spanish Immigration (1878-1936).

◊ The Platt Amendment.
◊ Three Racial Wars Are Brutally Suppressed By The Republic's Governments.
◊ The Rise Of Liberalism And The Demise Of Conservatism.

◊ General Gerardo Machado y Morales And How Cuba's Political Future Was Defined By His Presidency's Travails (1925-1933).

◊ In Bellevue Hospital, New York City, Dr. A. M. Santos-Buch Makes A Controversial Decision And Returns To His Country of Origin.

PREFACE
A HELPFUL EXPLANATION

This story is written largely to answer questions about our interesting family posed to me by my insistent three sons. I chose to write it in English for its easier adaptability by the sons and daughters of Cuban émigrés in the United States of America, and elsewhere. Perhaps it will explain issues of importance to all of them, no matter what their political stripe is today.

For this 87-year-old American of Cuban Criollo origins, revealing signal events of my life through the lens of the tragic history of what was our ancestral island home is exciting. These events date from the early sixteenth century Spanish Conquest of the Indies to the fall of the Euro-Criollo Culture with the Castro-Communist onslaught by the mid-twentieth century. It is clear today that what was once a predominant Criollo-European civilization is finished, and new demographics strongly indicate that a return to its pre-existing influence is very unlikely in this new twenty-first century. Cuba has been firmly transformed into another clone of populist political systems seen in myriad Latin-American nations in modern times.

For many contemporary young readers, this account may appear to be a chronicle of the lives of interesting and entertaining characters who seemed to have had a significant role in the history of a failed civilization. The historical journey documented here is flawed for other reasons. There are large gaps in the history of the early centuries and elsewhere, where faulty eyewitness accounts, erroneous interpretations, and recalcitrant "implicit" bias obscure events. Furthermore, there is a lack of reliable documentation and other proofs. As far as some of these early gaps are concerned, I assume that some of our family founders conducted their lives with lackluster duty and their stories did not break through the fog of history, and so these personages are not a prominent part of our story.

I have tried to deduce how historical events happened from knowledge gained by onsite observations. For example, I used the heraldic crests, or "coat of arms" emblems, of the Cossío and Céspedes knights, to identify their "casonas" when I visited northern Spain.

Coat of Arms used during the "La Reconquista" campaign.

Similarly, I visited Cuba's battlefields to better understand how the geography governed battle plans. This technique revealed that the most important battle of the 1898 Spanish-American War in Cuba took place on the right flank of the final assault on San Juan and Kettle Hills at El Viso and Caney, where an entire elite five-hundred-strong Spanish trooper regiment was fiercely wiped-out by Cuban Patriots and American Forces in a matter of three hours or so in July 1898. The right flank had to be secured before the final frontal assault on the Hills could be carried out successfully.

When the battle was finished, all dead and fatally wounded soldiers, horses and mules, strewn on the adjacent grounds, were interred there in unmarked graves by "guajiros"(peasants). This is how casualties were routinely disposed in the embattled island through the war years. Much later, urban sprawl covered some of these umarked and hallowed grounds.

Many of the Cuban soldiers fighting against the Spanish were from the mountain peasant class of the isolated eastern lands. When they were born, there were no registered birth certificates of them, and when they died, no registered death certificates. As far as the Spanish Empire was concerned, these men and women did not exist, ever. The disposal of the dead and the fatally wounded that received coup de grâces was primitive. When the high-end suburb of Vista Alegre of Santiago de Cuba was developed many years later, the bones of these forgotten men and women were discovered by surprised builders of the foundations of the well-to-do mansions. These observations reminded me of the horrific battles of Culloden in Scotland (1746) and of the Gallipoli Peninsula in Turkey (1915-16). Only the higher ranked officers were identified and given preferential treatment and disposal to family members.

Even though I have tried to confirm historical facts and events, much of this narrative is based on information passed by word of mouth by my elders, information undoubtedly no different than that passed on from a tribal chief to another, full of fury, images, whimpers and loud sounds over the course of five centuries plus. As the book moves to modern times, the principal characters are hammered by bewildering "truths" professed through many personal encounters and these so-called truths are frequently deceived by labyrinthine political views or turgid logic.

Parsing much of this "information" is intellectually seductive, either too pleasing or too horrifying. Most of it may, indeed, be truth. The reader will find many footnotes throughout for clarification of some obscured points. Many important explanations will be missed by not reading these footnotes. In addition, illustrations with detailed captions will help to further explain the two parts of the narrative.

It is important for the reader to understand that I am using critically spaced events of Cuba's journey to modernity as metaphors for how these events affected the story of the Cuban peoples as a whole. I believe that the reader will come to better understand how these events came about using this device.

Importantly, however, during these centuries of "historically silent years," the ancient founding families formed an influential mass of interactive "Criollos" that developed a strong culture based on a closed society and strong family ties.

According to the 2016 Wikipedia, the Criollos "were a social class in the caste system of the overseas colonies established by Spain in the sixteenth century, especially in Hispanic America, comprising the locally born people of confirmed European (primarily Spanish) ancestry. The Criollo class ranked below that of the Iberian Peninsulares, who were permanent resident colonists born in Spain. But Criollos were of a higher status/rank than all other castes: people of mixed descent, Amerindians, and enslaved Africans." Wikipedia's definitions are correct and the reader should keep them in mind in this narrative.

The Criollo political center was the isolated populace of the far lands of eastern Cuba, some six hundred-plus miles away from the Spanish governor's administrative center in Habana. This Criollo civilization was initially centered in the "encomiendas" of the eastern lands. In our story, the encomienda of interest is "La Caridad de Macaca," situated in the vast lands adjacent the Golfo de Guacanayabo.

This settlement was the base of our family ancestry and the foundation of its Criollo culture. The story told here is about them and their demise. Indeed, Cuban Criollos had a formidable overdeveloped sense of autonomy from the "Mother Country," reinforced further by tardy official communications between the power site of Imperial Spain in Habana and the distant Criollos of the eastern lands, the so-called "Interior."[1]

It is important for the reader to keep these facts in mind because I do refer to the Interior and Criollos throughout this narrative.

1. "Interior" also implies uncouth or coarse

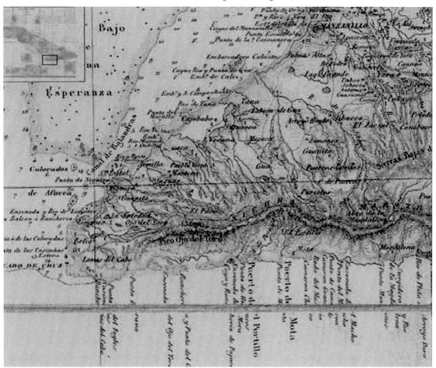

Map of Macaca Encomienda. Macaca, marked by the arrow, is found just north of Pueblo Viejo near the coast.

It is self-evident that the further away from the Spanish governor's fiats in Habana, the more freedom the ancient families of the east had. Criollos made many decisions of all types without fear of the Spanish boot. While the isolated eastern lands developed a relatively free and autochthonous culture, Habana, about six hundred miles west, famously grew pro-Spanish and faithfully toed the Colonial Empire's edicts.

Criollos intermarried frequently as you will detect by examining their doubled identical surnames. Take, for example, the full name of a personage, "Ana Tamayo y Tamayo." Criollos attached the mother's family name last, as it is done in Castilian Spanish, whereas in English, it is customary to place the mother's family name right after the given name(s). Often, Criollo marriages were with first cousins. The widespread inbreeding is not solely genetically important, but it is also a unique type of acculturation of European and native values that produced a people with a deep understanding of their land, their customs, and their mode and style of living, which was not to be challenged or disturbed. The Criollos' freedoms were defended to death later, as you will learn.

The ancient Criollo families did not long for Spain or Europe or, for that matter, the United States of America. They became, through and through, self-sufficient Cuban Nationalists with the sobriety of Mercantilists, and their survivors are so to this day. Criollo's exceptional culture was easy to discern. They lost the lisp of Castilian Spanish, they used native words of Taino or Siboney Amerindian origins, and words of an autochthonous Afro-Cuban dialect. Criollo music was theirs and no one else's. Their music was an evolving derivative of the English "contra dance" but rhythmically Caribbean and African, warm, romantic and vibrant.

Significantly, the Cuban "Trova" started in the nineteenth century in Santiago de Cuba, the capital city of the eastern lands, later to become the province of Oriente. Nuestra Señora de la Caridad del Cobre (Our Lady of Charity of El Cobre), Cuba's acknowledged patron saint who made her appearance in Santiago de Cuba Province in 1612, is an undisputed Criollo icon that has nothing to do with Spain. To this day, even recalcitrant Criollo free thinkers who shun the traditional pro-Spanish Cuban Catholic Church, pray to "Cachita"[2] in difficult times.

Meaningfully in this regard, the printed paper money of the young Republic, from 1902 up to the era of the 1959 Cuban Revolution, featured five eastern Criollo patriots while none from the western lands are represented, with the lone exception of left-of-center Marti. Importantly, Marti is buried in the fabled Santa Efigenia Cemetery in Santiago de Cuba in Oriente Province, not in

2 . Cachita is the intimate diminutive of Caridad, a name very popular with Criollo women and in Cuban lyrics.

Republican paper money collection. From top left: General Maximo Gomez, Jose Marti, the principal civil intellectual mentor of the 1895 War of Independence, General Antonio Maceo, and General Calixto Garcia. From the top right: Vicente Aguilera, who contributed immensily to finance the 10 Years' War, and President Carlos M. de Céspedes, Republic of Cuba in Arms, 1868-1874.

Habana, his birth site. Ironically and deeply troubling to the surviving Criollos of today, the Cuban Communist dictator's tomb, Fidel Castro, the son of a Spanish Imperial soldier who fought against Cuban Nationalist insurgents, is also buried in the Santa Efigenia Cemetery, close to many Criollo heroes of the Wars of Independence honored there.

This is a different history of Cuba. It is also the story of our family. For other accounts of the Cuban people, there are a multititude of history books that you can consult in your local library and elsewhere. A reader interested in "the Cuban Story" should beware that many books offer a high degree of historical bias, some quite hysterical and strident, and (most) are poorly documented.

The rise of these storied accounts does not give much significance to the Criollo civilization and its demise. Almost all modern accounts of Cuba's Republic are heavy on Spanish cruelty, genocide of the Amerindian native population, odious slavery, the American yellow press and the Hearst publications, Yankee Imperialism, the exploitation of the masses by rapacious and insensitive capitalists, the cruel and despicable actions of an unsavory bourgeoisie and the rise of liberal ideals that addressed "social justice."[3]

These dramatized accounts have a generalized proclivity to blame someone else, principally the Gringo or the Gallego[4], which distorts and renders his or her message somewhat unbelievable.

The story of our family's passage from the first decade of the sixteenth century to 1960 severely challenges many of the stereotypes that are so abundant in Cuban history books from all sides of the political spectrum. The tale told here is refreshing indeed, but don't expect to find detailed minutiae of Cuban history. History's trivial details have a tendency to obscure macro-socioeconomic movements or the causative effect of rebellions. Here, the reader will find an overview with anecdotes that represent the sentiments, triumphs, and troubling failures as truthfully as I perceived them from my family personages and my own experiences. As this account unfolds there are different narratives dispersed in time and space.

Anecdotes are useful to portray character and personalities. More importantly, I tried to use our family's triumphs and vicissitudes as examples of the effects of political and economic policy that shaped centuries of our history.

This journey will trace different characters and how they were greatly influenced by the Spanish Empire and the American Civil War, how they met in the eastern lands of Cuba, how the violent repression of Racial Wars produced a political backlash that resulted in the rise of a "unique and violent type of autochthonous Liberalism,"

---

3. Jesuit Luigi Taparelli of Sicily introduced the concept of "social justice" in the 1830s in the Roman Catholic Church, based on the St. Thomas Aquinas' precept that Princes and Kings may enforce Lord Jesus's evangelical principles as Edicts or Secular Laws. This was a radical departure from Jesus and St. Paul's teachings, which advocated the separation of Church and State. Interestingly Jesus never really preached social justice and the Taparelli proclamation was based on a very loose interpretative corruption of the Good Samaritan parable in the era of widespread demonization of the Industrial Revolution. Karl Marx published the Communist Manifesto February 21, 1848, after Father Taparelli's popularized proclamation. With the decline of Christianity over time, modern usage of social justice, even by Pope Francis in the twenty-first century, is closer to Socialist "distributive dogma" than how Taparelli originally intended it.

4. Gringo: The disparaging designation of a United States citizen by Spanish speaking peoples. Gallego: The disparaging ethnic designation of a Spanish citizen regardless of regional Iberian origins by Latin Americans and Cubans in particular.

how the evolution of an unsustainable and warped economy originated, and how and why a young Republic veered to the Left by 1933. It will also trace how this development clearly defined the country's populist future that reigns today, how they suffered through the Cuban Revolution of 1959, and how this family finally flourished in the United States of America.

Some chapters may be perceived as somewhat disconnected and each may seem autonomous to the others. They are not. In the course of historical events, convergence happens in exciting, and to sometime unpredictable, tragic ways. This history is chronologically written as remembered, occasionally having to imply the degree of reality or truthfulness.

To aid the readers, there is a glossary at the beginning of some chapters because ancient Spanish and some Cuban terms are no longer in use in modern times. For example, Afro-Cuban terms, like "ñangara," which means, interchangeably, "occultist, con-man or Communist," are translated in the glossary and are used frequently. My own knowledge of Afro-Cuban terms is translated in the course of several chapters.

The modern chapters portray my zigzags in education, my Harvard and Cornell years, and my early scientific career and political thoughts as I stumble through American academia and the Cuban Revolution. These chapters will give a sense of how the impacting political upheavals modulated the life of a young man trapped in these vortices.

Although I helped the M26-7 movement and Resistencia Civica in Cuba, my revolutionary participation was short and I was not able to keep up with the details of the rapidly developing military skirmishers in the field, nor with the depths of the political conspiracies, or with the organization of the urban guerrillas pari passu. In this book, my coverage of these important events is wanting in many respects but the information is valuable because I was able to obtain it from letters and directly from members of revolutionary cadres in the United States who had risked their lives by venturing into rebel-occupied territory on secret missions. The incomplete information I gleaned in those heady days was the only guidance I had at the time and governed my "revolutionary" efforts. Eventually the FBI closely watched my activities and though I was aware of their vigilance, I made a costly mistake that led to a Senate investigation of my activities with the Fair Play For Cuba Committee. The Senate Judiciary Committee exonerated me in a public hearing that was televised nationally. Subsequently, I defected from Castro's revolutionary organizations and became an American citizen.

The reader is referred to other authors who have reported on these events with great accuracy. The reports from 1956 to 1960 by Ruby Phillips, Bob Taber, Andrew St. George, Jay Mallin, Herbert Mathews and Juan Clark stand out for your use. The violent years of the Castro-Communist dictatorship and the eventual capitulation of the American Republic under President Barack H. Obama are not covered in this book. These years have been reported by many worthy authors who participated in these fateful events and who have devoted much time and effort to elicit the truth as best they could. My effort here is focused on events that affected our family right up to the few months after the failed Bay of Pigs invasion and the disaster of President John F. Kennedy's decision to betray and abandon the beached Cuban Rebel Brigade, thus sealing their fate.

For students of the years 1960 to the early decade of twenty-first century, I highly recommend the two-volume account of the Castro-Communist takeover of Cuba, *Castro's Revolution, Myth and Reality*, by Professor Juan M. Clark, as well as the detailed and well-researched treatise of Frank Pais' life and times by Professor José Alvarez.

Part 1

The Violent Country

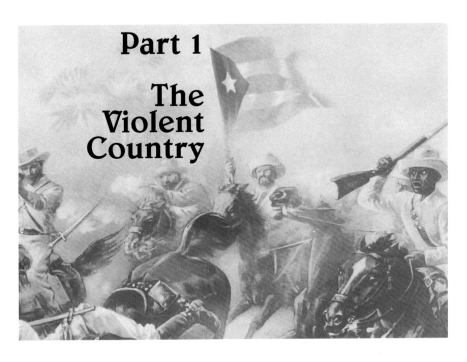

"What is life? In a little while, Crow Foot will leave you. Whither we cannot say. From nothing we came. Into nothing we go. What is life? It is as the flash of a firefly in a summer night. It is as the breath of the buffalo on a winter day. It is as the little shadow, which runs across the grass and is lost in the sunset."

Anonymous American-Indian lament found scribbled in a discarded note in The Adirondacks, New York, 1989

"We come and go, just like ripples in a stream."

- John V. Politis

"A nation that forgets its past has no future."

– Winston Churchill

CHAPTER 1.

◊ The de Céspedes of La Caridad de Macaca and the Cossios of Camaguey Establish a 16th Century Colonization Strategy.

◊ Suppression of Rebellious Amerindians. Afro-Cuban Slavery Is Introduced.

◊ How the Declaration of Independence from Spain and the Emancipation of Slaves By Eastern Criollos Was Done.

Glossary :

Céspedes — short grass savannahs or trimmed lawns

Un lugar — a place

Jarrones — large jars

Payes — rustic tenant Spanish peasant

Casona — manor

Caballero or hidalgo — knight

Caserío — settlement, village

Campeador — surpassing in bravery

Encomienda — a large estate granted by Spanish kings

Caballería — land measure of 33 acres

Caridad — charity, also a given name

Macaca – native Taino word for "La Sierra Maestra," the escarpment of the mountain range of southwestern Oriente Province in Cuba

A Differing View of Cuba's History

Cacicazgo — Taino or Siboney chiefdom

Caney — Taino or Siboney, village or settlement

el-Ándalus — Islamic kingdoms of medieval southern Spain before the Reconquest by Christian kings

Gachupines — First generation sycophantic Cubans of Spanish parents

Peninsulares — recently arrived Spaniards

Reconquista — Defeat of Islamic Spain by Christian armies

Batey or casco — central administrative and residential buildings of a large farm, hacienda, or ranch

Mambí — Cuban Criollo rebel

Manigua — thick brush and undergrowth of the Cuban jungle.

Pueblo Viejo — old village

Filibuster — a vessel engaging in unauthorized warfare against a foreign country

Carol, my wife, turned the car from the Medina del Pomar highway in northern Burgos and followed a paved road with the sign "Céspedes." She knew we were three kilometers away. It had taken some time leafing through different sources of information to finally find it in a very detailed Michelin map of Spain. Carol remarked how short the trees were and I guessed that we were above the frost line at this altitude. In a very short while, we came to a big plateau and there, on the vast green plain, was an agglomeration of five, maybe seven, stone and mortar homes with no electricity. Consulting Google on our smartphone, we found that Céspedes had twenty-seven inhabitants.

There was a rather quaint primitive church of uncertain, very old age, somewhat separated from the center of "un lugar de Céspedes," the ancestral origin of the famous heroes of the Ten-Years War of Independence of Cuba. I guessed that perhaps only about five families occupied the buildings near a public plaza with a running cold-water spring in a fountain. From here the villagers filled "jarrones" with water to transport to their homes and washed their clothes. Almost all of the "payeses" wore wooden clogs which, curiously, had carved heels. We were told that these northern Burgos villages received three to six feet of snow from November to March. Pigs, cows, and lambs occupied the first floor of these homes to warm the upper floor.

There was no knight's "casona" with the de Céspedes crest anywhere to be found. When we asked where the de Céspedes casona was, none of those we interviewed could give us a hint. I deduced from this that the de Céspedes became "caballeros or hidalgos" after they migrated from this poor and inhospitable "caserío," the place of their ancestral origin, probably as part of the retinue of a powerful hidalgo. I could visualize our enterprising ancestral relatives eager to leave this forsaken, cold and miserable land. They would join a small, hurriedly mustered fighting force led by a famous nobleman who was intent on facing hordes of fierce Moors, the occupiers of most of Spain for about eight centuries. After all, we were in northern Burgos, the land of the victorious "campeador" El Cid, Rodrigo de Vivar, (1043-1099.) Violent clashes of Spaniards and Moors had happened all around us in the course of nearly eight centuries of Islamic Occupation.

Why not? It seemed to me a reasonable deduction. All we had to do to support this idea was to document that there was such a landed gentry near Céspedes who might have ordered the recruitment of young "payeses" under his fiefdom.

I looked at my Michelin road map and noted that the Towers of Medina del Pomar of the Conde de Frias was four kilometers from Céspedes, close enough for the de Céspedes to gain the favor of their liege, in this case, Count Frias. Perhaps they became great warriors and favorites. Or maybe they were more cerebral and became the Count's scribes or treasurers. It did not matter, because after taking the definitive step to leave Céspedes, they were rewarded with knighthood by the king of Spain in the sixteenth century. Knighthood was characteristically awarded to warriors with significant battle victories over Islam.

Later, early in the sixteenth century, they indeed became the Spanish King's Men in San Salvador de Bayamo, in the eastern lands of Cuba. There are records of a Captain de Céspedes who successfully beat off French corsairs in battle near the largest river of Cuba, the navigable Rio Cauto, near the city of Bayamo, in 1512.

The de Céspedes warriors moved from their primitive ancestral origins in "un lugar de Céspedes" in northern Burgos to finally settling in the conquered Islamic Kingdom of Seville, in el-Ándalus (Andalucía). It was through a circuitous route across hazardous terrains, treacherous rivers, and unforgiving mountains. It probably took more than two centuries to do and it was achieved with military victories in a territory of some six hundred miles in breadth. In Seville, the de Céspedes were again recruited to join the great adventure of colonizing an immense encomienda of the King of Spain bordering the Gulf of Guacanayabo, Cuba, in the sixteenth century. Of course, much later, they led the Cuban people to independence in the mid-nineteenth century.

The first stepping-stone to glory may have been servitude under Count Frias, four kilometers from where I was standing.

We decided to drive there to investigate the place. We needed to locate a knight's casona in Frias with the characteristic de Céspedes crest. As it turned out, it paid off. We found the ruins of a knight's casona with the de Céspedes crest and amazingly, there were several de Céspedes families living in the Towers of Frias, including young Alejandro de Céspedes, who was photographed next to his Cuban relative, me. At the time, I reflected that his genes and mine were separated by almost half a millennium. The de Céspedes casona in Frias was "la mas rancia" (the oldest and of highest rank). The de Céspedes became Marqueses de Villafranca later, and today, the area of the casona is known as Villafranca.

I estimate that Captain de Céspedes actually set foot in Bayamo for the first time circa 1509-1510. It is probably of great significance that the first de Céspedes on record was a successful warrior, a captain of Imperial Spanish troopers. The de Céspedes in Cuba at that time were indeed loyal Spanish king's men and were rough and ready, aggressive warriors of the successful liberation war (La Reconquista) against the nearly eight-hundred-year-old Islamic occupation of Spain. We suspect, but could not confirm, that the future mayor of Santiago de Cuba, Hernán Cortes, was the recruiter of the de Céspedes warriors.

Carol, my lovely wife, and I had cracked a mystery and that night, as we went to bed, we both felt that we had solved an important issue about our famous ancestral origins and slept in wonderment.

The principal anchor of the Criollo de Céspedes family, Don Juan Antonio de Céspedes, came from the medieval bastion of Osuna in the Kingdom of Seville during the Reconquista. He and his wife, Maria Conde, voyaged to join the other family adventurers in San Salvador de Bayamo sometime between 1509-1517. Near Osuna, there is an adjacent area named "El Carrión de Céspedes." Carrión means "flesh" in English.

A Differing View of Cuba's History

The conquest and Europeanization of Cuba was undoubtedly proceeded by the colonization of vast agricultural units, called encomiendas. This system was used in continental Spanish America as well. The Spanish Kings rewarded the de Céspedes participation, which by all estimates, was accompanied by the harsh suppression of Siboney and Taino Amerindian natives who refused Spanish colonial enslavement and rebelled.

The death of Chief Guamá in battle, and the capture and execution of his warrior wife, Casiguaya, are well documented. The capture of the Taino Chief, Hatuey, who sailed from Santo Domingo to warn his brothers of the character of the Spanish Conquest and who had actively organized a brief armed skirmish with the Spanish militia, was executed by fire near the river Yara. Hatuey's bravery became a national symbol for Cuban Criollo patriots later. Friar Bartolome de la Casas was the first to publish this ethnic genocide in 1511.

Hatuey burning at a stake.

The long-term violence ultimately reduced the general native population of circa 120,000 to a handful in present day Cuba.

This period of totalitarian edicts with the purpose of changing widespread religion and ethnic cultures was also taking place in Spain itself, particularly after the edicts of King Phillip II. Later, his son King Phillip III took brutal control following the Moorish Revolt of 1567 and exiled Jews and Muslims alike. These events in this violent age, after all, were not unusual or unique to the Conquest of Spanish America or to Moorish Spain. They were happening in rapid cruel succession all over Europe during the Reformation and the Counter Reformation and would continue for over 150 years following the discovery of America in 1492. Although there is no documentation of the degree of the de Céspedes participation in this form of ethnic cleansing, there is little reason to try to exonerate them because they were loyal Spanish warriors of great repute. It would be absurd to say that they were not partly responsible for the violent ethnic cleansing of eastern Cuba.

To add to the debacle was the introduction of African slaves in Cuba during the next two centuries to perform the labor the rebellious native population refused to assume under the Spanish boot. One may well surmise that there was much to be sorry about and very little written of this awful period. The awakening of liberalism in Spanish America, and particularly among the de Céspedes family, happened in fits and starts in the early decades of the nineteenth century, as you will learn from this narrative. One may wishfully characterize this awakening as atonement and redemption from the incredible excesses inflicted on native Cubans and the enslavement of Africans the previous three centuries.

The de Céspedes managed the sixteenth century Cuban encomienda, known as the Hacienda de Macaca, of 5,400 caballerias, circa 72,469 hectares or 179,075 acres. A spot of the western-most corner of the property was named Caridad de Macaca, where one of the earliest places of worship was built early in the sixteenth century. They also built a small "batey or casco" with several homes, with some serving as administrative offices. I was able to find La Caridad de Macaca in an ancient Spanish map. The label is very clear. Unfortunately, I was unable to purchase it, as some lost soul bought it before me. The map showed that it was close to the coast and overlooked the Gulf of Guacanayabo.

They owned African slaves. I don't know the number exactly but from conversations with my grandmother I estimate that between Carlos Manuel, the oldest, and Pedro Maria, the youngest, de Céspedes del Castillo may have owned as many as two scores of slaves (around forty), perhaps more, by the mid 1860s. My grandmother, Adolfina Cossío y de Céspedes, told me that by the mid-nineteenth century, African slaves in Cuba were not mistreated. They were housed and taught how to read and write and those owners and their slaves developed mutual respect and dependency. The Chile author, Isabel Allende, in her historical novel, *La Isla Bajo el Mar* compares nineteenth century slavery in Santo Domingo with that of Cuba and also states that the relationship of slaves with their owners in Cuba was benign compared to that of Santo Domingo.

The hacienda's size is equivalent to 26 percent of the land area of the smallest state of the United States of America, Rhode Island. There is an enormous gap in the documentation of this family from the times of the Conquest and the advent of the Age of Reason in the early nineteenth century. It is clear, however, that the de Céspedes ruled the encomienda for about 350 years with varying degrees of success and troubled failures. As the immense area was colonized and the primeval forest was cut down for wood and sugar cane, the encomienda was subdivided many times, not only to many family members, but also to other enterprising Spanish migrants and European adventurers who bought parcels of their property.

By the mid-1800s the oldest of the de Céspedes del Castillo brothers and sisters, Carlos Manuel, held his principal sugar plantation at La Demajagua, not far from the Yara River. He also owned the coffee plantation of San Lorenzo, near the Contramaestre River, in the easternmost lands of the old encomienda and other properties. His youngest brother, Pedro Maria, held a smaller plantation with sugar and cattle known as Macaca, just southeast of La Demajagua. Both brothers owned family homes in the city of San Salvador de Bayamo near the biggest river of Cuba, El Cauto. In these ancient times, El Cauto was navigable and adjoined the sea in the Gulf of Guacanayabo. It was an important commercial route and Bayamo prospered from the sixteenth to nineteenth century.

President Carlos Manuel de Céspedes

Carlos Manuel and Pedro Maria played major roles in the first war of independence, as you will learn later in this narrative. With the advent of the Ten Years' War of Independence, much was lost as their properties were confiscated by Imperial Spain and sold in public auction for a song.

*Major General
Pedro M. de
Céspedes*

Shortly before the war, the Cossio family had enjoined the de Céspedes by marriage and faced an uncertain future. The modern branches of our family were split in different directions by the war.

Curiously, the Cossios originated near Céspedes of Northern Burgos in today's Cantabria, Spain. There is no evidence they knew each other before the mid-sixteenth century when the Cossio family settled in Camaguey, much further west from the de Céspedes of Oriente in the East.

The Cossios were originally Roman conquerors who occupied the beautiful high ground known as La Degollada between two fast moving brooks with rapids, which merge as one, and head into the Cantabrian Sea[5]. There, the Roman Cossios built a large stone fortress. The fortress was immense "with moats and counter moats" in Roman military style, constructed with yellow granite and sandstones

5. La Degollada, the girl with the slit-throat, was named after the brutal execution of a young rebel Cantabria maid there.

that were rectangular, well cut and smooth, from a nearby quarry. The fortress protected the northern Roman ports of the Cantabrian Sea from the tribes of native savages.

Over the course of centuries, when the area was pacified after the Islamic occupation of Spain was defeated, the fortress was dismantled piecemeal. The Cossios built a beautiful Romanesque casona that bears the elegant and very large crest of this powerful family below on the other side of a Roman bridge. The rest of the stones were used to build many other Romanesque homes that dot the village as well as the arched stone Roman bridge, which is large enough to allow carts, carriages and cattle to cross it without difficulty. The place appears today like a beautiful postcard photo with the snow-capped Peaks of Europe in the background and the quaint brooks moving fast to their Cantabrian destination in the foreground.

In due course, this powerful family moved to a prominent casona bearing the Cossio crest in Santillana del Mar in the north with access to the sea lanes. Today, it is one of the best-preserved medieval casonas in all of Spain and is a popular tourist attraction, well described in my Michelin map.

It wasn't long before some of the young members were recruited to colonize the Province of Camaguey in Cuba in the sixteenth century. The migratory trail of the Cossio family is, indeed, long and arduous. Knighted and honored by the King of Spain, family members also undertook the quest of conquering America. After Camaguey, some members sought fame and fortune in Mexico. From Mexico, some members migrated to Alto Peru (now Bolivia), and from Peru, some moved to Tucuman, in northwest Argentina.

Once in Argentina, this two-hundred-plus year trek resulted in the loss of the accent on the last syllable and, instead, gained emphasis in the first syllable. From Tucumán, the Cossios settled in Buenos Aires, where they became prominent and powerful professionals and members of today's social elite. Possibly the most influential and prominent is Don Pedro Cossio, M.D., a justly famed cardiologist and father to Dr. Patricio Cossio, a close friend and collaborator in our research of Chagas Disease.

In the 1860s, there were six de Céspedes del Castillo brothers and sisters. The oldest brother, Carlos Manuel, was bestowed with the customary advantages of the landed gentry of the age. He received a thorough education, graduated from law school in Spain, and spoke French, English, Italian and a little German. He was briefly involved in a plot by General Prim to overthrow the Spanish monarchy, which failed.

He traveled extensively in Europe and eventually returned to his lands. Inspired by General Narciso Lopez's failed attempt to overthrow the colonial government in Cuba, he became a nationalist Criollo rebel and activist against the Spanish Empire. He was not alone. His youngest brother, Pedro Maria, joined him in his political activities. He recruited his cousin, Perucho Figueredo, who later, in a more difficult and violent time, wrote the Cuban National Anthem. With his cousins Francisco Castillo Moreno and Jose Fornaris, Carlos Manuel composed the beautiful romantic ballad, *La Gentil Bayamesa*.

Apart from the soirees among his young friends, serenading the young women of Bayamo, and composing plaintive, romantic ballads, Carlos Manuel and this group of youngsters spearheaded revolutionary activities with thoughts of a representative Republic, very similar to that founded in the United States of America. The American Founding Fathers found an avid interest group among the very rich intellectuals of the landed gentry of the City of San Salvador de Bayamo.

Carlos Manuel's political leadership was charismatic. In 1855, after Carlos Manuel defended, pro bono, a number of Criollos accused of anti-Spanish activities, the alarmed Imperial authorities took notice. The younger brother, Pedro, had become the messenger leader of the group. He defended and protested the execution of Don Ramón Pinto, who was charged with subversive activities against the Spanish Crown.

14

The Violent Country

It wasn't long before trumped up charges were issued and arrests were made and Carlos Manuel and Pedro, in chains, were sentenced to two years' imprisonment in a dank and ancient Trafalgar man-of-war anchored in the Bay of Santiago de Cuba.

Fortunately, Rafael Tamayo y Fleitas, their cousin, convinced the Spanish authorities to transfer the prisoners to house arrest in his home. Following their house imprisonment, they were transferred to the Spanish garrison and prison of Baracoa and after some months there, they were moved to the City of Manzanillo with instructions not to travel outside the city to keep them away from Bayamo and Santiago de Cuba.

This daunting experience made the two brothers more determined to organize the opposition against Spanish Colonial Rule and they planned an armed rebellion against the empire. After their release, they joined kindred spirits, who were among the most prominent landed gentry of Camaguey and Oriente, and armed an opposition that would result in the creation of a Republic in Arms with the purpose to negotiate with the empire and gain a free and sovereign Cuba. The motto of the Criollo Republic was "Fatherland and Liberty" (Patria y Libertad). Carlos Manuel and Pedro wanted a representative Cuban-Republican government, styled after that of the United States.

Most of the financing of the rebellion was by the contributions of their peers, the rich landed Criollo gentry, including, of course, the de Céspedes brothers and the likes of Vicente Aguilera and Ignacio Agramonte. Contacts in Cienfuegos, Trinidad, and Habana were made but the Western lands were not enthusiastic, particularly among the Habanero aristocrats who were fond of the Spanish Empire.

As is likely among Cubans to this day, division of opinions arose among the conspirators. Some wanted annexation with the United States, others wanted autonomy and an incomplete separation from Spain but the insistent Carlos Manuel and Pedro wanted a free independent and sovereign Cuba and a representative Republican form of government.

The discussions became acrimonious, but the de Céspedes brothers and their Bayamo compatriots prevailed in favor of a republic. Carlos Manuel was elected President of the Republic of Cuba in Arms in the First Guaimaro Assembly. A Republican government was formed and sworn-in. The government had to move from time to time in an instant to escape the Spanish Imperial armed forces, who were bent on trapping it to destroy it and kill all of its members. Its structure was organized like a mini-American government. It was remarkably effective and this undoubtedly had a great deal to do with Carlos Manuel's leadership and organizational skills.

Later, near the end of the Ten Years' War of Independence, the Second Guaimaro Assembly of the Republic in Arms deposed him. Some believe he was betrayed by his own compatriots in arms, and lost his life in a firefight when he was exiled to his Contramaestre San Lorenzo plantation without adequate escorts.

Carlos Manuel and Pedro grew suspicious of the commitment of their co-conspirators and decided to force the issue. In his distant Macaca plantation, on October 9, 1868, Pedro announced to his slaves that they were officially freed and that a Republic in Arms would be created. The following day, on October 10, Carlos Manuel in his sugar mill plantation of La Demajagua gave a moving and emotional oration by all accounts.

A written proclamation, the Declaration of Independence from Imperial Spain, was signed and Pedro de Céspedes, my great-grandfather, was a signatory with his older brother and many other patriots of different economic stripes. In the proclamation, it was announced that slavery was abrogated and their slaves were freed. The long-standing indifference to redress Criollo grievances by Imperial Spain is made clear in the Declaration of Independence of Cuba, October 10, 1868 (See Appendix).

Undoubtedly, Carlos Manuel's invocation was greatly influenced by President Abraham Lincoln's brilliant and moving Gettysburg

Address, widely publicized and read in Oriente, a mere five years earlier (See Appendix).

The rebellion had a very inauspicious start. In the very first skirmish against the Imperial Army, the Criollo insurgents and free slaves, commanded by Carlos Manuel de Céspedes, were forced to withdraw near the "caney" of the Taino "cacicazco" of the Yara River, not far from the site of the martyrdom by fire of Chief Hatuey. It was a disastrous encounter with the disciplined and well-trained Imperial Spanish Troopers and de Céspedes' ragtag militia under their battle flag.

de Céspedes Battle Flag

They withdrew from the field of battle, humiliated. Later, its residents torched parts of the city of Bayamo, which had been in the hands of the Republic in Arms, as news alarmed them that a large column of Spanish regulars and cavalry had arrived under the command of Count Valmaseda. In due time, Spanish regulars occupied it.

In the course of the Ten Years' War, the insurgency never was able to conquer and control a large enough space to claim statehood and independence from Spain and gain international recognition. The insurgency was soon forced to develop hit and run tactics of guerrilla warfare to avoid line confrontations. Even so, commanders like Donato Marmol, Ignacio Agramonte, and Máximo Gómez and others did engage the Spanish Imperial Army, toe to toe, in successful lightning-quick cavalry machete charges. A rising star, Colonel Antonio Maceo, emerged as a master of these lightning cavalry attacks followed by swift withdrawals that successfully plagued Spanish regulars[6]. Maceo and his brother, José, Calixto Garcia, Bartolomé Maso, and others quickly rose in rank and formed a fairly cohesive and imposing Army of the Republic in Arms.

But it was not enough.

The Ten Years' War floundered and the de Céspedes suffered major setbacks. It did, however, provide a dress rehearsal for the War of Independence later in 1895. The field officers of the Mambí Army gained enormous experience in leadership, troop movement, artillery placements, logistics, tactics, and overall strategy to successfully combat a better armed and disciplined Imperial Army twenty or more times their number. The mambí rebels were able to deal a severe blow to the Spanish Empire in the War of Independence, (1895-1898), as you will learn later in this narrative.

In the 1860s, Egmidio Cossío Serrano of Camaguey courted and later married Herminia de Céspedes y Tamayo, the daughter of now Major General Pedro M. de Céspedes and Ana Tamayo y Tamayo. Egmidio was a good looking young man, who was well known for his many affairs with women of any station and race. By all accounts, he was a very unsavory and pedantic character.

Photos of Herminia de Céspedes y Tamayo in her 40s show a taciturn, sad looking lady with marked characteristics of a possible indigenous origin, a possibility vigorously denied by my mother,

---

6. Maceo's cavalry attacks were mirror images of those of Confederate General J.E.B. Stuart charges of the American Civil War. It can be said that most of the successful Criollo Generals learned much of their tactics from the experience published in English of the American Civil War.

Herminia Greig Cossio y de Céspedes. I differ with her simply because the physical attributes of my great-grandmother are, in my mind, indisputably Amerindian. The notion of our ancestry being partly of Native American origins is supported by the family's history itself. The Tamayos are known to have conquered vast Indian lands through marriages of Indian chiefs' daughters of the Bayamo region very early on in the course of the Spanish Conquest of Cuba.

Ana Tamayo y Tamayo was orphaned when her parents, Esteban Tamayo and Ana Maria Tamayo, upon returning from their studies in Spain, were assassinated by brigands that pirated their boat near their "Tamayo" Cay. The infant Ana and her same-age slave Narcisa (a.k.a. Sisa) survived the ordeal. Sisa was freed and lived more than one hundred years to tell and confirm the story.

Sisa, the freed slave.

19

A Differing View of Cuba's History

In the early goings of the Ten Years War initiated by the landed gentry of Oriente, Emigdio joined the insurgency and gained the rank of lieutenant. Alone in La Caridad de Macaca, Herminia gave birth to a healthy and handsome boy, Randolfo. More than a year later or so after this child, she gave birth to another handsome boy, Pedro.

Later, when the filibuster side-paddle steam ship Virginius was captured and her husband, Major General Pedro de Céspedes del Castillo was summarily executed, all the de Céspedes women with their children were rounded up in la Caridad de Macaca in 1873, probably in December that year, and deported to "permanent" exile by the Spanish Empire to Kingston, Jamaica, in a British freighter.

The de Céspedes' lands had been confiscated and the penniless but proud aristocrat, Herminia de Céspedes y Tamayo, with little Randolfo and Pedro Cossio and in the "family way," set up a sewing sweatshop in Kingston to survive a very precarious future. She was joined in Kingston by several impoverished close relatives of the de Céspedes family that resulted in further penury to all of them. The never-do-well Egmidio Cossio never settled with Herminia, or helped in any way, and was eventually gone from our history.

My grandmother, Adolfina Cossio y de Céspedes was born January 13, 1878, in Kingston, and became a British subject by birthright.

She is the only relative I know who had survived small pox as a child but her skin was not scarred. She had an enormous impact on my upbringing and was instrumental in shaping my character and thought for the rest of my life. She was a handsome, beautiful woman and she loved me like no other.

Adolfina Cossio y de Céspedes
(Family photo heirloon)

CHAPTER 2.

◊ The Virginius Affair (1873) and How England and the United States Were Brought to the Brink of War with Spain.

◊ The Calamitous Course of the Ten Years' War of Independence (1868-1878).

◊ The Republic In Arms' Fateful Denouement.

◊ The Insurrects Sign an Armistice with the Spanish Empire.

◊ An Uneasy, Peaceful 17-Year Intermission.

Glossary :

Quitrín — elegant, nimble, uncovered, one horse, two-wheeled carrier, usually driven by a livered African slave.

Yarey — palmetto leaf strings used for tropical hats, baskets, etc.

Voluntarios — sycophantic paramilitary soldiers with extraordinary power; organized and sponsored by the Spanish Colonial Governor to subdue Criollo patriots in their cities and villages

A Differing View of Cuba's History

I was unable to find the exact reasons why Mr. Richard Hudson Beattie sailed to Santiago de Cuba from Jamaica. It is easier to understand why he traveled with his young wife, Isabel Brooks, to Kingston, Jamaica. Kingston was the Caribbean center of the British Empire under Queen Victoria and many Scots and their families populated the strategic and humming island colony, just forty nautical miles south of Oriente Province. Kingston, Jamaica, (not Habana) was the principal port of commerce of Santiago de Cuba during the reign of Queen Victoria (1837-1901). This explains why so many British subjects traveled the eastern lands of Cuba.

The Beattie ancestry hails from the small village of Dumfries, just some miles from Glasgow and the estuary of the river Clyde. When James Watt invented the rotatory steam engine, naval engineers out-fitted the shipbuilding industry on the Clyde. The Beatties were early steam engine engineers and designers, builders, fitters and installers — so good, in fact, that the Russian tsar in the 1850s hired the princi-pals of the family owned business and their engineers and moved all of them to St. Petersburg to modernize the Russian Navy, where they thrived successfully for over two decades, perhaps longer.

Young Mr. Beattie may have been left out of this scheme and sought fame and fortune elsewhere. This path may have guided him to visit the City of Santiago de Cuba from Kingston to seek a business or other form of employment. Because of his education in husbandry and agriculture, the rich dark soil of Oriente in Cuba may have looked pretty attractive to the recently married Scot, or it may have been that in the course of his adventures, he met and married the well-connect-ed and rich Maria Isabel Brooks.

The landed gentry Brooks family had established roots in Oriente during the time of the short-lived British occupation of Cuba in the 18th century.[7] In the summer of 1853, their son, Thomas William

---

7. During the American War of Independence of 1776, the high society ladies of the rich Habana merchants sold their jewelry and contributed the money to General George Washington, who wrote a letter acknowledging the receipt of the money and offering his most gracious thanks. It was not really a

Beattie Brooks, was born in Santiago de Cuba. Isabel had eight other children with Richard.

Thomas W. was duly registered in the Kingston British Colonial Office as a British subject. When his father was able to work for a sugar plantation owner of British descent, Thomas W. prospered, grew, and was educated by Jesuits in Santiago de Cuba, where he learned perfect Spanish and some French and was called "Don Tomas" by his servants. The family, over time, returned to Dumfries to work in the shipbuilding industry, possibly at Brown & Co., on the Clyde, the probable shipbuilders of both the Spanish Imperial frigate Toronado and the American Confederate blockade runner and later day Spanish filibuster, the Virginius. These vessels turned the history of my family upside down in seemingly unpredictable events.

Don Tomas graduated with a degree in engineering from the University of Glasgow and specialized in undersea cable communications. Soon after finishing school at age twenty-two and armed with a perfect command of Criollo Spanish, he traveled to his beloved Santiago de Cuba to manage El Cable Ingles (The British Cable Co.). Cable had just been laid from Great Britain to Jamaica, to Santiago de Cuba, then Cienfuegos, across the Island to Habana, then to Savannah, Georgia, and New York City and other connections north.

There, in the ancient city, he fell hopelessly in love with a beautiful Criollo landed aristocrat, who was already married. It was an impossible obsession. She was Clara de Céspedes, a.k.a. Clarita, the owner of an enormous farm that comprised the area from the City of Niquero to Cabo Cruz, which bordered the Gulf of Guacanayabo.

I can picture, with a degree of certainty, that on the morning of November 10, 1873, twenty-two-year old Thomas Brooks Beattie could not take his eyes off the two-wheeled "quitrín" drawn by a

---

demonstration of sympathy by the Habana rich for the Cause of Liberty, but rather a demonstration of Spanish antipathy for the English who had defeated Spain in many armed conflicts through the previous centuries. Furthermore, England had occupied Habana in 1762 for about a year, which was resented by the pro-Spanish Empire Habana rich.

black Arabian horse and driven by a liveried African slave. She was absolutely the most beautiful creature he had ever seen in Santiago, or even on the banks of the Clyde or Dumfries: classic refined features, jet-black hair carefully and casually arranged, accentuating the already famous de Céspedes beauty.

Clarita was also crying. Her horse clippity-clopped past him and she did not even acknowledge the removal of the large "yarey" hat as the quitrín passed by.

It was rumored that she had been the model for the statue of the Virgin Mary of Bayamo's Cathedral, still under the pain of the Spanish boot and in the throes of the Criollo insurgency, now five years going. Very disturbed by her outpouring of grief, he suspected it was deeper than she showed, and that something very wrong was happening. As a matter of fact, his freed Afro-Cuban servant had been downcast and unusually taciturn and silent that morning.

The entire city appeared under the spell of impending doom.

"Someday, hopefully sooner than you might think, we will meet again and you will be more receptive, Clarita, and you will smile at me, lass . . ." but the Scottish youth quickly dismissed his thoughts.

He had just arrived to the front door of his office, "The Cuba Submarine Cable Company," also known in town as "El Cable Ingles" on Marina Alta Street. It was in a one-floor Spanish colonial house, which was dwarfed by the enormous mansion of Don Andrés, Count Duany, that looked down on the quay and beyond to the shimmering bay.

He shivered as he recognized the side-paddled, over 200-foot-long, 491-ton steamship Virginius near her captor, the armed Spanish frigate, Toronado.

The larger, menacing, black English frigate, HMS Niobe, had elegantly out-maneuvered the other warships and had taken a position to advantage that squarely favored her against the smaller Spanish gunboats, the Tornado, Juaneta and others. British sailors had opened her portholes and uncovered ten black guns and calmly cleaned and worked them.

"Not good, not good at all." He worried as he watched Her Majesty's own marines lower a skiff with its complement of uniformed rowers and her master and commander, Lambton Lorraine, into the placid waters of Santiago Bay.

Illustration. The Virginius under pursuit by the Toronado.

His Majesty's Acting Vice-Consul Theodore Brooks, his uncle, had sent a message to him by hand the night before. It asked to meet with him, Commander Lambton Lorraine and the Governor of Santiago de Cuba, General Juan Pedro Burriel, at the Governor's Palace. Tom Beattie had personally handled Ted Brooks' cablegrams in strict confidence ever since the arrival of the Tornado, with her prize, the Virginius, and her entire crew, on November 1, 1873.

The arrival of HMS Niobe, flying her huge Cross of St. George flag, was the result of Uncle Brooks' feverish series of cablegrams to Commodore A. F. R. de Horsey, Her Majesty's Commander of West Indian Naval Forces in Kingston, Jamaica. De Horsey had ordered Lambton Lorraine, Commander of HMS Niobe, to immediately sail to Santiago some forty nautical miles away.

Cablegrams from Emil G. Schmitt, the Santiago American Vice-Consul, to the American Consulate, had gone through his hands and he now knew that the American hero, Captain William Baker Cushing, a decorated Civil War and Apache War veteran, and commander of the USS Wyoming and its 30-pounders, was steaming at full speed from what is today Panama City, heading to Santiago's bay.

The mission of the warships was to halt at all costs the massacre of the Virginius expeditionaries and crew, many of whom were English and American citizens. Don Tomas handled the messages with secrecy and care and now he had to face Governor General Burriel, the master of their lives and enforcer of civil order of the City of Santiago de Cuba, an Imperial Spanish tyrant like no other, even in this savage age.

The filibusters were tried under Habana's Captain General Dulce's decree of 1869: "All vessels captured on the high seas near Cuba with men and munitions should be treated as pirates and their crews immediately executed." The decree was clearly illegal according to that era's International Laws of the Seas.

The crew (Cuban Criollos were regarded as Spaniards) were not allowed their Consulate defense attorneys under vigorous protest. As a matter of fact, there were no defense attorneys to represent any of the prisoners. The arrogance of the local voluntarios was palpable in the ancient city. Their hatred was vehemently made known to the Santiago population of all persuasions.

When the Virginius, flying the American flag and carrying a United States registry, was captured, the crew had already thrown overboard an enormous cargo of Remington repeaters and ammunition and other accouterments destined for the embattled Cuban rebels fighting the Spanish Empire. On board was my great grandfather, Major General Pedro de Céspedes Castillo, who along with the eldest de Céspedes brother, Carlos Manuel, had been one of the signers of the Cuban Proclamation of Independence, October 10, 1868, at Carlos Manuels's sugar cane plantation, La Demajagua. There were three other outstanding veteran mambi generals with distinguished battle records captured with Don Pedro: General Bernabe Varona, General

Jesus del Sol and Brigadier General George Washington Ryan, a decorated American Civil War veteran.

They were summarily executed by firing squad in great ceremony against the ancient wall of the city's "abattoir" in Matadero Street, close to the Bacardi Rum Distillery and about half a league from the Santa Ifigenia Cemetery. The Spanish troopers failed to kill the generals on the first volley and the platoon officer, a Captain Gonzalez, with great discomfort, delivered a coup de grâce with trepidation.

Their bodies were decapitated. Their heads were placed on pikes, and paraded that night in the streets by a drunken mob of voluntarios, gachupines and peninsulares and many more pro-Empire Santiagueros. The city was exultant; a few closed their windows and doors in abject dismay, horrified by the furious spectacle. Confused and bewildered, freed Afro-Cuban ex-slaves seethed outrage and they held their heads high in defiance, out of admiration and respect of the mambi generals. They cried, proudly, and unashamed.

In the following days before the arrival of the HMS Niobe, the captain of the Virginius, Joseph Fry, a veteran of the Confederacy and Annapolis graduate who was under the employment of the Junta Revolucionaria Cubana based in New York, was executed together with thirty-seven of the crew and passengers. Twelve more were shot the day before the arrival of Commander Lambton Lorraine and a total of fifty-four were buried in a common grave under a simple mark in the Santa Ifigenia Cemetery. Among them lay what was left of my great grandfather, Major General Pedro M. de Céspedes and his fellow generals and conspirators.[8]

Commander Lambton Lorraine, his executive officer and two others of his command entered El Cable Ingles office and Tom Beattie and Ted Brooks met with a somber and brisk conver-

---

8. Today there is a simple monument of the common grave in Santa Ifigenia of the "Martyrs of the Virginius." In my youth, I visited the grave often with my grandmother, Adolfina Cossío y de Céspedes. I named my first yacht, a Maine Lobster down east motor vessel, Virginius, to honor this event in our family history. My son, Charles J, named his Grand Banks yacht, Niobe. Both vessels were anchored in Norwalk, Connecticut, proudly and defiant.

sation. Ted Brooks had secured a meeting with Governor Burriel at mid-day. The party proceeded on foot for a short distance to the Governor's Palance at Marina Alta and Carniceria streets and were admitted to the spacious and luxurious waiting room of the governor's office. Shortly after their arrival they were shown to the governors' office and there, Burriel with marked affectation, introduced himself and his military command, which included Captain Gonzalez, who had directed the execution of the Virginius crew and passengers and ordered the decapitation of the four insurgent Cuban generals. Tom Beattie acted as the official interpreter of Commander Lorraine.

It was a terse and unambiguous moment. In simple and straight-forward language, Commander Lambton issued his famous ultimatum: "Immediately stop further execution of the Virginius complement or, by order of the British Admiralty, Niobe will reduce Santiago to rubble."

It was not received lightly and the exchange was loud and intense. Burriel invoked Captain General Dulce's decree and pointed out that the executed men had been court martialed and condemned to death by firing squad, fair and square. Sir Lambton pointed out the Virginius was an American freighter flying the American flag when it was boarded and captured in the high seas under protest and contrary to International Laws of the Seas. He pointed out that among the executed men were many British subjects and that there was no evidence of war materiel when the crew of the Spanish Empire gunship, Toronado, boarded her. He further indicated that the Virginius capture was of great international concern and that he had received information that the USS Wisconsin, an American Navy light cruiser under Captain Cushing, was steaming to Santiago to protect imprisoned American citizens awaiting further execution.

Burriel indicated with bravado that neither the HMS Niobe nor the USS Wisconsin were enough to reduce the Spanish Navy moored in Santiago Bay or defeat the Imperial Army of Spain, which, at this time, numbered around 54,000 seasoned veteran soldiers of the Criollo insurgency. The discomforting meeting was adjourned for two days.

On the arrival of the USS Wisconsin two days later, the executions were stopped. Captain Cushing announced to Governor Burriel that the entire American Atlantic Squadron under Vice-Admiral Dewey was being mobilized and ordered to the Spanish Main in the Caribbean. Tom Beattie, again, was the interpreter. Cushing was deliberate and clear. The demand was made for the immediate release of the prisoners, the conveyance of the Virginius to the Wisconsin and reparations for the families of Captain Fry and the executed crew.

After a short number of days, the Spanish Empire Governor agreed to almost all demands with the notable exception of payments of reparations when it was established that the Junta Revolucionaria Cubana of New York, which supplied the Insurgency, indeed had bought the blockade-runner and filibustering Virginius, and had previously scored several incursions against Spanish Cuba.

The survivors of the crew of the Virginius were received as heroes in New York City. On route home, the Virginius, which had suffered much damage inflicted by Spanish boarders on capture, sank in a storm near Cape Fear, on its way to New York City without loss of life.

The loss of the cache of arms and ammunition, and the execution of the four generals, dealt a lethal blow to the Ten Years' War and the Criollo insurgency never recovered after the Virginius affair.

Afterwards, a number of severe reversals happened in succession:

Captured by Spaniards, the oldest son of the president of the Republic in Arms, Oscar de Céspedes y de Céspedes, was executed when his father refused to surrender to save his son's life. General Ignacio Agramonte, a giant intellect and a strong right-of-center conservative mambi leader, was mortally wounded in the Battle of Jimaguayú and captured in Camaguey Province.[9]

9. There are several conflicting interpretations to explain why there is no identifiable grave of General Agramonte we could find in our extensive search. The "official" view is that the body was correctly identified but it does not show where it is buried. The "controversial" Criollo interpretation holds that the body

31

A Differing View of Cuba's History

The measure of Agramonte's loss to the higher cause of Cuba's Independence is immense. It is comparable to the loss of Colonel Frank Pais of the urban insurgency action groups in Santiago de Cuba in 1958, as you will learn later in this narrative. Agramonte had leadership and intellectual qualities unequal among all of the insurgents, and importantly, he had conservative political ideals that countered Jose Marti's left of center views.[10]

Soon afterwards, the delegates of the Second Assemblea de Guaimaro deposed President Carlos Manuel de Céspedes of the Republic in Arms, during which he was accused by his political detractors of "abuse of power." In an unexplained and heavily criticized maneuver, Major General Calixto García enforced the decision to depose President de Céspedes with his troopers and escorted him, humiliated, to his hacienda of San Lorenzo. He sought refuge in his San Lorenzo hacienda, deep in the Sierra Maestra Mountains near the Contramaestre River with a small complement of guards, possibly under Lieutenant Quintín Banderas.

It was not long before a Spanish column of regulars found him alone and unguarded when escorts had gone on patrol, and approached the house. In the short firefight with de Céspedes, a young Spanish trooper with pink sweaty cheeks and clear blue eyes, a mere eighteen years old, shot him dead while yelling in a hoarse voice, "I killed him, I killed him."

The impact of the rifle shot lifted the body. It tumbled backwards, awkwardly, like a broken mannequin, and fell deep in the steep ravine where the Contramaestre River makes a gentle turn on the grounds of the ancient Macaca Ecomienda as it flows to join the majestic El Cauto and exits into the Gulf of Guacanayabo. He is buried in the

---

was cremated in the battlefield of Jimaguayú and his ashes dispersed there by sympathetic peasants before Spanish and Cuban officials could retrieve them. The Agramonte family refused to speak with me about this issue. These two unresolved conflicting versions remain a troubling mystery today.

10. The reader is referred to the Appendix contrasting the writings of Marti with those of Agramonte.

Santa Ifigenia Cemetery of Santiago de Cuba. [11]

Later, an Armistice was signed between the feckless leaders of the Republic in Arms and Spain in 1878, which ended the calamitous Ten Years War.

The eastern territories had suffered much and poverty was rampant. The governor's capital, Habana, and adjacent territories were unscathed.

Slowly, defeated, and broken in spirit and in wealth, the Criollo exiles began their return to their homeland under the sneer and contempt of voluntarios, peninsulares, and gachupines and many other Spanish sympathizers. The insolence and arrogance of the voluntarios against the Criollos was heavy across Santiago and Camaguey.

La Demajagua and San Lorenzo had been confiscated, the land was sold, and Pedro's Macaca plantation was in somebody else's hands. The surviving brothers and sisters fled Oriente and settled in Habana. They were looking out for themselves and would not help others who were less fortunate.

The sugar plantations around Media Luna and its sugar mill, now named Isabel, were no longer in the hands of the de Céspedes. The once powerful family, which had opened up the lands and had survived more than three hundred and fifty years of triumphs and vicissitudes, was greatly diminished. In fits and starts, they began to prosper, some significantly so.

Others, possibly misguided, or with less luck and lesser fiscal acuity, did not do so well. Pedro de Céspedes' family did not recover and struggled mightily to see better times through fortunate marriages as you will see later in this narrative.

Herminia de Céspedes y Tamayo and her family readied to leave Kingston since they were allowed by the Armistice to return from

11. The body of Carlos Manuel de Céspedes was first taken to the Bayamo Cathedral where it was mourned by the city. Later it was taken to Santiago for burial at Santa Ifigenia. After the establishment of the Republic, the Cuban government and donations of family members erected a beautiful, magnificent monument in the burial site. The site is in good state today.

exile to Media Luna in 1883.

La Caridad de Macaca near Media Luna and its vast territory now belonged to Don Thomas W. Beattie and his wife, Isabel, who along with his two sons, Richard and Arthur, had acquired the sugar mill, the lands and assets in auction. They had great plans for the ancient encomienda. They also ran a small steam ship, the Anita, along the coastal townships of the Gulf of Guacanayabo from Cabo Cruz to the City of Manzanillo. The landscape of the powerful had changed and greater challenges loomed ahead.

Adolfina, five years old, a pretty girl with fair, smooth, white skin, bright, intensely intelligent black eyes and spectacular long and smooth black hair that reached her thin waist, stood firmly holding her mother's hand among the Anita passengers leaning on the safety bars. The Sierra Maestra Mountains stood brightly under the eastern sun in the background, beckoning them home.

With her sons Randolfo and Pedro at her side, Herminia shuddered and quietly sobbed as the ship approached the quay of Media Luna, keenly afraid of what the return home might bring to her greatly impoverished family.

CHAPTER 3.

◊ The Successful 1895-1898 War of Independence Financed by Jose Marti Is Launched.

◊ Marti Joins General Maximo Gomez's Staff and Is Killed in Battle.

◊ The Spanish Empire Makes Critical Mistakes and Enforces Brutal Reconcentration Camps of the Interior's Peasants.

◊ General Weyler Is Recalled.

◊ How the United States Department of War Designed A Battle Plan By Following Admiral Mahan's Naval War Precepts And By Recruiting Two Experienced Criollo Generals.

◊ The Critical Battle of El Viso/Caney Is Won By Mambi and American Soldiers Under General Garcia and General Ludlow.

◊ Spain's Atlantic Squadron is Destroyed by the American Atlantic Fleet at the Entrance of Santiago de Cuba's Bay.

◊ How a New Constitutional Republic Was Born in America (1902) Under General Leonard Wood.

A Differing View of Cuba's History

A God our help in ages Past
Our hope for years to come
Our shelter from the storm and blast
And our eternal Home"

Elizabeth Finlay Greig,
Age 11, Year 1874
Crosspoint Embroidery
Signature of our Family's Heirloom

Glossary :

Clan – A tribe of genetically related Scots.

Sept – A maternal separate branch of a Clan member.

Shire – range.

Hato – The largest area unit of the Spanish language.

Medio – Middle.

Trochas – A military line of small fortresses.

Guardia Rural – A Cuban Republic Army unit during the years
of republican government operating in the
countryside and in the manigua.

Caballería – Equivalent measure of 33 acres.

Casona – A manor.

Manigua – Cuba's thick jungle and underbrush

Red and green squares are typical of the beautiful Clan MacGregor tartan. The western highland MacGregors, north of the Clyde, came to quarrel with the Stuart King, James VI, in 1603. He sentenced the entire MacGregor clan to death. The MacGregors' ancient foes, the Campbells, massacred the MacGregors and their septs wherever they were found. The result of this persecution was power and wealth for Clan Campbell. Historians have described it as a veritable genocide. The sentence of the diktat stood until 1774 when it was stricken from statute books.

In the course of these violent events, some survivors of the extermination left the western highlands north of Glasgow and began to establish themselves east, principally around Aberdeen and its shires. Some migrated to Norway across the North Sea.[12] Today, there are very few of them left. Greig is a sept (or branch) of Clan MacGregor. As the surviving members integrated with English rule, a fair number of them resided in the cities and villages around the shires west and north of Aberdeen. Most of these MacGregor are Anglican, merchants, professionals, farmers and property owners. Generally, they do not belong to the Kirk (Church of Scotland) preferred by the Highlanders and the majority of Scots.

My great-grandfather was George Greig, a successful Angus rancher of good repute from Middle Third, Strichen of Aberdeenshire. He is in Scotland's Angus Register. Like many Scots who excelled in husbandry, George was awarded third place with a prize Buchan cow at a fair in the shire in 1874. He married Jean Finlay, Clan Farquhar, and as it was determined by the economics of the day, he had nine children, eight males and a single daughter, Elizabeth.

My grandfather, Charles Finlay Greig, was born in 1870. We have an 1874 Greig heirloom embroidered by Elizabeth F. Greig, his sister, when she was eleven. In this treasure, the initials of her loved ones include many Fs, and this made me suspect that Charles' grandmother

---

12. Edward Grieg, Norway's famous composer, is a MacGregor.

was a Finlay, not Williamson as believed by some of my relatives, because the middle initial usually represents a mother's surname. This notion is reinforced by the existence of a photograph with a handwritten Finlay surname. My sister Enid confirmed all of this on a family visit to the homestead in Aberdeenshire. A discovered family photo shows stern looking parents, dour Scots, God-fearing, hard working and prosperous. Charles' brothers, Richard and William, on the other hand, show pleasant and engaging broad smiles.

We know one brother and a cousin struck out for Toronto, Canada, where they settled in the New World and prospered. Soon after graduating in architecture when he was twenty-two years old, young Charles Finlay Greig decided to test his luck with his Canadian family and arranged to take the SS City of New York from South Hampton in 1892.

On board, Charles met Don Tomas Beattie Brooks and his wife Isabel. In the week and a half voyage to New York they formed a strong friendship that was to last until his untimely death in 1907. Don Tomas convinced Charles to come with him to Media Luna and work for his sugar mill as his principal accountant. It took little time for the adventurous Charles to make the decision to go with the charismatic Cuban-born Scot and forsake his brothers in Canada.

The long trip from New York to Media Luna's quay in the Gulf of Guacanayabo in Oriente Province was uneventful. Young Charles rented a room in a Cuban home and he began the difficult task of learning Spanish. Don Tomas would inspect his lands on horse back and young Charles took advantage of these trips to get a better idea of Don Tomas' varied business and agricultural enterprises.

Alone riding his horse, Charles approached the clear waters of the Vicana River. There, on a riverside rock combing her jet-black smooth hair, was the most beautiful creature he had ever seen, the petite Adolfina Cossío y de Céspedes. She knew English – Jamaican British schools had taught her well.

He was completely and hopelessly charmed and vowed to pursue

La Zafra

her for marriage. She responded warmly, in awe of the handsome giant, blonde northerner with the easy smile and piercing steel-blue eyes. His attractive Scot's brogue fascinated her, and for the first time in her peripatetic life, she found peace and love in his arms.

It was not easy, he found out, to marry this splendid lady of a well-known family who had opened the land several centuries before. The problem Charles faced wasn't so much a cultural clash as much as a quasi-political problem. After all, Herminia de Céspedes y Tamayo, in Kingston for many years, had learned to ingratiate all British and Scots who were well to do.

The embattled de Céspedes family had suffered and lost greatly under the Spanish boot. The Spanish dominated Catholic Church had sided with the empire and not with the insurgency. In fact, it was common knowledge that the Catholic Church had passed information obtained at confessions to Spanish authorities to protect what the de Céspedes believe was an illegal occupation of the tragic island. It was firmly believed by the mambises that many arrests followed by summary executions by firing squads had resulted from this form of espionage by the Spanish priesthood. The de Céspedes family squarely shunned the Catholic Church and the majority of its members were viewed as "Free Thinkers."

Charles' Church of England was nowhere in sight of Media Luna, or, for that matter, of Manzanillo, the nearest city. The age of the bride was less of a problem – fourteen and fifteen-year-old girls were commonly married to older, well-to-do gentlemen in this age. The de Céspedes agreed to a civil marriage and ceremony without much fanfare in Media Luna, which was well attended by the Beattie family and many Ten Years War mambi veterans in 1893. Charles pointedly registered the civil marriage with the British Colonial Office in Kingston, Jamaica.

Adolfina and Charles were a strikingly beautiful couple in Media Luna. She appeared more mature than her age suggested, and soon after marriage, she was in the "family way." Richard Beattie could not get his eyes off her and visited the couple as often as he could; he declared his intentions much later, in difficult times, after Charles' death, as you will learn later.

Her first-born in 1894 was a beautiful son who was properly baptized Charles, like his father. The odious Spanish Empire required by imperial edict a Roman Catholic Church baptismal certificate archived in the public records. Young Charles was also registered in Kingston, Jamaica, as a British subject.

The family prospered in this pastoral setting until early 1895 when news slowly reached Media Luna that the insurgency had survived, that it was organizing actively and had gained momentum, money, and strength in the United States. A renewed Junta Revolucionaria Cubana in New York, under the leadership of Jose Martí, had recruited the famed Generals Máximo Gómez and Antonio Maceo and other principals. Rumor had it that it was now well financed by rich donations from prosperous exiles and many commoners alike.

A Financial Genius

Some of the petitions for insurgency financial support were rejected out of hand. Some of the rich approached by the Junta offered well-thought-out explanations for their refusal to give or otherwise support the insurgency. To my knowledge, the most prescient anecdote involved the Cuban leader José Martí and Don Andrés, Count Duany, in his elegant Ansonia Hotel suite in Columbus Circle, New York, not far from his stable of horses, one snowy Manhattan afternoon, as told to me by Andrés J. Duany, his son.[13]

Don Andrés Duany was the scion of one of the most prominent families of the ancient city of Santiago de Cuba. Educated in Paris and famously wealthy, he was a Cuban Andrew Carnegie with homes in Santiago de Cuba and Habana, apartments in New York and Paris. He was a member of high social circles in all of them, and had an uncanny knack for succeeding in business ventures when others, mere mortals, failed miserably.

Cultured and supremely polished and civilized, he ushered in José Martí and his other two companions, all known by the international press. Martí and his companions, in their own inimitable style, presented their case for a free Cuba and pointed out why it would be politically correct for Duany and his wife, Carmen de la Torre, owner of vast sugar cane lands and sugar mills in the north of Oriente Province, to make substantive donations to the cause of the insurgency.

Don Andrés responded in measured sentences. It was a devastating commentary reflecting his clear understanding of the future of Cuba as he saw it in that cold fall of 1895. He said that the immigrant and demographic changes in Cuba would ultimately determine its future, that the immense immigration of Spanish nationals would

---

13. The family name is derived from the Irish O'Duane who came early on to Jamaica at the turn of the 16th and 17th centuries. They achieved prominence as architect/engineers of Spanish Empire military fortresses. El Morro of the entrance of Santiago Bay was redesigned and rebuilt in 1702 by O'Duane, which later became the phonetic Duany.

bring anarchists, Marxists and socialists who would overwhelm the Nationalist Criollos, impose their ways over them, and take control of labor unions and political parties. He said that the disenfranchised freed slaves seething with rage for not being able to join the mainstream economy would join the anarchists and the Marxists, and that the so-called War of Independence would facilitate military intervention by the United States to protect their economic interests, and that all of these developments would finally result in Communism.

The Cuban patriots nervously sat through his analytical predictions and were unable to offer a convincing riposte. Martí did not effectively defend the concept of creating a Republic as envisioned by the Bayamo Mambí patriots.

When one studies Castro's Cuba today, it is clear Don Andrés was predicting the ordered but failed Communist state that was to come in the 20th century and hold sway into the following century.

Don Andres' uncanny sense of foretelling major events in 1895 was not limited to predicting the Communist takeover of Cuba. In 1928-29, he foresaw the advent of the Great Depression and sold all of his major capital investments before the financial debacle, which included the Santiago Ice Company and assorted real estate holdings before the collapse of Wall Street.

Oh yes, he lost some, but he was poised for a come back. Later, he bought all of them back at greatly reduced prices.

Much later, when the Rockefellers, the United Fruit Company, and Fidel Castro's Spanish father bought the cheap land adjacent El Hato del Medio, his immense hacienda, he foresaw that his neighbor land grabbers would cheat their fences. He documented all of this and took them to the Supreme Court by hiring the best and brightest Habana lawyer of the day, Mr. Jose Antolin del Cueto. He won the case, of course, and got richer. For his great efforts, Don Andres named one of the townships in the center of El Hato del Medio "Cueto" to honor his lawyer. The opposing defense lawyer, Mr. Marcane, also gained equal status from this famous trial and the port village of Marcane to the north was named after him by the townspeople. His Hato del Medio plantation railroad had a terminal in Cueto and another in Marcane.

I met Don Andres when he was 90-plus years of age and I was taken by his absorbing conversation and I sensed that I was speaking with a giant intellect.

Marti and his Cuban patriots silently cursed him and left without a penny. Despite difficulties in financing the uprising, the Cuban patriots were ready to infiltrate the coast of Oriente and start anew. This time they were sure to win and did.

In Oriente, Criollos were restless and consumed with hatred and there was talk of revenge. The de Céspedes, once again plagued by their demons and their anxieties, feared for their safety. The peninsulares, and worse, the voluntarios, held open contempt for the "Englishman" as well as his young wife, who hailed from a race of "troublemakers," and worse, were secret "mambises." As for Adolfina, she had absolutely no love for Spaniards, none whatsoever. She saw no redeeming qualities in Spanish people and they were of no use to her. Life hurriedly became rather uncomfortable for the young married couple.

Charles looked for a safe haven for his family away from the vortex of the impending insurgency. Through his connections with his Canadian brothers and the good efforts of Don Tomas Beattie, he applied and was offered a good job in the Bank of New York in Manhattan. He planned to leave Media Luna as quickly as circumstances demanded.

Boarding the Beatties' Anita and finding their way to Santiago de Cuba with their savings such as they were, the couple with the little infant, Charles, found passage to Savannah, Georgia, and arrived in New York City by train, possibly early in the summer of 1895.

A Differing View of Cuba's History

They eventually settled in a rented home in Montclair, New Jersey. It was a wood-frame house with four bedrooms, living room and ample corridors that overlooked the hilly countryside and a partial view of New York City's skyscrapers and the splendid Statue of Liberty. He commuted to Manhattan and his job at the Bank of New York. He did well in the bank, and in the following years, Charles found financial tranquility as his family grew. [14]

With 1895 came the bloody Cuban War of Independence, which was to last until the end of the Spanish American War in 1898. It was financed by the gigantic efforts of Jose Marti who was able to get contributions from exiled but sympathetic Cuban rich and the large numbers of hard working Cuban émigrés in Tampa, Key West, New York, and Latin America, principally in Mexico and Venezuela.

Adolfina could hardly manage her household, let alone have time to ponder the rapidly developing events of the Cuban War of Independence and the "ancient animosity" between America and Spain that many believe exists to this day.

A few of the veterans of the Ten Years' War criticized Marti's efforts and nicknamed him "Capitán Araña" because he lacked battle experience. This was a most unfair designation.

He was to prove his courage under battle with General Maximo Gomez's forces in Oriente Province but was killed in a firefight with superior numbers of Spanish regulars in Dos Rios. It was an irreplaceable loss. He was taken to the Santa Ifigenia Cemetery of Santiago de Cuba where he is buried and honored by his compatriots.

The Spanish Empire struck back at the insurgency in 1896 with an increasing force of continental regular soldiers of the line. The

---

14. In Montclair there followed two pregnancies with one survival: Adolfina gave birth to Carmen in 1897, another year of great upheaval. The beautiful infant died of intermittent fevers and enteritis a year later in 1898. The next child in 1899 was a healthy red-headed girl, a Scottish lass if ever there was one, named Elizabeth, who lived to be 104. She became an American citizen by birthright, although I am sure she was also registered in the British Consulate, as her father did with all of his children. George A. Greig was born in 1901, who at age of three months died of dehydration that followed a gastro enteric disease of unknown cause. In 1902 Richard Greig was born, a very healthy and thriving son who survived to his senior years.

historian Pedro Roig has documented that by "February 1898, when the last contingent of 7,186 men landed in Cuba, a total of 203,449 troopers made it the largest European army ever to cross the Atlantic to America."[15]

Mambi attack on Spanish Fortin

Wikipedia says this of General Weyler: "In 1895 he was given the Grand Cross of Maria Cristina for his command of troops in the Philippines. In 1896 when rebellion was in full swing in Cuba, Weyler was named governor with powers to suppress the insurgency and return the island to political order and the sugar industry to greater

15. Young Winston Churchill alongside a comrade in arms, both recent graduates of the Royal Military Academy of Sandhurst, obtained permission from the Spanish Governor General in 1895 to observe the nascent hostilities in the manigua near Trinidad in the center of the narrow and long island. It was their first exposure to flying bullets fired by insurgent guerrillas and their tactics. Churchill initially sympathized with the Cuban insurgency but gradually changed his mind, possibly because of his penchant for Empire. He again changed his mind after many years and looked on with sympathy of the efforts of the rebels.

profitability."

Governor of Cuba, General Valeriano Weyler y Nicolau, launched a highly successful campaign that reigned-in some of General Máximo Gómez's and General Maceo's successes. This was done by partitioning the narrow Island of Cuba from north to south with multiple lines of many small fortresses (las trochas) that slowed or sometimes impeded the light cavalry movements of the Cuban Liberation Army to take the fight to the Province of Habana from east to west into the heart of Spanish imperial power.

In addition, a very important Weyler strategy was the construction of many field concentration camps to isolate the peasantry and other logistic supporters of the guerrillas. The so-called "reconcentration camps" had been used with some success in the Spanish campaign against Filipino nationalist guerrillas. General Weyler, a veteran of the Philipino rebellion, made masterful use of the camps, which were purposely designed to starve and kill the Criollo logistic support base of the Cuban Liberation Army. These camps were principally operated in Oriente Province where the guerrillas had held the Imperial troopers in check. Conservatively, more than 175,000 Criollo peasants died in these camps in less than two years. Significantly, the majority of the casualty count was in Oriente Province in the East.[16]

In the interim, a New York newspaper reported that Evangelina Cossío, Adolfina's first cousin, was captured with documents and money for the insurgents and incarcerated in a Habana prison. She escaped in a cause celebre financed by the New York Herald Tribune, was welcomed as a beautiful heroine rescued by a handsome American reporter, and was on the front pages of America's newspapers. Adolfina and Charles never got to see her in New York. After her release, Evangeline continued working for the Cuban insurgency until the

---

16. My father, Dr. Santos-Buch, was a pro bono physician to Doña Serrat, a Catalonian immigrant and a survivor of a reconcentration camp erected some four "leagues" from El Caney and her testimony to me was difficult to believe. It was to the letter a confirmation of the Spanish atrocities. Weakened by starvation, she lost her husband and three children in the camp to dysentery and other upper respiratory infections. In gratitude to my father's attention, she gave her Santa Ifigenia Cemetery vault to him, which is our immediate family's final resting place.

Reconcentration camp liberated campesinos
(Family photo heirloom)

defeat of the Spanish Empire at war with the United States in 1898.

General Valeriano Weyler's campaign strategy was very effective and some of the insurgents withdrew from the fields of battle of the west and regrouped in Oriente Province to reconsider their plans.

During 1896 and 1897, the international press discovered the concentration camp atrocities and seriously condemned them. International pressure from the United States and most European countries forced the resignation of General Weyler and another governor of Cuba was appointed. General Valeriano Weyler y Nicolau was received with a hero's welcome in Madrid with pomp and ceremony. He was decorated and widely acclaimed throughout Spain.

The "reconcentration camps" were slowly dismantled and the financially and physically crippled Criollo peasantry returned to their burnt homes to start again. With its newly found logistical support, the insurgency successfully attacked the lines of forts and took the fight to the western provinces near the Capital.

In Montclair, this news was received well; letters from Media

Luna indicated that America was about to intervene by declaring war on the Spanish Empire. The issue was settled when the American pocket battleship U.S.S. Maine, on a peaceful mission and anchored in Habana Bay, exploded without explanation. An investigation concluded that the explosion occurred outside and beneath the hull of the Maine and sabotage was suspected.[17] A state of war between Spain and the United States of America was declared shortly after.

PREPARATION FOR WAR AND STRATEGIC PLANS

Portrait of Admiral Mahan (Family photo heirloom)

The American war strategists were well-versed with Admiral Mahan's concepts and recommendations. The mainland was not to be attacked. They correctly deduced that to defeat the Spanish Empire in its colonies, the seas around the Philippines and Cuba had to be under the control of the American Pacific and Atlantic fleets to enforce an iron-clad blockade before ground troops could land near highly valued strategic targets.

Americans correctly saw that the war would not be won unless ground and mounted troops were used in coordinated landings that required the cooperation of the Philippine and Cuban insurgencies.

This coordination was gained when courageous messengers with strategic plans to facilitate troop and cavalry landings were delivered by hand to General Francisco Makabulos in Northern Luzón Island of the Philippine archipelago and to General Calixto García of the Criollo insurgency in the area of the Provincial Capital of Oriente Province,

17. Ironically, later, in the 20th century, a study by Admiral Hyman G. Rickover, the father of the American nuclear navy submarines, concluded that the explosion occurred by carbon gases in the closed coal stores of the battleship.

Santiago de Cuba. American strategists also selected generals Máximo Gómez and Calixto García as their preferred field officers to jointly battle the Spanish Army with the American Expeditionary Force. American officers were also preselected to land in Cuba and become observers with the mambi general staffs.

General Máximo Gómez had favorably impressed the American War Department when he showed daring and innovative planning in capturing the garrison of the Múcaras Fort at the western entrance of Santiago Bay during the Ten Years War. He had held the fort for several days in open defiance of the Morro Castle's batteries on the opposite side of the bay entrance and the superior numbers of Spanish forces.

General Gómez was also known for his expertise in artillery deployments and troop movements under fire.

He was regarded by the War Department as the best field officer of the Cuban Liberation Army by far. Gómez was assigned the important task of cutting off the Empire troops' efforts to relieve and supply the Santiago Spanish garrisons under attack.

General Calixto García's high reputation rested principally on the ferocity of his successful frontal assaults of several garrisons of Oriente Province, like Holguin and Tunas (See Appendix). He was courageous, quick and nimble in close, man-to-man combat. He was very tall and his troopers idolized him when they saw him unperturbed in a seemingly desperate situation, which he invariably would win.

He was assigned to be the "Point of the Spear" with his mambi division of about 1,500 well-armed troopers to operate with the specialized American regiment under the command of General William Ludlow.

The Atlantic Royal Spanish Navy was not prepared for war. A squadron was readied as best and fast as possible. The Spanish Imperial Squadron was placed under the command of Admiral Pascual Cervera y Topete, an able veteran, and well known and respected by American strategists.[18] The Spanish war ships were faster than the Americans but they outgunned the Spaniards with bigger, more powerful cannons. The American gun crews were also faster and more accurate.

Out of coal in Puerto Rico, Cervera's squadron finally refueled in Santiago de Cuba. Because of pure luck rather than good military intelligence, the American Atlantic Fleet and the Tampa troop ships arrived near Siboney Beach just east of Santiago, almost at the same time that the Cervera Squadron entered Santiago Bay to the West.

Cavalry Charge at Desmayo, Camaguey

(Family photo heirloom)

The entire Squadron was bottled up in Santiago de Cuba Bay and a blockade was established as previously foreseen. To complete the blockade, Lieutenant Hobson, commanding the Merrimac, sank his ship under heavy fire near the narrowed entrance of Santiago Bay. However, the current and the momentum of the ship carried it away from the channel and the plan failed. The Spanish fortress' firepower had damaged Merrimack's steering capacity. Hobson survived his ordeal.

The hastily organized American Expeditionary Force of roughly 15,000 soldiers and cavalry landed with little opposition in Siboney and Daiquiri Beaches some twenty kilometers east of Santiago. A

18. By far the best account of Admiral Cervera heroics, who survived this ordeal, is Luis Gómez y Amador's "La Odisea del Almirante Cervera y Su Escuadra". It is highly recommended because it is a lucid, fair and balanced naval record.

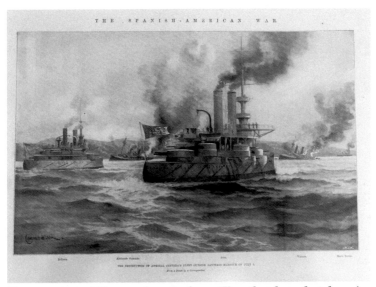

Destruction of Cervera's squadron (Family photo heirloom)

coordinated pincer maneuver by the Cuban insurgent General Máximo Gómez surrounded the western and northern approaches to the city. The Spanish imperial army did not breach the encirclement and the intended reinforcements failed to reach the Provincial Capital.

Santiago was isolated and under bombardment. The siege brought hunger, doubt, despair and fear to the population as sporadic rounds hit several portions of the ancient city.

Under the gallant Admiral Cervera, the squadron fired up the boats and steamed to certain destruction, one by one, as they exited the narrow mouth of the bay, and the cannonade from the more modern and better-armed American fleet sank or incapacitated, every one of them.

Importantly, as the survivors swam ashore, Cuban guerrilla snipers picked off the drowning sailors in a terrible and cruel act, later condemned by both sides.

A naval task force with small vessels rapidly attacked the city of Cienfuegos to disrupt the communications provided by under sea cable from Santiago de Cuba. They failed in their assigned mission.

Generals Ludlow and Garcia before the El Viso assault
(Family photo heirloom)

The Battle for Santiago resulted in the disabling and sinking of the entire Spanish Atlantic Navy, the bombardment of the city, and the American ground troops' triumph of the San Juan Hill and Kettle Hill Battles.[19]

A key Spanish fort, El Viso, under attack principally by Cuban insurgents under General Calixto García, had to be taken to protect the northern (right) flank of the American and Cuban frontal attack by foot soldiers on the embattlements of the high ground of San Juan and Kettle Hills.

El Viso/El Caney became the sites of the bloodiest battle between Cubans under General García and Spanish Empire troopers under Brigadier General Joaquín Vara de Rey. Together with American

19. The site of Kettle Hill is obscured by modern urban sprawl. The confiscated Sacred Heart Convent and surrounding houses are atop the Hill today. No monuments honoring this battle are found.

Official photo of Brigadier
General Joaquin Vara de Rey
(Family photo heirloom)

forces under U.S. Army Brigadier General William Ludlow, Cuban troopers finally defeated the Spanish brigade-sized garrison. The elite, five-hundred-trooper strong Spanish garrison fought the insurgents and American soldiers to the last man, and their gallant stand delayed by several hours the final American frontal assault on Spanish garrisons and embattlements of San Juan Hill and Kettle Hill.

Like Lt. Colonel Armstrong Custer's 7th Cavalry Regiment destruction in the Battle of the Little Big Horn, the defeat of the Spanish Empire at El Viso/Caney Battle is the turning point of the land War of 1898.

Spanish General Vara de Rey was awarded the highest honor bestowed to heroic warriors under fire, "La Cruz Laureada de San Fernando" and received honored commendations for his heroism from his Cuban and American counterparts.

There were many American, Spanish and Cuban Criollo casualties. A regiment of African American "Dog Soldiers" and the Rough Riders of Teddy Roosevelt fought gallantly and well. Many of the elite Ivy League recruits in the Rough Riders Regiment shed their blood in the skirmish with Spanish troopers.

The first American killed in the Spanish War was Columbia College graduate Hamilton Fish, a wealthy young New Yorker, in an ambush at Las Guasimas. Roosevelt had been able to recruit over fifty men with backgrounds similar to his own in the Rough Riders Regiment.[20]

20. The core of the Rough Riders aristocrats was mustered from graduates of the Ivy League colleges of Northeast America. They were not sycophants of so-called imperialists who professed to take care of the colored masses worldwide. They were, indeed, young adventurers, much like Winston Churchill's action

A Differing View of Cuba's History

As the Battle of Santiago was won, Admiral Dewey in the Pacific subdued and surrendered the Pacific Spanish Imperial Navy in Manila Bay, the Philippines.

The short-lasting Spanish War started and ended in 1898 and with the American Occupation of Cuba, peace and order ensued.

The effete and ignorant Secretary of State, John Milton Hay, in a letter to Colonel Roosevelt, called it "a splendid little war" in a monumental overestimate: In realistic terms, it was the end of a long-armed process for independence from Imperial Spain beginning with the Ten Years' War of 1868 and ending with the War of Independence of 1895, started by Criollo patriots who paid an immense price in destruction, confiscation of properties, misery, exile, countless lives and ravaged fortunes. Colonel Theodore Roosevelt understood this very well.

The mischaracterization by Secretary Hay is a lasting, disjointed disservice to Cuba and America's heroes who together had shed their blood unto the island's soil for the higher cause of liberty.

The United States had come into the process late, when there was a virtual standoff between the Imperial Spanish troopers and the Criollo insurgents. It was the daring and decisive strikes by the Criollo insurgency cavalry by Generals Maximo Gómez and Calixto García that weakened Spain's Empire Expeditionary forces and allowed the ease of the American landings by cutting off Spanish army reinforcements.

In modern times, the ridiculous sobriquet, "a splendid little war," became a rallying call by the worldwide Revolutionary Left to underline American arrogance and capitalist expansionist plans for "the take-over of Hispanic America." It has been attributed to President Theodore Roosevelt in a glaring historical error. The reader will come across it many times in the perusal of the Cuban story.

After the signature of a peace treaty and some costly missteps,

---

to observe the Cuban Insurgency for Liberty. They advocated clear Liberal ideas compelled by General Weyler's atrocities and nothing more.

The Violent Country

Harvard graduate General Leonard Wood, M.D., a veteran of the Indian Wars, was early appointed governor of Oriente Province for the period of rapid reconstruction and prosperity that followed. Other American generals and their civil counterparts in Habana and other venues were slow and feckless and did not do as well as Wood[21] and were dismissed by Washington later.

General Leonard Wood's widely recognized successful role in the appeasement of Santiago de Cuba became the paradigm of American occupation forces in Puerto Rico and the Philippines. His success was directly related to his ability to appoint Cubans and even Spaniards in key positions in the transition years and to his iron hand.

Importantly, as you will see later in this narrative, during the America occupation justice was not brought to the voluntarios and other officers of the Spanish Imperial army guilty of atrocities against mambi troopers, their officers and the peasantry of the interior. The voluntarios and many Spaniards who had played major roles in the Weyler atrocities never paid for their heinous deeds, and furthermore, faded away from the public eye and, later became part of a prevalent odious anti-American opposition in the general population that severely hampered the road to democracy during the free Republican Government years.

A very important gesture of gratitude, primus inter pares, was honoring General Calixto García, his general staff, and his Cuban Liberation Army in a grand parade, jointly with General Wood, through Santiago's main streets. This helped to restore the honor of Criollo patriots after their disdainful and arrogant omission from the initial surrender ceremonies of the capture of the city at the end of hostilities.

Later, the Cuban army was reduced and re-organized by General

21. "Leonard Wood, Rough Rider, Surgeon, Architect of American Imperialism" by Jack McCallum is an excellent source of the Harvard educated MD and celebrated soldier. The Constitution of 1902 is regarded by some scholars as the best of several written in the Republic's short and violent history. The 1902 Cuban Constitution is parallel to that of the successful US Constitution. Of interest, Wood developed a brain tumor, which was partially resected by famed Dr. Harvey Cushing of the Peter Bent Brigham Harvard Hospital without success.

Wood and Cuba's mambises and the peasantry was redeployed to their countryside homes. A "Guardia Rural" was mustered and armed, the depleted public treasures of Oriente were restored within the year, sanitation and sewerage facilities were constructed, public water service was designed and built, and streets in ill-repair for centuries under the Spanish boot were paved.

Oriente's public coffers, depleted by the rapacious Spanish authorities, were again filled to the satisfaction of Cuban authorities and native businesses prospered.

None of these achievements would have happened if Don Emilio Bacardi Moreau, the Santiago patriot whose son, Emilito, had gallantly fought with General Antonio Maceo's cavalry in the Western Front, was appointed by Wood and later elected mayor of Santiago.

Don Emilio's input in the reconstruction after the cruel and bitter war and that of his Cuban and Spanish allies was invaluable and memorable.[22] Later, General Wood was named governor of Cuba and moved to Habana, where, as was his style, he again recruited prominent Cuban intellectuals and politicians who helped write the Cuban Constitution of 1902. He surrendered the embattled island to the freely elected government of President Estrada Palma in Habana on May 20, 1902, and a newly representative republic was born in the Western Hemisphere.

Don Tomas Beattie, back in his holdings, again offered work to young Charles F. Greig and plans were made to move back to his property in La Caridad de Macaca in 1903.

Charles moved decisively. The first thing he did with his considerable savings was to buy a prefabricated British-designed bungalow via a Montgomery Ward catalogue to ship to Manzanillo as fast as possible.[23] It arrived in Media Luna that summer ready to be

22. The best book par excellence documenting the patriotic efforts of the famous family is "Bacardi and the Long Fight for Cuba" by Tom Gjelten.

23. The bungalow design had been in use by the British in India for a long time because it was cool and airy. The Greig bungalow in Media Luna still exists today. Don Tomas and Clarita indeed did marry fulfilling his youthful prediction and it is believed she had two issues who died a few months after birth.

assembled.

The trip back to Media Luna was long, difficult and hazardous with the three children who were a tiring handful. The oldest, Charles, was the calming soul to four-year-old Lizzie and the infant Richard. At the Media Luna quay, the family was received with open arms by Ana Tamayo y Tamayo, Herminia de Céspedes Tamayo, Randolph and Pedro Cossío y de Céspedes, and other family members. Don Thomas Beattie and his sons, Richard and Arthur, were also in the receiving line of the Greig family. To the dismay of the attendants, beautiful Adolfinita, with tears streaming down her face, announced that she was in the family way again. Herminia had made arrangements for temporary lodgings in Media Luna.

The services of the freed slave Narcisa (Sisa) were acquired and gradually their confusing excitement subsided and Charles was again a dynamo in the Isabel Sugar Mill. He noted the simple burial site of Don Tomas' wife, Isabel, constructed near the mill and learned she had died of cancer. To his surprise, he was ordered by Don Tomas to ride to the large farm holdings of Clara de Céspedes to accompany her during her visit by way of a quitrin trip to Media Luna from the casona at Belic, some six hours away. He rapidly deduced that Don Tomas' intent was to marry his long-time muse, Clarita, now a widow.

It wasn't very long after their arrival that Charles began to assemble the bungalow with the great help of local laborers, masons, and carpenters. Charles thrived in adversity and his serious, older son and namesake was by his side at every opportunity.

There is every indication that Charles was thoroughly enjoying his job with Don Tomas and Richard. The youngest brother, Arthur, was now in Media Luna, working in their enormous holdings. The mill employed a very efficient administrative team and it was apparent to Charles that sugar was king and the mainstay of the fledgling Cuban republic.

George Greig Cossío was born in the bungalow in the summer of 1904 without any difficulties. He was as fair and handsome as his father, sharply contrasting his coloring with the swarthy Spanish-looking Richard, who was a highly active and curious lad, handsome and enterprising in other ways. Gradually, Charles and Adolfina became familiar with the quirks and issues of the bungalow and learned to use all of its facilities. They settled in this pastoral setting surrounded by sugarcane fields and fruit trees. The issue of schooling was arranged with grandmother Ana and Adolfina's sister in law, Elvira Esturo, Randolph's wife. Home schooling, under the illumination of kerosene lamps, was a very serious business with this family.

The family progressed as planned. Charles bought four caballerias from the de Céspedes family for $400 and Don Tomas allowed him to use another six adjacent caballerias, all planted with sugarcane. Eleven-year-old Charles, the oldest and sturdiest, even though home-schooled, worked on the small sugar cane farm with his father, who was otherwise very much occupied with the business. Life was looking good in these brief golden and peaceful years of the young Republic.

In the fall of 1906 Adolfinita announced that she was pregnant again. She could sense that her child was strong and healthy and she was happy and looking forward to the new addition to her thriving family. She noted that little Charles, now thirteen going on fourteen, was a handsome, muscular lad, devoted and hard-working, who was rapidly progressing in his home schooling. She asked herself, "What will he be in this brutal land?" She dismissed these disconcerting thoughts frequently by paying attention to running her busy house-hold. Besides, she found great comfort with her faithful ever-loving Scottish giant at her side.

He was at his prime at thirty-seven years of age. She was twenty-eight years old and in splendid health.

The idyllic setting was to change in a fleeting, tragic moment.

An Early Death

The moonless night over Manzanillo was hot and humid. There was no breeze coming through the hospital window. Charles Finlay Greig jack-knifed on the soiled hospital bed, was on his side, and from time to time, hiccupped coffee-ground vomit on the towel Adolfinita brought to his parched lips. He was sweating profusely and tried to hold his gaze on her ministrations. It was a losing battle; he could not hold his constant vomiting. He laid on the soiled bed covered with sweat and tried to focus on the kerosene lamp hanging from the sill of the hospital window. He tried to warm his numb hands, rubbing them weakly. What was wrong?

How did this get started? What did Dr. Sanchez say?[24] He couldn't remember. He did not want to remember.

Suddenly, he jerked up and projectile-vomited into the porcelain washbasin with a splash of bright red blood. With a sardonic smile and awful pallor, he rolled up his eyes and died, falling from the hospital bed.

Adolfinita brought her hands to her face, screamed, and collapsed.

Following Charles' death by a few weeks, on July 14, 1907, Adolfinita, with the ever-present Richard Beattie at her side, easily delivered in Manzanillo a beautiful baby girl with alert steel-blue eyes and fine Scottish features, to be named Herminia Adolfina Greig Cossío y de Céspedes (a.k.a. Lala, my mother to be).

As she laid with Herminia on her breast, the indomitable Adolfina shivered involuntarily as she contemplated an uncertain and defenseless future.

---

24. Dr. Sánchez is Celia Sánchez's father, Fidel Castro's companion and secretary in the Sierra Maestra Mountains during the Cuban Insurrection 1956-1959. Charles Finlay Greig was interred in Manzanilo's cemetery. A family member discovered at the end of the 20th century that local authorities had destroyed his tomb.

CHAPTER 4.

◊ The Cultural, Political And Economic Impacts Of A Massive Spanish Immigration (1878-1936).

Glossary :

Clan – A tribe of genetically related Scotts.

Sept – A maternal separate branch of a Clan member.

Shire – Range

Hato – The largest area unit of the Spanish language.

Medio – Middle

Trochas – A military line of small fortresses.

Guardia Rural – A Cuban Republic Army unit

Caballería – Equivalent measure of 33 acres.

Casona – A manor.

Manigua – Cuba's thick jungle and underbrush.

Indenpendistas – Criollos who favored Independence from Spain.

Gachupines – First generation sycophantic Cubans of Spanish parents.

A Differing View of Cuba's History

Peninsulares – Newly arrived immigrant Spaniards.

Catalanes – Ethnic origins from Catalonia.

Gallegos – Spaniards from Galicia, also used as a derogatory term by criollos to designate all Spaniards.

Voluntarios – Paramilitary organization of pro-Spanish Empire sycophants used by Spain's Governors General to terrorize Criollo dissidents, often operating outside standing law.

Diezmar – The firing squad execution of ten (diez) randomly selected prisoners.

The Santos Rodriguez brothers, Angel and Manuel of Fermoselles, La Mancha, just on the border of Portugal, had decided to emigrate to Cuba, specifically to San Luis where others from Fermoselles, like the Guerra boys, had gained prosperity. It was 1890 and Spain's economy had taken a dangerous downturn and severely impacted the families of Fermoselles.

As Spain's economy declined and failed, it was a very good decision to leave and seek fortune in the then very prosperous Cuba. The city of San Luis was a communication and agricultural center near Boniato's Gap (Puerto Boniato) that allowed commercial traffic in a precarious dirt road, such as it was at the time, between Santiago de Cuba, the second largest city of Cuba, and the sugar mills, sugar cane plantations, and the wealthy land owners to the north.

By the 1890s, the Ten Years' War promoted by the Independistas in Cuba had been over for some time and Spain had gotten rid of the troublemakers, particularly those irksome de Céspedes, Agramontes and Maceos. Other troublemakers who had actually believed in a republican representative government for Cuba were either in voluntary exile or dead.

An armistice had been signed in 1878 and Criollos, who had sought safety and tranquility in the United States, Central America, and elsewhere, were slowly returning to their homeland to start again. The Spanish Empire had confiscated the properties of Cuban patriots and Europeans bought large arable land tracks, businesses and homes at very favorable prices. The large land holdings of the de Céspedes, Aguilera, Agramonte and those of many other dead patriots were put up for public auction bidding in *The New York Times*. Americans and Europeans pounced on them.

The war, in spite of all of the terrifying calamities, had only engaged a small proportion of the native population estimated at the very most, optimistically, around 20 percent.[25] The overwhelming majority of Euro-Cubans, particularly around the governor's city of Habana, greatly favored the iron rule of the mother country. There was political order in this new era of relative peace under the Spanish boot.

The Ten Years' War had brought another salutary result, which was the eventual abolition of slavery initiated by the government of the Republic in Arms. The Colonial Office in Madrid had reluctantly supported this major proclamation by the Independistas overtime. To the shame of Spaniards and their island supporters, Cuba's slaves were officially freed by Spain very late in 1886.[26]

Ten of thousands of freed Africans entered the labor market. The large injection of foreign money and cheap labor produced a booming post-war economy on the island. Like hundreds of thousands of

25. This figure is much lower than those quoted by several different authors. My mother, Herminia Greig Cossío, believed that those higher figures were inflated by patriotic fervor and were not based on fact.

26. Brazil was the last of the European colonies in America to free African slaves. Brazil's slaves were freed at the turn of the 19th century.

their compatriots, the Santos Rodríguez brothers wanted to tap into the booming Cuban economy.

Since Cuba had been a Spanish colony, there were no legal impediments to Spanish emigration, and so began the largest transfer ever of a people and their culture in the millions to the embattled island.

From the end of the Ten Years' War in 1878 to 1936, just before the Spanish Civil War, not less than three million Spaniards migrated to Cuba, significantly changing the demographics of the native island population, which in the 1870s stood at about two and half million, if that.

Maturin M. Ballou in his *History of Cuba* (1854) did a "statistical account" and estimated the total population, including slaves, at 1.5 million in 1854, based on numbers compiled from the previous five years. In the archives of the Cuban Research Institute, Professor Nicholas J. Quintana's study also estimates that three million Spanish immigrants came to Cuba by 1936.

These figures are not out of line.

The bulk of Spanish immigrants settled in the governor's city of Habana and the outlying cities and villages of the western Habana Province.[27] The uppity Spanish immigrants had become the majority of Euro-Cubans in a few decades and they became the most important sector of the Cuban population since they were economically prosperous and politically savvy. Voluntarios, peninsulares and gachupines boasted rights, which Criollos believed they did not have and had not earned.

It is now quite evident that during this period, most Catalonian

27. When the Spanish Empire decided to avoid British and French privateers that raided their gold laden galleons as they navigated to Santiago for careening and provisions for the long trip home, Habana and the East Coast of Spanish Florida was selected as the safest route of choice to cross the Atlantic Ocean early on in the 16th century. The City of Habana prospered at a very rapid pace in the 16th and 17th centuries, out stripping the rest of the Island in architecture, Spanish culture and teeming wealth. Habana was the Spanish Governor's City and later, USA General Leonard Wood's Governor headquarters during the American Occupation years (1898- 1901). Today, Habana in spite of the assaults of time and the deplorable Communist regime, the magnificence of the capital city is quite impressive.

immigrants went to Oriente Province where earlier Catalans had already established deep roots, as early as the first decades of the 18th century. Another enormous group comprised of Galicians, immigrated to the Western Provinces, principally to La Habana, on the north shore facing the Florida Straits.

On the other hand, Castilians like the Santos Rodríguez of Fermoselles, Basques, Andaluces and Asturianos were about equally divided between east and west and formed a distinct minority.

Seeing all of these developments, Cuban Criollos watched with great alarm and suspicion the arrival of droves of "peninsulares" who, along with "gachupines," firmly believed they were a step above them and were determined to impose their Spanish culture. The feared Criollo-hating voluntarios, a para-military organization subsidized by the Spanish boot, had been formed from disaffected peninsulares who greatly influenced the Empire Governors General over time and ruled with an iron fist by the non-too-subtle demands of the financially important newcomers.[28]

Angel Santos Rodríguez and his brother Manuel, upon arriving in San Luis, Oriente Province, immediately set up two stores. Manuel ran the general store and Angel managed the other, La Borla. La Borla sold bolts of fabrics from the United States, Japan and China. The northern Oriente Province Port of Antilla was thriving.

The wives of the wealthy Spanish bourgeoisie and the newly landed gentry of San Luis were his principal clients. As time passed by, the general store was sold and the intellectual Manuel Santos Rodríguez moved to Habana in 1898 to look for a more cultured

---

28. Voluntarios: A Spanish government subsidized para-military force headquartered in Habana with units distributed in the six Provinces of Cuba. The Voluntarios were sycophants of Spanish Imperial Rule with almost autonomous powers used by the Governor General to contain rebellious behavior in the cities. Voluntarios rarely fought the Insurgency in fields of battle. By far the worse act of the Voluntarios was to force the sentencing of ten Habana medical students accused of defiling the burial monument of one of the directors of the Voluntarios. They were guilty of nothing else than horsing around the cemetery with no ill intent. None of the students were in the Insurgency. All ten were selected from their class randomly (diezmar), and after being declared innocent in the first court hearing, the Voluntarios forced a retrial and their immediate execution by firing squad in Habana, 27 November 1871. It was not Spain's finest hour.

European-based ambience. The more pragmatic, hard-working Angel Santos and La Borla, on the other hand, did well in San Luis and prospered financially and socially, both with rich Criollos and the recently arrived nouveau riche Spanish immigrants.

Don Angel rapidly developed a circle of friends in San Luis who socialized in the tiny "Plaza Mayor" on weekends. He was a very serious and generous man, utterly honest and formal, with a bushy dark upper-lip moustache that called out for respect and confidence. You could say that he was a distinguished – if rude – Castilian with strong and taciturn features, probably reflective of the arid Fermoselles and La Mancha, cooled by the meandering El Duero River and bordered by the fine vineyards nearby.

This was a man who was listened to and was known to be a careful analyst and truthful, not prone to giving in to the easy exaggerations of the loud native-borne "Criollos" who habitually moved their hands to closely emphasize every idea that crossed their minds.

Don Ángel was rapidly taking a curious admiration of the United States of America's entrepreneurial inventiveness and confounding vitality and exceptionalism. Most of his commerce with America was by ship from Nipe Bay in the north or from Santiago in the south of San Luis and the merchandise was shipped to Savannah, and then by rail to Atlanta or New York. Another United States-bound shipping port was Manzanillo on the Golfo de Guacanayabo in southwest Oriente. The commercial and communication hub in San Luis in central Oriente Province was, after all, America's news.

Don Ángel was beginning to entertain the idea of educating his children in the United States and not in Habana or in Europe. This was an almost heretical idea among the Euro-Cubans of his day and certainly among the "peninsulares." Needless to say, the concept was anathema to voluntarios. Don Ángel Santos Rodriguez's newly found friend, Don Luis Mestre, of the drug store just down Main Street a ways, was also a well-respected and recent Catalonian émigré, who publicly praised the formidable achievements and discoveries of the

"Colossus of the North," as the leftist Cuban liberal Jose Martí tagged the United States. They began to look into its educational system, which was deemed better than that of Great Britain, France, or Spain.

The years following his San Luis arrival were marked by prosperity, and by and by, Don Angel met Señorita María Buch Rodríguez, who, not even in his wildest dreams, would he ever think of marrying. Indeed, María Buch Rodríguez was everything else that he wasn't.

The Buch family first arrived in Santiago de Cuba from Catalonia, Spain, in 1770, when Santiago Buch y Molas emigrated from the village of Calella in the Province of Gerona, which has a northwest frontier with Andorra and a southeast frontier with France. At this time, Santiago was beginning to wax and wane in importance to Habana, which was rising and predominating.

The Germanic names like Buch were part and parcel of many Catalans in large numbers who were to make Santiago their lasting home. Don Santiago Buch became very rich and it is said that at the end of his life, he owned more than one hundred African slaves. It is important to know that Don Santiago's consequential family came to be widely recognized for its intellectual and financial contributions to the development of Santiago de Cuba and the city of Holguín.

The Buch are contrarians – even to this day – but some easily integrated with Criollos and Spaniards and entered mainstream Santiago. They developed a well-founded reputation of being very intelligent, persistent, and immensely interested in education in a city, which lacked good secular schools and failed to sponsor the fine arts.

The Catholic Church in Santiago was fanatically adherent to the cause of the Spanish Empire and received generous financial support from it and held to the notion that the only schools worth their salt were theirs.[29] The belief that the Catholic Church was the

---

29. When I read a collection of letters of the Catholic Nuns of "Siervas de Maria" order to their relatives in Spain during this period I was amazed by the deep hatred expressed by them against the Mambi insurgency.

key to salvation was a powerful inducement to attend their schools because the majority of Criollos, of all sorts of racial lineages and social standing, did not attend them.

The Spanish Empire had given monies to the Roman Catholic Church and their schools for centuries, and had not promoted a public school system for Criollo children.[30] Following the temerity shown during the Ten Years' War, Criollos questioned the meaning of salvation.

"Salvation, exactly, from what?" they averred. And the answers they learned were not very satisfactory. In face of their violent history, they often thought that perhaps God had long left their beloved "island in the stream."

Don Luis Buch Rodríguez changed all of that in ancient Santiago de Cuba. By the late 19th century, the intellectual leader by force of his strong personality in this very challenging family was the mambí Colonel Don Luis Buch, a self-educated veteran of the Ten Years' War (1868-1878) and later, a veteran of the War of Independence with General Calixto García (1895-1898).

He spoke Italian and German, as well as English. To the chagrin of Spaniards and other devout Roman Catholics, he read the Bible, was a Third-Degree Master Mason, and like most of the veteran officers of the Ten Years' War, he was a free thinker. He distrusted the Catholic Church, which had sided with the Empire.

Don Luis had established a well-deserved reputation even among Spaniards, who vehemently swore never to support the Republic in Arms. He, along with his brother Antonio, was a consultant for the occupying American Forces under Colonel Leonard Wood (1898-1902) at the end of the Cuban-Spanish-American War of 1898, and assuredly met Colonel Theodore Roosevelt. His brother, Don Antonio Buch, recruited by Wood, was a brilliant engineer graduate of the University of Paris who designed and built the Charco Mono Dam

---

30. The Catholic Church support of statist tyrannies has a long history since the condemnation of the Magna Carta by Pope Innocent III.

that supplies Santiago de Cuba with water to this day.

He liked to hunt and was a sharp shooter with his Remington repeater to the delight of Wood. His home had a library that was the envy of many well-to-do. He was, during his times, the image one may have of a friendly, husky sort of a person. In this antiquated colonial city, he was a man for all seasons, a man you would like to have by your side facing any kind of challenge or danger and who stood by you, and yet, a man of change. He liked and admired the progressive ideas of Theodore Roosevelt developed during his presidency.

At the end of his busy and tumultuous life, Don Luis founded a secular school modeled after a French military school named Juan Bautista Sagarra, in honor of another mambí who believed in secularism and military discipline that Criollos sorely lacked. This action broke the Spanish Catholic Church monopoly of Santiago's school system.

The secular school quickly became known for its extremely high, no-nonsense, scholastic standards and its discipline.[31] If you happened to have a Buch somewhere in your ancestry, you were mandated to attend the Juan Bautista Sagarra School at the great risk of becoming very well-educated.

Don Luis Buch also founded the first medical emergency service of Santiago de Cuba with his own money and other family contributors. To this day, a bronze plaque "Emergencia" (Emergency Clinic) commemorates this notable contribution with his name. There are other luminaries in the Buch family, as you will learn later in this narrative.

María Buch Rodríguez, his first cousin, moved easily in this family circle, where, if you did not have it in you, you became something of an oaf or, worse, an intellectual pariah because you

---

31. Curiously, Dictator Raul Castro entered Juan Bautista Sagarra School and was in my class but lasted only two or three months because of his inability to cope with both the academics and the discipline. He was later admitted into the Jesuit safe-haven for the pampered well-to-do Spanish-Cuban children, La Escuela de Dolores, to be with his older brother, Fidel Castro. Fermín Sarabia and I were his Sagarra school monitors.

did not have the facile word or well-constructed phrase to actively participate in the mental gymnastics of vociferous and passionate family reunions, replete with recluse savants, engineers, M.D.s, lawyers, mathematicians, poets, scientists, avant-garde intellectual hermits, syphilitic patriots, musicians and tubercular writers. This was the dynamic Buch "clan."

Doña María was on the plump side with sparkling brown eyes, severely worn white hair, a soft and warm bosom, a million-dollar heart of kindness and understanding, and a teacher's patience. I remember her well and miss her to this day.

She was, of course, well read and very bright. She wanted to be an actress (she was not pretty), she played the piano (none too well) and she sang (hardly), played in community plays, and would recite Shakespeare's *Cordelia* by heart to us, the dumfounded and ignoramuses, all of her mesmerized grandchildren.

She had an extensive library with the most recent English and Spanish plays. Like her cousin, Don Luis, she became a teacher, not in Santiago de Cuba but in San Luis, not in the antiquated, slow paced, gossipy provincial capital with street vendors in horse-drawn carts filled to the brim with fruit and other produce, but in the needy countryside, close to her own people, who looked to learn how to read and write and master the mechanics of arithmetic, all sprinkled with a heavy dose of burning patriotic fervor.

And so, Don Ángel Santos Rodríguez, the taciturn and dower Castilian from La Mancha, met Doña María Buch Rodríguez, the vibrant and energetic Oriente Criolla, who was to raise five healthy children and bring excitement, controversy, and light into his sequestered and peaceful life in San Luis.

The third child was my father, Dr. A.M. Santos-Buch. He absolutely hated his given names for the rest of his life. It was a little bit like the complaint in Johnny Cash's plaintive song, "A Boy Named Sue." His was Angel Maria. His initials stand for Ángel María.

CHAPTER 5.

◊ The Platt Amendment
◊ Three Racial Wars Are Brutally Suppressed
◊ The Rise of Liberalism and Twilight of Conservatism

Glossary :

Afro-Cuban dialect:

"*Como un teinda derechito, Bruca Manigua*" – Understand me straight, Jungle Witch.

(Most of the Afro-Cuban dialect is translated in the text when necessary.)

At the onset of the Republic, the capital city of Habana, the previous quarters of the Spanish Empire's governor generals and the headquarters of the dreaded voluntarios, was a largely uninvolved spectator of the Ten Years' War, other minor conflicts, the War of Independence and General Weyler's atrocious concentration camps.

She now stood unscathed, thriving, and beautiful. With the reins of power still in her hands, she was a poor witness of the destruction, casualties, civilian deaths, hunger, misery, and slow reconstruction that was going on far from the capital in the eastern provinces.

It was harshly obvious to the Criollos in the rest of the island that the spoils of war and victory in Santiago were about to escape them to be squandered by the politicos, Spanish mercantilist barons and questionable members of the insurgency in the capital city. The insurgents' brilliant officers, who together with Jose Martí had finally defeated the empire, were dead or were too exhausted and old to be much of a force as Cuba formed political parties and organized a government under the fiats of America's pro-consul, General Leonard Wood, who favored the Euro-Cuban bourgeoisie of mostly Spanish descent. Deep in their hearts, they disliked the "American Occupiers."

General Wood held a weary eye on the uncouth Criollo veterans. The result of all of this was that the frustrated insurgency was disfranchised from the halls of power dominated by slick Habaneros with pro-Spanish sentiments.

The trials and tribulations, accentuated by the reigning violent environment and the outburst of short-lived revolutions and rebellions against the public order in the so-called "years of the republic," severely affected all Cubans, some more so than others, as you shall see in this narrative. It is, therefore, necessary to summarize Cuba's republican travails here.

We start with the Cuban and American efforts to establish a transitional political platform directed by General Leonard Wood, under the aegis of the 1902 Constitution and the Army Appropriations Act approved by the U.S. Senate in 1903.

Even when the Constitutional Assembly appointed by General Leonard Wood met in 1901 before the transfer of power to President-Elect Estrada Palma in 1902, a glimpse of the development of the failed political system that plagues Cuban politics to this day was predicted by some.

The Violent Country

The most vocal of interested American politicians of the day was Connecticut's Senator Orville H. Platt, who effectively argued in the Senate that Cuba's insurgents poorly understood what a representative republic was all about because they had been under the boot of the Spanish Empire for more than four hundred years.

He pointed out that there were no democratic institutions in the length and breadth of the violent island. He spoke of the politically and financially important conservative ex-members of the voluntarios and the equally violent and politically important left-of-center members of the insurgency forces. Spaniards who wished to be permanent residents of Cuba were allowed to do so and they controlled the island's economy.

Spaniards became Cuban citizens in a blink of the eye. In fact, the number of Spanish immigrants increased several fold from the turn of the century to shortly after 1936. Thousands of anti-American and anti-Criollo "voluntarios" had seemingly "faded away" into Cuban businesses and society with guile and effectiveness and were immune to prosecution for war crimes by a de facto amnesty imposed by America's pro-consul, General Leonard Wood. The ex-voluntarios were to exercise significant political power in the young republic.

Aggressive American investors were allowed to develop their businesses and that was added to the disparate, dangerous mix. Senator Platt further showed that there was an immense gap between the "haves" and "have nots" and he foresaw that civil unrest would ensue if nothing was done to prevent it. Senator Platt's arguments resonated not only with his constituency but also broadly in the Senate and in the House of Representatives. In 1901, the senator successfully introduced an amendment to the Army Appropriations Act, which financed and regulated the withdrawal of U.S. troops from Cuba.

Senator Platt and his colleagues from both sides of the aisle were keenly aware of the history of violent takeovers by a variety of interest groups that arose in the heat of the defeat of military occupations, such as that of the Spanish Empire. They knew that dictatorships often follow popular revolutions. Their guiding principles, taught in the U.S. Military Academy at West Point, was in the history of the French Revolution and Robespierre's Reign of Terror after the guillotining of the French king. They were determined to do all they could from the American side to prevent such horrific development.

General Leonard Wood, a Harvard graduate and the American de facto pro-consul, was very much aware of this violent possibility. Tragically, Senator Platt's misgivings and predictions were borne out right up to the Cuban Revolution of 1956 and the present day Communist dictatorship of the Castro brothers' dynasty, Fidel and Raul. As it often happened in Communist states of the 20th century, Cuba's history was changed and re-written to conform to a state-directed narrative of "imperialism," "expansionist policies," "manifest destiny," and Wall Street capitalist shenanigans that plague modern historians.

A brief summary of the history of the Platt Amendment, taken from the liberal version of Wikipedia in 2011:

The Platt Amendment of 1901 was a rider appended to the Army Appropriations Act presented to the U.S. Senate by Connecticut Republican Senator Orville H. Platt after much debate. Approved on May 22, 1903, it stipulated the conditions for the withdrawal of United States troops remaining in Cuba at the end of the Spanish-American War and defined the terms of Cuban-U.S. relations until the 1934 Treat of Relations. The Amendment ensured U.S. involvement in Cuban affairs, both foreign and domestic, and gave legal standing to U.S. claims to certain economic and military territories on the island that included present day Guantanamo Bay Naval Base.

During the Spanish-American War, the United States maintained a military arsenal in Cuba to protect private property and to mediate

Spanish-Cuban relations. In 1899, the McKinley administration was set to avert a national military dictatorial government in Cuba following the end of Spanish control.

In an effort to turn Cuba into a 'self-governing' country, American General Leonard Wood established a rural guard composed of ex-mambi fighters to maintain public order, reduce theft, and protect private property. General Wood, using the financial resources of the Cuban treasury, oversaw the development of sanitation systems, road works, and an education system. The right to vote was only extended to literate, adult, male Cubans with property at least worth $250, which excluded and disenfranchised a large portion of the Afro-Cuban population and women from participation.

The Platt Amendment received the strong support of the American Secretary of War, Elihu Root. It passed the U.S. Senate by a vote of 43 to 20. Though initially rejected by the Cuban Constitutional Assembly, the amendment was eventually accepted by a vote of 16 to 11 with four abstentions and integrated into the 1902 Constitution.

The amendment stipulated that Cuba would not transfer Cuban land to any power other than the United States, mandated that Cuba would contract no foreign debt without guarantees that the interest payments could be met from ordinary revenues, and permitted U.S. intervention in Cuban affairs when the United States deemed necessary. It also prevented Cuba from negotiating treaties with any country other than the United States that would either 'impair or tend to impair the independence of Cuba' and from allowing 'any foreign power or powers to obtain by colonization or for military or naval purposes or otherwise, lodgment in or control over any portion' of Cuban territory.

The Platt Amendment restricted Cuba in the conduct of foreign policy and commercial relations. It established that Cuba's boundaries would not include the Isle of Pines until its title could be established in a future treaty. Cuba also agreed to sell or lease to the United States 'lands necessary for coaling or naval stations at certain specified points to be agreed upon.' The amendment irrevocably leased the grounds of the Guantanamo Naval Base to the United States and provided for a formal treaty detailing all the foregoing provisions.

After U.S. President Theodore Roosevelt withdrew federal troops from the island in 1902, Cuba signed the Cuban-American Treaty (1903) outlining the role of the U.S. in Cuba and the Caribbean. Tomas Estrada Palma, who had early on favored outright annexation of Cuba by the United States, had now flip-flopped as an avid nationalist Republican and became the first elected President of Cuba on May 20, 1902."

President Teddy Roosevelt also signed a commercial treaty that, for all intents and purposes, rendered Cuba a favorite commercial client state of the United States, giving the financially strapped island great advantages, particularly with the principal all-important yearly sugar cane harvest and sugar exports that were favored with higher prices over other foreign competitors of the U.S. market.

These treaties and commercial advantages were severely criticized by resident Spaniards, ex-voluntarios, anarchists, Communists and their fellow travelers and misguided Cuban nationalists. Most liberals and the rising number of anarchists and socialists who emigrated from Spain in the previous decades also opposed what they considered American expansionism that, later, was further codified as "American Imperialism" by internationalists and the global liberal press. A lot of this was fueled by the bitterness of the defeat of the Mother Country, Spain, by the insurgency, and particularly, by armed American interventions.

To better understand the nature of the Cuban political conflicts following the defeat of the Spanish Empire in 1898 one has to view the rapid development of essentially two different ideologies: Conservatism and Liberalism.

On one hand, the majority of the mambi soldiers of color, despite of some very important exceptions, were attracted by the center-left and the outright political left that gained acceptance at the turn of the 20th century. On the other hand, conservative mambi soldiers were attracted by the traditional views of private property, free enterprise, and the free market ideas principally promulgated by the likes of de Céspedes and significantly more by Ignacio Agramonte during the existence of the Republic in Arms, that are prevalent in the United States and Europe.

Unfortunately, the core beliefs of José Martí, the strongest intellectual force of the War of 1895, did not detail a plan of a free republican government. If you review his writings, you will note, either in speeches or in his evocative lyrical writings, vague platitudes short of specifics on how the future government of Cuba ought to be after the defeat of the Spanish Empire. He dedicated more time to lash out bitterly against the "Colossus of the North" and its "Manifest Destiny," which he claimed was the warped and discredited notions of a small group of American thinkers of the mid-19th century.

It is safe to say that Martí failed to understand that American "exceptionalism" and its capacity to change had rapidly moved away by the 1890s from its discredited retrograde beliefs. After all, Colonel Teddy Roosevelt was initiating the Progressive Movement, as we know it today during his presidency. The Cuban Constitutional Assembly and the budding politicians had to go at it alone without direction (other than General Wood's) and as the phrase goes, "on the fly."

Both sides made drastic mistakes.

When you review the leaders of the young republic of 1902, you will see a diverse group of vocal contrarians. Popularity of a political figure during the days of the early republic hinged greatly by their degree of participation in the Ten Years' War and in the War of Independence of 1895-1898. Some of the Cuban veteran histories were accurate and others greatly exaggerated, with the passionate characteristic of Cubans in general. One has to keep in mind that a political figure might be a liberal and a famous combatant against Spain at the same time. On the other hand, another political figure may be a non-combatant conservative and have politically accepted credentials on the basis of having aided the insurgency at the great personal risk of imprisonment, exile, or summary execution by firing squad.

The exclusion in the first presidential election of a significant part of the Afro-Cuban population, based on literacy and property restrictions, only increased the animosity of Afro-Cubans principally in Oriente Province.

The first presidential election was soon followed by the Rebellion of "Los Negros" near the end of the Presidency of Don Tomas Estrada Palma in 1906. Los Negros insurgency radically sought an African Republic with the exclusion of all other races, which was contrary to the principles of racial and religious equality and tolerance of the Constitution of 1902.

Already there were members of the Constitutional Assembly who espoused precepts of modern "liberalism" and sympathized with Los Negros insurgents. The Rebellion of "Los Negros" took place principally in Oriente with the largest Afro-Cuban population. There were tentative steps to form a Liberal Party "with teeth" in opposition to Conservative president Don Tomas Estrada Palma.

The poorly organized rebellion was short-lived and violently suppressed by the guardia rural and elements of the Cuban army. It was poorly documented by the press, which greatly under-reported the number killed and wounded. However, this was not the only racial armed conflict of the young republic.

In truth, the political leaders of the Liberal Party throughout the subsequent Cuban governments from 1902 to 1933 always argued from the start that it was "easier to win political power by armed insurrection than by the ballot box" and they regarded subversive violence as the best option available to them to fundamentally reform Cuba. Afro-Cubans were attracted to this idea historically and this conflict between conservatives and left-wing liberals characterize most Cuban political conflicts to this day.

The Violent Country

Under the aegis of the Platt Amendment, the United States intervened by landing troops principally in Oriente Province on several instances to bring peace, order, and compliance with the Constitution of 1902. What was quite evident is that Cuban politicos of all stripes did not believe in or defend the Constitution of 1902, even though it was a mirror of the U.S. Constitution which has survived over two centuries and has been defended to the death by Americans in many conflicts. It is not a mystery that Cubans just did not have it in them to do likewise.

Habanians continued to enjoy great prosperity and they were exempted from serious armed conflict, at least for a while. Habana's immunity was to change drastically under the Castro brothers later.

Ironically, the easily corrupted government officials and the financial advantages provided by the government of President Teddy Roosevelt catapulted the economy, further widening the economic gap between the "haves" and the "have nots." In spite of the penury and calamity of the Great Depression of 1929 and the very low price of sugar dictated by President Franklin Delano Roosevelt during World War II (1941-1945), the Cuban economy managed to bounce back with furor later, but too little of that prosperity filtered to the have nots of the war-ravaged "interior" of Cuba.

The Cuban economy was almost entirely dependent on the once-a-year harvest of its sugar cane crops and its ups and downs correlated with the price of this commodity worldwide. President Teddy Roosevelt was well aware of this and he sought to stabilize the Cuban economy by regulating the amount of sugar cane America bought preferentially over other competitors, even to the detriment of the American sugar beet industry.

With the ensuing years, politics and WWII greatly impacted the Cuban man of the street. It is a paradox that the young republic reached a standard of living higher than Spain and was only second to the United States at the onset of the Cuban Social Revolution of 1959. Half a century later all of that was gone under the Castro brothers and

A Differing View of Cuba's History

Cuba's economic standing in Latin-America is only higher than that of Haiti, which was ranked last in this hemisphere by 2012.

The racial and economic divide was too great at the end of the Spanish War. The Afro-Cuban rebellion of 1906 of Los Negros was followed by the "Racial War" of 1912, which was blatantly supported by a violent Liberal Party in opposition to the Conservatives in power. The racist insurgents torched and partially destroyed the village of La Maya in Oriente Province and there were many skirmishers between "insurgents of color" and army troopers and cavalry.

American troopers provided guns and some intelligence to the Cuban Army, under the command of generals José de Jesús Monteagudo and Pablo Mendieta, both veterans of the War of Independence of 1895-98, who harshly suppressed the Racial War of 1912. A lieutenant, Arsenio Ortiz gained his violent reputation for his handling of "los negros" prisoners, many of whom did not survive the ordeal.

The following faithfully reflects the sentiments of the politically disfranchised Afro-Cuban Insurgents during the early years of the young Republic.

Sentiments of Afro-Cuban Drums

Yo son Karabali

Negro de Nación

Tanto maltrata

Cuerpo ta'furieh

Sin la liberta

No pue'o vivir

Yen-yere Bruca Manigua

Como teinda derechito

The Violent Country

Múdenle caba

Con mi corazón

Yen-yere Bruca Manigua

I am Karabali

Black of an African Nation

Mistreatment was so great

My body is furious

Without Liberty

I cannot live

Listen to me, Jungle Witch

to understand me straight

The world finished

My heart

Listen to me, Jungle Witch

By Arsenio Rodríguez – Matanzas, Cuba, 1937.

(Author's Afro-Cuban translation)

Later, in the third and last racial Chambelona War of 1917, the now Colonel Arsenio Ortiz gained the sobriquet of the "Jackal of Oriente" (el "Chacal de Oriente") for his unauthorized hangings of the rebellious peasantry from "guásimas" of the tropical forest. The very mention of his name aroused a mixture of fear and awe among the Santiago bourgeoisie. Ortiz was never prosecuted for his racist crimes.

The carnage and repression of the Chambelona by the Cuban army under the conservatives produced a political backlash across all layers of Cuban society. Significantly the backlash now included the heretofore "uninterested" Habaneros. The intelligentsia, academics, businessmen and landed gentry were appalled by the racial wars and their violent repression.

Lynching of Afro-Cuban Rebel in the last Racial War

(Family photo heirloom)

The Liberal Party thinkers were greatly mobilized and politicized kindred spirits. This development was no different from what was happening in the United States under the Keynesian economists of the New Deal and politicians who followed President Franklin Delano Roosevelt and the Democratic Party.

In elegant soirees at Habana and Santiago mansions, the intelligentsia explained the merits of an agrarian reform, advocated for Roman Catholic "social justice," and the usefulness of redistributing wealth by a strong centralized government and discussed Marxism-Leninism.

They dismissed Stalin's 1937 trials as an aberration or a required and necessary political violence and supported the Republican side of the Spanish Civil War. In the United States the turn to the political left produced the "New Deal" and in Cuba it produced a variety of "liberal" political parties with diverse exotic names, always containing a modifier implying "Revolutionary."

President Alfredo Zayas y Alfonso (Family photo heirloom)

In the center of the elite movement was Don Alfredo Zayas y Alfonso, an aristocrat and intellectual. As soon as he was the acknowledged leader of the Liberal Movement, he removed the aristocratic "y" from his name and avoided the "Don."

When the Liberal Party presidential candidate, the well-spoken Alfredo Zayas y Alfonso, an avowed populist, received more votes than the conservative candidate Mario García Menocal in 1916, the Chambelona War ensued, again principally in Oriente Province.

The Chambelona War was an armed conflict between the two political ideologies, conservatives versus liberals. General Menocal ruthlessly subdued the liberal insurgency in 1917 and assumed the presidency by a close vote.

When the populist Zayas was elected in 1920 in the next presidential cycle and became president the following year, liberalism, which was espousing a modified version of redistribution of wealth and an agrarian reform program, had found strong and lasting support throughout all of Cuba.

By this time, the price of sugar dropped from 22 cents to 3 cents per pound globally, issuing the greatest Cuban recession ever, followed by the world's Great Depression. The hard times facilitated the rise of even many more radical groups and among them was the "ABC" and "La Joven Cuba." Cesar Reynel Aguilera describes in his book, *El Soviet Caribeño*, how other Communist activists flourished during this period.

It is useful to give a short account of La Joven Cuba because, although short-lived, it illustrates how well the prevailing revolutionary environment of the country provided the substrate for its development under the charismatic leadership of Antonio Guiteras Holmes and how he contributed to the later rise of "A Sergeant Named Batista" as the power behind the effete and corrupted central governments of the late 1930s.

Antonio Guiteras Holmes was born in Philadelphia, Pennsylvania, of a prominent, well to do family of Cuban origins. The Guiteras were originally from Habana and had settled in Cuba in the early 19th century.

Antonio's close relative, Dr. Juan Guiteras, professor of medicine of the University of Habana was a leading researcher of yellow fever, who along with the Scot-Cuban physician Carlos Finlay and the team of American physicians, established that the striped mosquito, Aedes Egypti, transmitted the disease and that the infectious agent was a non-filterable virus. Their investigations, which used human subjects for the first time in the history of western medicine, was a seminal and definitive study of the dreadful disease. It led to a vaccine and control of the insect vector by appropriate measures that kill the larvae of the striped mosquito in stagnant water pools.

Dr. Guiteras was associated with the prestigious School of Medicine of the University of Pennsylvania in Philadelphia. Later, another Guiteras, also professor of medicine of the University of Pennsylvania, became one of the editors of the famous *Journal of Experimental Medicine* for many years.

Despite his illustrious background, Tony Guiteras became a Marxist revolutionary in the course of growing up.

The Violent Country

It is useful to quote Wikipedia's brief biography here:

"Antonio Guiteras y Holmes (22 November 1906 in Philadelphia – 8 May 1935 in Matanzas Cuba) was a leading politician in Cuba during the 1930s.

"*A proponent of revolutionary socialism, he participated in the Ramón Grau San Martin government installed after the popular overthrow of the autocratic right wing Cuban President Gerardo Machado y Morales in 1933. In 1931, Guiteras established the Union Revolucionaria group. Guiteras's political beliefs were nurtured in the volatile political climate of the 1920s. He first became widely known as a student leader and associate of Julio Antonio Mella, a young Communist revolutionary. He believed that the liberation of the people would be achieved through violent confrontation with the established authorities, but simultaneously held firm to the ideal of democracy. Antonio Guiteras was named Minister of the Interior under President Dr. Ramón Grau San Martin. Many reforms were introduced, including a minimum wage, minimum labor regulations, academic freedom, and nationalization of important sectors of the economy. After the 'government of 100 days,' Guiteras became even more radical and founded La Joven Cuba, a political organization driven by anti-capitalism and the progressive nationalism of José Martí.*"

In Wikipedia, the account Cuba: A New History of the leftist historian Gott summarizes Guiteras' beliefs and methods as follows:

"*Guiteras's views reflected an eclectic mix of revolutionary influences, from Auguste Blanqui to Jean Jacques Jaures. He drew inspiration from the Mexican and the Russian Revolutions of 1917, the Irish War of Independence and Augusto Sandino's guerrilla movement in Nicaragua. He shared the anti-Imperialist politics of the age and drawing on anarchist roots, he advocated rural and urban armed struggle, assaults on army barracks, and the assassination of policemen and members of the government. He was a firm believer in direct action, the propaganda of the deed, derived from Blanqui and the Spanish anarchists, and was much criticized by the Communists for his*

85

voluntarism and his predilection of violence. Guiteras was fatally shot by Batista troopers along with his Venezuelan comrade Carlos Aponte in Matanzas Province in 1935."

Guiteras's figure grew taller after his assassination and La Joven Cuba became the example to follow by future Cuban Revolutionaries. It served as a template very much like Saul Alinsky's "Rules for Revolution" did for the far left in the Democratic Party in 2012 American politics. La Joven Cuba would provide a helpful guide to young revolutionaries who organized the successful underground against the dictatorship of General Fulgencio Batista in 1956.

The rise of liberalism under President Zayas and his followers ushered kindred revolutionary groups to the La Joven Cuba and the ABC, frequently captained by young Spanish émigrés, in the breadth and length of the violent island.

Ironically, it finally was the triumphant election of General Gerardo Machado y Morales in 1925, a liberal who used conservative economic principles in governance and later was labeled a "right winger" that defined the irreversible turn to the left of the young republic opposition during his presidency. It had to do with the history of the 1933 revolution against him and his reforms.

It is not easy to parse the events of 1933. Much has been written and much has not been critically analyzed. It is much more illuminating to understand 1933 Cuba when the principals are examined with clarity in the proper historical context when you use their publications on the tragic events that did away with Machado's presidency.

CHAPTER 6.

◊ Gerardo Machado y Morales and the Definition of Cuba's Political Future By His Presidency (1925-1933)

"Oh! Cuba hermosa, primorosa
porque sufres hoy tanto quebranto?
Oh! Patria mía,
Quien diría
que tu cielo azul nublara el llanto"

Oh! Beautiful, graceful Cuba
why do you suffer today
so many transgressions
Oh, my Fatherland
who would have foreseen
That your blue sky
Would be clouded by tears

From Eliseo Grenet's "Lamento Cubano", 1932.
(Author's translation)

A Differing View of Cuba's History
"In 1933, Tony Fenner died for me"

From the lyrics that celebrate an anti-Machado American volunteer, sung by Gilbert Roland in the role of Guillermo Montilla, a fictitious and surviving member of a Cuban Revolutionary Group in John Huston's 1949 film "We Were Strangers" which romanticized the failed tunnel attempt to blow up President Gerardo Machado in Habana's Colon Cemetery.

Glossary :

Cacique — native Cuban tribal chief

Botella — sinecure, also bottle;

el interior — all territory comprised outside the Habana
    boundary

Partido Independiente de Color — Independent Party of Color

Ñangaras — Afro-Cuban for con-men, cultists, Communists. It
    is still used by Cubans of Criollo origins today.

Gerardo Machado y Morales was born in Camajuani, in the Province of Las Villas, in the "interior," about half way between the capital city of Habana and the center of the island. It is disdainfully said by his detractors that he had difficulty reading and writing because of his defective schooling.

It is clear that when Governor Weyler adopted his system of Las

Trochas and concentration camps to isolate the peasants who helped the Cuban Liberation Army, young Machado rustled cattle of pro-Spanish landowners and the Spanish Imperial Army with equal success. He distributed some of his prize among the local peasantry, as well as the Cuban Liberation Army. His brother, Lorenzo, was a colonel under General Calixto García with a distinguished combat record in Oriente.

An intelligent and fast learner, good looking and apportioned with great cunning and a quick sense for nimble improvisation in combat, he joined the mambí army in Santa Clara and rapidly was commissioned with the rank of brigadier general in July 1895 for his leadership and merits gained in war. He was the youngest and one of the bravest generals of the entire conflict that ended in 1898. He served in the Constitutional Army in the Province of La Villas in the early years of the republic.

Brigadier General Gerardo Machado y Morales

His penchant for the welfare of poor Criollo peasants and disfranchised Afro-Cubans led him to side with Don Alfredo Zayas y Alfonso and the Liberal Party's armed confrontation against the conservative forces of General Mario García Menocal in the Racial War of 1917. One of the most telling consequences of the lamentable tragedy was the killing of the renowned mambí General Quintín Banderas in this fratricidal conflict. He was the most prominent casualty of this conflict. His death was described as an assassination caused by his fervent support of the "Partido Independiente de Color," which openly disregarded the 1902 Constitution.

Brigadier General Mario Garcia Menocal

(Family photo heirloom)

After initial victories, the Liberals lost to the greater firepower of the Conservative forces that used half a dozen water-cooled tripod Colt machine guns provided by American army units to field test their efficacy. They had reached Santa Clara shores by stealth.

General Machado did not give up and continued the fight despite great many casualties until he realized his "cause was unsustainable" and he surrendered.

There were no reprisals, and he was not strung up, because President Menocal rapidly proclaimed a general amnesty after Machado's surrender. He survived this ordeal and was discharged from Cuba's army.

He dedicated his postwar period to managing his ranch successfully. In these difficult economic times he became an accomplished businessman and earned some spare capital. In the Cuban press, he was regarded as a rich landowner, even though his "finca" was a sliver of land when its size is compared to the enormous landholdings that, for centuries, had a stranglehold on the peasantry and the general economy by the landed gentry. The gap between arable land ownership and the dispossessed peasantry was firmly in his mind, always. His harsh experience in the fields of battle imbued him with an uneasy mixture of fear and respect of Spain, the U.S.A., and their respective acolytes.

His bravery in the Racial War was legendary among the disfranchised and the peasantry of the Province of Santa Clara. He was an unwavering nationalist, which was fueled by the action taken by the United States Army against his troopers, who were pitilessly machine gunned down in the field of battle. He also greatly resented the lack of clear and balanced reporting of the Chambelona massacres by the editors of the Habana mainstream media of the day. He described them as desk-bound pro-Spanish reporters and effete foreign intellectuals, most of whom had not participated in the Wars of Independence in any capacity.

It was true that the press did not cover much of the Chambelona war and it opposed the Afro-Cuban rebels' political goals on constitutional grounds and, sometimes, on grounds of unequivocal racial prejudice. A hurtful ditty that ridiculed the Chambelona war was composed and popularized in Habana's bistros, which further rankled and dismayed the bloodied combatants of both sides.

It is fair to say that Machado's psyche was indelibly sensitized by the very real threat of a possible armed American intervention and by the ease the opposition was mustered by an ultraliberal mainstream media. These two lingering threats were to dog him during the last years of his second presidency, as you will learn later in this narrative.

He sensed his rich popularity among the populace of Las Villas and Santa Clara provinces. He therefore decided he had a future in politics and joined the Liberal Party. He served as Interior Minister under the Presidency of José Miguel Gómez, a mambí general and liberal compatriot himself.

Later, he successfully supported Don Alfredo Zayas' Liberal Party candidacy for president and delivered the Provinces of Santa Clara and Las Villas in his presidential election. When Zayas, a profligate, big-government president, ended his ruinous four-year term, he decided to run as the Liberal Party presidential candidate.

His political platform severely criticized Zayas for his progressive measures that resulted in rampant corruption and his administration's widespread use of patronage, sinecures, cronyism, and liberal economic policies, all of which ushered a severe drop in the price of sugar, the mainstay of the Cuban economy, to one-half cent on the pound. In the mix, he had witnessed important inroads a few Communists had made in the newly formed Popular Party and publically blamed President Zayas for allowing the political organization of well-known "ñangaras."

Like many in Cuba those days, he clearly underestimated the strength of the strongly organized, albeit still small group, of underground revolutionaries, principally, communists and anarchists, many of them foreigners, principally French, Spanish, Mexican and other South American immigrants, who wanted to fundamentally change Cuba's political panorama.

These groups would receive major support from President Franklin D. Roosevelt later and play a major role in organizing the violent opposition to Machado in his ill-gained second term, as you will learn later in this narrative. You see, the Cuban Constitution of 1902 did not permit re-election to a second term. Nevertheless he sought a two-year prolongation of his presidency, which was ending in 1929, and his Congress offered it to him fair and square on a silver platter, with terrible consequences for the future of Cuba.

The two-year prolongation of his first term became a four-year term in due time, also approved by Congress, a Constitutional Assembly, and the Supreme Court. It was a remarkable mistake because he misjudged the strength of a violent opposition and the rapidity with which his previous supporters abandoned him politically.

In 1924, his opponent in the Conservative Party was his old nemesis, mambí General Mario García Menocal, a Cornell graduate. The newly constituted Popular Party was too small and disorganized to challenge his campaign significantly. Further, his timing was perfect because the

The Violent Country

backlash of the Racial Wars had its full effect on the general electorate at this juncture (*Vide supra Part I, Chapter 5*) and he had won the support of the peasantry and the politically disfranchised Afro-Cubans, who saw him as their trustworthy champion.

He won by an overwhelming national majority to become Cuba's fifth president on May 20, 1925. He had an unchallenged and clear mandate to complete his promised reforms. *Time Magazine*, a liberal publication, noticed and portrayed him on its front cover.

When he named his cabinet, he had previously secured their "word of honor" from all of his ministers and secretaries concerning the urgency of fighting the reigning corruption of all branches of government. He promised them he would monitor their activities closely. They delivered. And so did he.

Next, he met with the loyal opposition "across the aisle" in the Senate and the House of Representatives – individually, eye to eye – to muster support for reformative measures in education, public works, transportation, taxation, the treasury, and importantly, tariffs.

His initiatives to obtain a majority of support from Congress were met with successes. Importantly, his support in Congress was deeply indebted to the influential Senator Clemente Vázquez Bello of his own Province of Santa Clara, who was President of the Senate – the equivalent of the Majority Leader of the U.S. Senate – and the leader of the Liberal Party and commanded the respect of the loyal conservative opposition.

It can be safely said President Machado's first term ushered what we should regard today as the meteoric rise of Cuban Modernity.

Many of his successes are attributed to the close relationship he rapidly developed with U.S. Republican President Calvin Coolidge.

President Coolidge, an Amherst graduate, was a "small- government Republican conservative." He was a student of Adam Smith and it is fair to say he was a firm sponsor of Smith's ideas of laissez faire economics and self-regulation. Remarkably, Machado had found a kindred spirit in Coolidge. President Coolidge visited Habana during Machado's presidency and when he left he let it be known to Machado that he was to face further political difficulties during his governance and wished him luck.

President Calvin Coolidge visits President Machado.
(Family photo heirloom)

Vice-President Coolidge reached the presidency after President Warren G. Harding died in office in 1923. Coolidge was rightfully elected in the next cycle and served his presidency a total of six years from 1923-29. Machado learned greatly from his close contact with the laissez faire and conservative American president and both became close friends. They often spoke at length by telephone.

It was not a coincidence that Machado's reform measures for Cuba neatly mirrored those sponsored by President Coolidge. The Machado program was based on two general combined principles: fiscal prudence and pro-growth measures, including:

1. *Measures to Reduce the Size of Government.* All departments of the Central Government in Habana as well as those of the provinces were ordered to clean up sinecures, patronage and

other political abuses and to significantly reduce their payrolls.

2. *Efficient Management in Government.* Appointments to all departments were based on proven managerial competence and honesty, regardless of party affiliation, and they were to be regarded as collaborators, not as adversaries.

3. *Independent Oversight Commissions.* An independent oversight commission was empowered under the impeccable direction of banker Don Joaquín Gelats to oversee the awards of the best bidders for Public Projects and Works, which included education, water conservation, provincial roads, schools, etc.

4. *Elimination of Partisan Judges.* The Justice Department was re-organized to eliminate partisan adjudication and care was taken for the appointment of truly independent constitutionalist jurists.

5. *Monetary Policy Based on Parity with the Dollar.* The treasury was carefully monitored and monetary policy was based on the dollar.

6. *Protectionist Tariffs.* The approval of a new law governing new tariffs with the intent to protect domestic industry and agriculture from foreign competition and "dumping" and other predatory practices by foreign governments and industries.

7. *Fair and Appropriate Taxation with Efficient Collection of Tax Revenues.* Taxes previously ear-marked for non-productive populist measures were diverted to finance public works, principally the construction of the Central Highway.

8. *Modernization of Land Communications and Roads.* The engineering and building of a Central Highway that interconnected the length and breath of the largest island of the Caribbean. For the first time the Eastern Criollos and the western pro-Spanish population were free to interact freely, which resulted in the growth of domestic markets of the war-ravaged interior of the island.

9. *Strengthening Cuban/America Relationships and modifications of the Platt Amendment.* Foreign relations were largely in the hands of President Machado and President Coolidge, which included plans to abrogate the Platt Amendment. (Abrogation of the Platt Amendment was not to happen under Machado's presidency.)

As these measures took effect, Cuba began to "take off" in visibly exciting and promising ways. The first eight objectives were famously carried out with frenetic intensity. President Franklin D. Roosevelt's Special Envoy, Mr. Summer Welles, sabotaged the ninth objective and the American intrusion of New Deal policies had nefarious lasting results to this day.

The new tariffs and the Central Highway were tenets of the laissez-faire economic plans developed during his first term. Businesses prospered in this new environment, as did agriculture and new start-up industries in the underdeveloped interior. The bustle of economic prosperity and change was palpable to all. Tariffed imports like eggs, meat, coffee and other commodities were greatly reduced and in turn, Cuba became a significant exporting nation of these same commodities abroad and was on its way to self-sufficiency.

Significantly, even though specific taxes were raised slightly, a generally accepted "no-no" during a recession, the national foreign debt was cut from a $90 million deficit owed to the Chase Bank by nearly $40 million at the end of his presidency. This was due to an increase in revenue as a result of a phenomenal increase in business, industry, and agriculture.

Importantly, as promised in Machado's campaign, tax collectors ceased to be bribed and sinecures were greatly diminished as the result of independent oversight with clout. The habitual patronage that followed previous administrations was also held in check, albeit not completely abolished.

The armed forces were reorganized by appointing officers who had demonstrated unwavering obedience to the 1902 Constitution and included recent graduates of the National Military Academy in Managua and the National Naval Academy in Mariel. He increased the budget of both academies and supervised the appointments of their faculty.

Machado demolished an old wooden Spanish Imperial headquarters in the center of Habana and built modern auditoriums, classrooms, and laboratories for the new National University quarters that marvel visitors today.

He finished building the Capitol building with the two chambers modeled after that in Washington, D.C., which had started and stalled under President Menocal, and added the luxurious décor of its salons and corridors that mesmerizes tourists today.

He supplied all public schools throughout the island with books, pencils, paper, etc. He appointed independent judges in the Supreme Court and in all the appeal courts in the provincial capitals.

He sponsored international meetings in Habana that were very successful and well received. Habana's great architects designed and critically expanded the city westward with magnificent suburbs that rivaled the western world's classical cities.

In a very short time, Habana became America's darling city. A huge number of socialites, Hollywood stars, world intellectuals, musicians and many other celebrities visited fabulous Habana. Indeed, Habana seemed to be the center of the Americas, a place to be seen and to meet. Habana exuded dynamic power, magnificent palazzos, beauty, culture, sports events, vibrant music, and of course, beautiful women.

Importantly, the war torn "interior" began witnessing significant public works that were completed for the first time in centuries in their dilapidated provincial capitals and rural areas. The Oriente peasants delighted on the newly traced rural roads and their trains of mules, replete with their produce, clippity-clopped to markets of interior cities and villages and reached their market destinations quickly.

Initially, there was no apparent stopping these developments during his rule. Life, to him, could not have been more promising or better. At the start, his old Conservative enemies initially cooperated with Machado's initiatives and tendered significant support.

The star of Machado's public works, however, was the Central Highway Project that united the entire island in a network of roads of the interior, but delays and difficulties funding the massive initiative created a great deal of anxiety in his presidency. He began to toy with the idea of amending the Constitution to provisionally add two more years to his tenure to finish the project.

All of these significant achievements came to an end, however, first slowly, during the disastrous U.S. presidency of Herbert Hoover, and then abruptly, during FDR's presidency in 1933.

Machado's bubble was also collapsed by a confusing world that had changed radically and created global forces that would not yield to collective reason or common sense. These forces were rightfully described as unstoppable violent "movements." To world observers, violent political movements were the power technique of the day, naturally and effectively sponsored by disfranchised and economically strapped populations and seemingly managed by populist political leaders who tapped the unleashed vortex and furies.

There were many ongoing examples worldwide for all to see. Only a precious few of the political elite understood what was going on worldwide. Visionaries, like Winston Churchill, were ignored.

In Spain, the Anarchist Party was growing to an extraordinary size, and in a short time, just before the onset of the Civil War in 1936, it became the largest political party of the Iberian Peninsula. The Spanish Civil War was the symbol of the final struggle between Nationalist Socialist/Fascism and International Communism. The Brown Shirts and Adolf Hitler gained unstoppable rising popularity and were about to deal a deathblow to the floundering, mismanaged, and ruinous Weimar Republic of Germany.

In México, the Institutional Party of General Lázaro Cárdenas was about to confiscate American-owned oil fields and Washington, under FDR, had yielded to the takeover. In Italy and in Argentina, Mussolini and Juan Perón were about to gain power and enforce similar statist economic reforms, underscoring the concept of Nationalist Socialism.

France had elected a Socialist Government and in Russia, Stalin had consolidated an iron-handed nationalist Communist dictatorship. In China, the war lords of old were severely challenged by the peasant Communist Mao Tse-tung who showed a winning populist hand.

Under the approving umbrella of FDR's leadership and his Good Neighbor Policy, governments changed to military pseudo-populist dictatorships in Haiti, Santo Domingo, Colombia and Venezuela. Cuba was to follow suit in 1933.

In the United States, the economy had collapsed in the Great Depression. Keynesian politicos, headed by FDR and his cronies, veered the American Republic to the left. In Cuba, the "left of center" ABC underground movement grew rapidly, even before Machado's petition to add two years to his presidential tenure.

This growth was directly related to the socialist/liberal movements happening across the world at large. The economist and ABC revolutionary, Joaquín Martínez Sáenz and his co-revolutionary, Jorge Mañach, grew in stature as they fervently and eloquently espoused Keynesian economics for the island under the guise of Martí's teachings, using him as a venerated "apostle," even though there is little about these economic reforms in Martí's writings. The American Progressive-Democratic Party took notice and liked what it saw and heard in Cuba. Keynesian terms like the left of center popularized "pump priming the economy" and "deficit spending economics" were discussed frequently in the Cuban mainstream media of the day.

When Herbert Hoover succeeded President Calvin Coolidge in the next cycle, Machado's relationship with the U.S. presidency soured. Herbert Hoover was really a Republican in name only. Hoover's presidency was characterized by dismantling the small/fiscal prudent mantra Coolidge had so successfully used during his six-year tenure. Hoover's solution to avert the Great Depression was to raise taxes and "invest" government treasure in social measures to appease the social furies but those measures did not create lasting well-paid jobs and dangerously increased the national debt.

In a short time, Hoover became an anti-trade president and an isolationist, who refused to negotiate with President Machado. *The Wall Street Journal's* contributor Alan Reynolds wrote: "President Hoover raised taxes in 1932 and expanded the number of brackets to 30 from 23. The top rate skyrocketed to 63% from 25%. But the highest capital gains remained at 12.5% until Congress enacted the tapered tax in 1934. Yet since the capital gains tax grew in tandem with raised income tax rates, the top income tax bracket increased to 79% in 1936" under Franklin Delano Roosevelt with disastrous results.[32]

The Great Depression under Hoover worsened significantly, and subsequently, FDR created a recession that lasted a long time and was relieved only when the U.S. entered World War II in December 1941, because of the enduring giant war effort.

When Hoover realized that Machado's tariffs protected startup agricultural and industrial initiatives in rural Cuba, hurting America exporting interests, he raised tariffs on Cuban sugar and other imports. A counterproductive tariff war ensued between the two countries and Cuba stood to be badly hurt by America's measures.

When the Democratic Party and FDR were later empowered by the American electorate in the next cycle, Machado faced a type of interventionist America that was not to employ the military as in the past, but rather, used deceit and economic and political ruses and measures. These policies and ruses created the demise of Machado's presidency and also the demise of a series of feckless succeeding governments under the iron hand of the Cuban military and the heavy weight of American New Dealers in the White House. It was, of course, the left of center President Franklin D. Roosevelt and his Assistant Secretary of State for Latin American Affairs, Mr. Sumner Welles, who promoted and brought down President Machado's mandate and his presidency.

32. *The Wall Street Journal.* "Hillary Parties Like It Is 1938." September 3, 2015. Page A13.

The Violent Country

FDR's Cuban interventionist policy was based initially "to appease the crisis" created by the gruesome sporadic violence of anarchists and also by politicos, who axiomatically accepted the dictum "political power was best attained by acts of violence" in open disregard of the Constitution of 1902. In 1931, these rebellions by small and disorganized political groups, including conservative and centrist politicos with remarkably ill-defined agendas, were suppressed by the national armed forces that defended the 1902 Constitution.

The leaders and participants were captured, tried and rapidly released by Machado's presidential pardons and voluntarily exiled to Santo Domingo, the United States, and other places. The intervention of the Constitutional Army resulted in a minimum of casualties and order was momentarily re-established.

In the interim, Machado's petition for a two-year addition to his tenure was approved by a supermajority in Congress. Importantly, the Supreme Court also accepted the petition. When the jurists reconsidered the options, the petition was amended and again approved by Congress and the Supreme Court for a second presidential term that would encompass a longer, four-year period. It was an extraordinary legislative "triumph."

But it was not to be. Machado was overjoyed, but the outcry and opposition that followed was deafening and widespread. As it turned out, the presidential second term extension provided the violent opposition with the so-called "moral" grounds to depose his government by violent means in open disregard of the Constitution and the approvals of the Congress and of the Supreme Court.

The alarmed Cubans of the street looked with sympathy to the violent leftist revolutionary groups who wanted change to avoid a Machado dictatorship. Many were treading in unchartered waters and misunderstood the revolutionary agendas of the times. There were very few calls to defend the Constitution and those who wanted to defend the Constitution were cowed by the populist demand for change.

As a result, towards the end of his presidency, Machado faced larger, better organized, dangerous and now, underground, opponents distributed the length and breadth of the tragic island. Indeed, contrary to the ill-defined political agendas of the failed politicos, the long-standing revolutionary groups, like "La Joven Cuba" and the "ABC," had clearly defined socialist objectives and adopted violent methods tried in Ireland and in South America with success.

In Machado's "My Eight-Year Struggle," he credits the National University Student Organization as the most formidable and violent opponent he had to face. He attributed the students' violence to a few anarchists and communists who had hijacked their ideals. There were many confrontations between the government and the police and students, some with lethal consequences. In reality, when the results of the violence of the revolution that deposed him are examined, it was the ABC and La Joven Cuba and the non-commissioned Army officers under Sergeant Fulgencio Batista who took over the power of the Armed Forces with the tacit approval and encouragement of Mr. Sumner Welles, FDR's point man in Habana.

Importantly in this regard, the revolutionary university students were not represented in the Pentarchy that followed Machado's fall. Indeed, they rightly believed they had been betrayed and that their demands and proposed objectives had been hijacked.

The first extraordinary blow to Machado's political power was dealt when his close friend and mentor of his first and second terms, Senator Clemente Vázquez Bello, president of the Senate and leader of the Liberal Party, was assassinated in front of his Santa Clara home.

Machado's government retaliation was violent and unforgiving. Many of the underground opposition were killed, wounded, tortured, or imprisoned. Some were pardoned. However, by this time, with the aid of a liberal press, Machado's political advantages were rapidly reversed and his downfall was generally predicted when the intervention of Mr. Sumner Welles in Cuba's internal affairs was clearly understood by the entire populace. Importantly, the landed gentry and the rich and the well-to-do believed that America was coming to their safety.

The Violent Country

The second major blow to his presidency was dealt when Sumner Welles secretly met for negotiations to depose Machado with ABC leaders Joaquín Martínez Sáenz and Jorge Mañach without his knowledge or authorization. When Welles met with the underground opposition leaders, he liked and was comfortable, with what he heard. Martínez Sáenz and Jorge Mañach used Keynesian terms that mirrored exactly what the New Deal was all about. The secret meeting with the ABC and other minor underground groups produced a document demanding Machado's resignation and the creation of a provisional transitional government to succeed him. Machado was presented with these written demands by Welles, who told him – in no uncertain terms – that the United States favored his resignation and the creation of a provisional government followed by elections to take place when peace and order prevailed in due time.

As "suggested" by America's pro-consul Welles, Machado tendered his resignation to Congress and sought political asylum in the United States in August, 1933. The violent revolutionary reaction that followed Machado's resignation did not last too long.

In Santiago de Cuba, Desiderio Arnaz, the freely elected mayor and my father's University of Maryland classmate, just barely escaped the furies of the anti-Machado rabble in arms and reached asylum in the United States to join his family. A Machado enforcer was captured and brutally assassinated in the streets of the provincial capital. Similar violence was enacted in several important cities of the "interior." In the capital city, the *Habana Herald*, a New York Herald controlled newspaper, was raided and destroyed. However, most radio stations and newspapers were spared by the furies of revolutionary zeal.

Significantly, no one of importance and power – other than the Constitutional Army Officers – stepped forward to defend the Constitution. Machado and his family escaped by hurriedly flying to Nassau, Bahamas.

The third and gravest blow to Machado's reforms happened when non-commissioned Army officers organized a rebellion lead by Sergeant

A Habana newspaper is sacked by a mob.

(Family heirloom photo)

Fulgencio Batista Zaldívar. In a bold and rapid move, the Army rebels surrounded the great majority of the Army's Constitutional Officers quartered in the Hotel Nacional in Habana and many of them were killed and wounded in an asymmetric firefight.

Batista and his sergeants took total command of the armed forces shortly after this massacre. Following Batista's takeover of the Armed Forces, America's gray eminence, Summer Welles, met with the able and cunning young sergeant Batista who received America's blessing to become the real power behind several succeeding "civil" governments over many years. Many regarded Batista's insurrection as the triumph of "class warfare" against the privileged and the powerful, caused by "unsustainable inequality and abuse of power" in the armed forces. Later, *Time Magazine* dutifully portrayed Batista on its front page.

A non-commissioned soldier declares victory.

(Family heirloom photo)

Astonishingly, Machado's army and political supporters had vanished rapidly. Under the guidance of Mr. Welles and now Colonel Batista, several underground organizations tried to form a transitional government to prevent an outright American military intervention to bring some semblance of peace and order. This provisional government was known in the street as the Pentarchy. However, the reality was that a new power was dominating with the tacit blessing of the American President, FDR: the leaders of the Sergeants' Revolt were in command. Under pressure from FDR's proconsul Welles, Don Carlos Manuel de Céspedes Quesada was named Provisional President and the Pentarchy was dissolved (See Appendix).

Don Carlos Manuel de Céspedes Quesada, the son of the great Mambi patriot but sorely lacking his charisma and strong character, was designated provisional president by Mr. Welles to form a cabinet.

It was a blatant show of forceful American intervention in the internal affairs of Cuba at this time. De Céspedes indeed named a Cabinet of his distinguished peers but, in a matter of days, his entire government resigned under pressure by the intransigent Colonel Batista. The de Céspedes presidency had lasted barely one week.

The succeeding appointed "transitional" governments rapidly voided the Platt Amendment treaties, passed the right of women to vote and the right to divorce, and businesses were required to employ 50 percent Cuban borne citizens to avoid the control of the economy by Spaniards. Voter income and literacy restrictions were abrogated to increase the electorate with previously disfranchised minorities. Armed forces' salaries were raised. A law was passed which virtually abrogated the rights of an employer to fire an employee. Many other progressive measures were enacted in a very short period.

The populace warmly received many of these welcomed measures. However, taxes were raised, patronage and corruption flourished, teachers received salaries of non-existing schools, deficit spending became the rule of the day, and Cuba's foreign debt, which had gone down nearly 45 percent under Machado, sky-rocketed in record time. "Deficit spending" was the economic rule of the day.

Even though labor was re-organized, the Communist Party increased its membership. Some were given Cabinet seats for toeing the line and good behavior. An extraordinary law was passed, the Ley de Coordinación Azucarera, which socialized the free sugar market and its production by owners and sharecroppers. The state was to regulate what different sugar planters could legally mill in each of the once-a-year sugar harvests. The law affected the small planter worse than the large landowner.

It was the end of the relatively laisez faire Machado economy. Poverty grew and upward mobility was again interrupted to the general population. Government was by fiat and Congress was powerless.

Significantly, many of the leaders of the ABC left for the U.S. in self-imposed exile. Antonio Guiteras and his companions were killed in an asymmetric firefight with Batista's soldiers. The University students were also under surveillance and under control by the secret police for the time being.

In due course, there were a total of six appointed presidents of Cuba between 1933 and 1940, about one president every year, who, without much disguise or guile, kowtowed diktats issued by America's ambassadors in Habana or by America's client strong man, now General Batista.

This state of affairs changed when clean and free elections gave the island's presidential mandate to a populist General Fulgencio Batista Zaldívar for a period of four years (1940-1945).

When one reviews these complex developments, there are left two very important irreducible observations:

1. At the end of the day, conservatives were powerless and out of political worth; the multiplicities of political parties, such as they were, all embraced left of center policies and it was difficult to distinguish one from the other. They said the same things and had similar platforms. Politics was centered on personalities, not on substance.

2. It is quite evident that all political participants, the armed forces and the majority of civil society, had thrown the concept of a governing Constitution right out the window. None of those of importance or clout truly believed that an effective representative constitutional government like that of the United States was possible. The importance of the concept of a Cuban Constitution and its defense as well as its obedience was not part of the national angst of the time. The Cuban Supreme Court decisions were never regarded as the last word that must be obeyed and they were manipulated effectively by the powers that be at any given time, almost frivolously.

Indeed, the day of the "cacique" reigned, and the people at large had become "the product of their times."

Later, under the mandate of a constitutionally elected President

A Differing View of Cuba's History

Batista, the famously regarded progressive Constitution of 1940 was written by a well-represented Constitutional Assembly of all political stripes, including Communists, and was approved by a supermajority of a legitimate Congress and the Supreme Court. It was an unexpected and remarkable achievement.

The people of the street, however, looked on the proceedings of the Constitutional Assembly with some curiosity but with more cynicism, even greater skepticism, and lesser understanding. (In sharp contrast, the less minutae-laden but philosophically grandiose American Constitution was widely distributed and read, defended to the death and Supreme Court decisions defended). It was not widely read then and was all but ignored but by a few scholars, even now. Among the stipulations of the 1940 Constitution was for the government to proceed with the break up of the vast land properties that had oppressed peasants and entrepreneurs for centuries since the beginning of the encomienda system of colonial times. It never was to happen under the Constitution of 1940.

The result of the controversial stipulation of redistributing parts of the productive lands owned by the very few to the many landless peasants was to give rise to a secret organization of a powerful cabal of wealthy landowners at risk, with terrible political consequences, as you will learn later in this narrative (*Vide Infra Part II*, Chapter 5, pages 128-129).

The 1940 Constitution was to receive the same ill respect the Constitution of 1902 received from the politicos, the armed forces, civil society and the rich and powerful. The modern Constitution of 1940 was incompletely enforced and the minority rich landowners (circa 7 percent of the population in 1956) were happy and secure . . . for the time being.

Given these circumstances, it is not surprising that a relentless era of unchecked corruption, marked principally by widespread distribution of "botellas" (a.k.a. sinecures) in undisguised patronage, prevailed from 1933 to 1959, under many blurred administrations undistinguished from one another. Officials and private sector executives who refused to be part of the good old boys' club were ridiculed for their "stupid" devotion to simple honesty. It was easier to the up and coming to participate in the

108

corrupted vortex.

Even the top echelons of Cuba's presidential administrators trafficked in drugs at the end of these "republican" years.

Gradually, this cynical and shameful environment was too much to bear by the general public. Commerce and the general economy were warped by corrupted officials at all levels when the envisioned intention long before was to have an honest, self-regulating free market based on fair and square competition.

These are the years that preceded the advent of a profound social revolution because the nation was now readied to take desperate and violent corrective measures that would plunge Cuba into the abyss of Communist rule, under the direction of a cruel and unforgiving populist, Fidel Castro Ruz, the son of a veteran anti-mambi Spanish Empire soldier and today's Supreme Leader of the Cuban People. By force of arms, he was to found a ruling family dynasty, which still receives homage worldwide today because it defeated the United States of America's efforts to depose it.

It was said that on the occasion of his Cuba trip in the 1970s, the former Spanish president, Felipe González, a socialist, presciently joked to Fidel Castro during his Habana visit that he should take the historical opportunity to title himself "King of the Cuban People in Perpetuity," modeled after triumphant medieval kings who wielded absolute power by force of arms.

Cuba's powerful armed forces in the Americas was possibly second to that of the United States at this time and had established armed initiatives with the support of the Soviet Union, its tacit protector, in Angola, Argentina, Nicaragua, Venezuela, Colombia and others.

González's joke was not far off base. Fidel burst-out laughing, and regally waving his cigar, dismissed his entreaty.

Part 2
Modernity

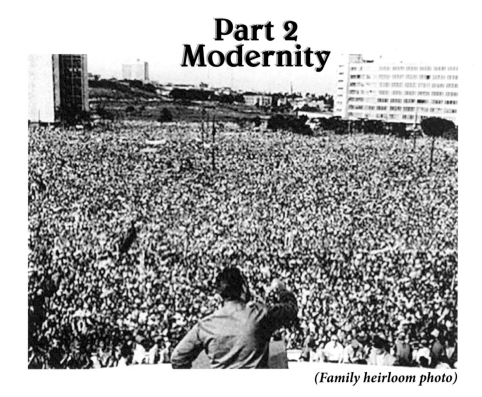

(Family heirloom photo)

"All of this for what? Cuba today is a slave, energy dependent nation with invisible shackles, not likely to be free anytime soon. The story of Cuba is tragic."

Anonymous tourist, on his return home. July 2018. South Norwalk, Connecticut, USA

"We must always conduct ourselves as if Life is Just, as if Humanity is Grateful, as if Men are Good."

Commander Frank Pais, M26-7 Cuban Urban Guerrila Forces, June 1957. Santiago de Cuba

CHAPTER 1.

◊ In Bellevue Hospital, New York City, Dr. A.M. Santos-Buch Makes a Controversial Decision and Returns To His Country of Origin

In San Luis, Doña María Buch and Don Angel Santos prospered and parented their multitalented five children. Home schooling had been very productive and the children responded very well.

At the turn of the nineteenth century, the oldest son, Miguel Angel, showed great interest in becoming a medical doctor. Miguel showed no passion for his father's retail store, La Borla. He was particularly talented in bookkeeping and managing money so he worked in the business office. The next in line, a comely girl, Cusa, showed remarkable ability with the piano and the arts. Next was Angel Maria, and he was energetic, unstoppable, and passionate. He was a bright, lets-get-going, hands-on kid with a keen sense of humor, who actively worked with his father in the textile production side of the business. He was quick of mind, strong and agile. Dolores, a.k.a. Lola, was next and she leaned strongly to literature, history and the arts in general. The youngest son by many years, Ángel Luis, was an insecure and over protected soul in this challenging, enterprising family.

Don Ángel's friend in San Luis, Luis Mestre, after having an extraordinarily successful business with a patent medicine distribution enterprise throughout Oriente Province, was planning to move to the capital city, Santiago de Cuba, and expand further in association with the Espinosa brothers. He talked about sending his three sons to a Wallingford, Connecticut, college preparatory school called Choate with the hope of getting them into Yale College, an Ivy League school for the rich and powerful. Despite not being able to reach as high, Don Angel was quick to plan another version of an "American education" for his children.

The first step was to register Miguel in the School of Medicine at Habana University. He graduated later with distinction in the top third of his class. The next three siblings were shipped off to Eastern College, Manassas, Virginia, when their San Luis home schooling allowed them to apply and enter the college. Eastern College was selected on the recommendation of their oldest and brilliant cousin, Jesús Buch Portuondo, also known as "Chu." Chu was first in his class at Eastern College and had been accepted to attend the School of Medicine at the University of Maryland in Baltimore. María Buch's children idolized Chu Buch for his determination, patriotism, scholarliness and brilliant mind.

Ángel María Santos-Buch took Eastern College by storm. Master of an enviable academic record, he also engaged in athletics and was a pole-vaulter on the track team. To supplement his tuition, he got a job responsible for awakening students in the dormitories with an ancient bronze bell still in our family's possession today. The toll happened at six-thirty a.m. every school day, a job which gave Ángel María a perverse sense of enjoyment.

His roommate was Loys von Kreuter and on their first day, after a fistfight when the smaller but stronger Ángel María gave Loys a black eye, the two became inseparable friends for the rest of their lives. His mother, Victoria, was wife to Germany's military attaché in Russia, General von Kreuter. In his years at Eastern College and later in Baltimore, Ángel María became a devoted friend to Victoria von Kreuter and her son, Loys. She became his muse and advisor and he was her young apprentice and admirer. This relationship was to enrich his broad understanding of Europe and its place in world history and American politics. With his impressive academic record, particularly in organic chemistry and physics, the school of medicines of Johns Hopkins University and the University of Maryland accepted him. Jesús Buch, already in Maryland and breaking all of its academic records, prevailed over Ángel María and he entered its medical school. On graduation, his academic records were good enough to get an internship and residency in medicine in the famed Bellevue Hospital in Manhattan, New York. He blossomed at Bellevue from 1913 to 1915. In fact, at the end of his residency in 1917, Dr. Palmer, New York University professor of medicine, offered Ángel María a place in his practice in his Park Avenue office with the promise of great earnings from a large personal clientele.

What was Ángel M. Santos-Buch, M.D., to do? At age twenty-one and fluent in English, well-trained and able, worldly with Washington and New York connections, impeccable social graces, one would have predicted he would stay under the tutelage of the powerful Dr. Palmer. What motivated Dr. Santos-Buch's return to the pastoral and at the same time, violent, Oriente Province is a mystery to this day. His brilliant cousin, Jesús Buch Portuondo, inexplicably also returned to practice internal medicine in the history-rich Santiago de Cuba. For Ángel María, the decision was to start in the countryside and hang his shingle in the town of Contramaestre, near the river of this name not far from Dos Ríos and near the village of Jiguaní, where the Cuban Patriot José Martí had fallen under the fusillade of Spanish troopers during the very beginnings of the War of Independence he had fiercely sponsored.

It was a horse and buggy practice. He did everything under his newly acquired Habana University degree and License of Internal Medicine and Surgery. There were deliveries, appendectomies, lacerations to suture, and pneumonias, cancers and heart disease to attend as best he could. He was very busy and very well liked. The rich and powerful and the underprivileged of all races paid according to their incomes. It was much more than he anticipated and, no surprise, he was getting rich.

Yet, he longed for the basic science support he did not have. There were no clinical laboratories and no medical infrastructure.

He had to use a microscope and he had to do all the blood work and chemistries himself as well as other more elaborate laboratory techniques he acquired quickly to support his practice. The idea to create the first clinical laboratory in Oriente Province entered his mind at this time. He considered that his older brother Miguel may be interested too and he decided to explore a joint laboratory venture with him.

Current events made the decision easy. Unpredicted and dangerous revolutionary actions made up his mind to leave the countryside practice and move to the safety of the capital city. During the Chambelona Racial War, Dr. Santos-Buch was captured while attending the wounded from both sides, liberals and conservatives. The Afro-Cuban rebels exiled him to Key West because they feared for his life. He returned the long way, via Habana and then by rail to Santiago, to await the advent of peace and order when American troopers intervened in the conflict. This event was the last straw for him and he decided to settle in the more peaceful provincial capital of Santiago de Cuba.

With his brother Miguel, he wrote a business plan and indeed, created the first clinical laboratory of the provincial capital. They named it Laboratorios Santos Buch in 1918. It was remarkably successful. Part of the success was based on its location near the center of the old colonial city, San Basilio and Calvario Street, near one of the oldest Roman Catholic enclaves of the ancient city, Siervas de María Convent and the eighteenth century San Basilio Magno Chapel and Seminary. To expand their biologic products, such as immune sera, they decided to buy Chantilly, a thirty-three-acre farm in Cuabitas,

116

six miles north of the laboratory in Santiago.

The Chantilly purchase ultimately changed their business and their lives. The clapboard, two-floor, white frame house had a distinct French style with corridors around both upper and lower floors. The roof was made of zinc-plated sheets. French doors and shuttered floor-to-ceiling windows allowed an excellent vista from its perch on a gentle slope of an attractive hill. It had been built by an order of French nuns in the 1880s and was named Chantilly. West of Chantilly, you could see Villa Retazos, residence of Captain Manuel Cutillas and his wife, Olga Covani Bacardi. Behind the villa, you could not miss the terracotta roof of the Mediterranean palazzo retreat of Don Emilio Bacardi's Villa Elvira, named after his wife, Doña Elvira Cape. In 1926, Don Radames Covani Puccinelli, his wife, Doña Marina Bacardi Cape and their daughter, Marina Lydia and her husband, Luis del Rosal, occupied it.

Emilio Bacardi and Dr. Santos-Buch houses in "Los Cocos," an area named for its many coconut trees.

A Roman running fountain with a centered statue of a faun adorned the pleasantly manicured gardens. Other statues, all sculptured by Mimin Bacardi, daughter of don Emilio, were scattered in the park. The northern view showed the dense wooded footprint of "El Cocal" where Don Enrique Schueg, who was born in El Caney and was of French Swiss origins, found rest and solitude in weekend retreats in another clapboard frame structure of ample dimensions. French speaking Don Enrique was another important and brilliant financial officer of the Bacardi Rum Company, founded in 1862. Just beyond Villa Elvira to the west was the sharply rising slope of "La Loma Bacardi," a mountain with large reddish volcanic rocks, whose peak dominated the little village of "Cuabitas" eastward and the Charco Mono and the Chalon Reservoirs westward below. Several volcanic rocks, more than three to four meters wide, rolled below in the very distant past and now decorated the landscape of the spectacular Villa Elvira gardens.

The only railroad track from Santiago to Habana, some 750 "leguas" west, the equivalent of nautical miles, ran between Villa Elvira and Villa Retazos with its tennis court and separate garage. Habana, in 1926 the capital city of the Republic of Cuba, was relatively isolated from the "interior" in spite of the long-existing railroad between the east and the west. The newly created two-lane asphalted road ran east-west. It was 975 kilometers long and it took about fifteen hours via bus to travel from Santiago to Habana. The Carretera Central had been been almost completed by 1927 under President General Gerardo Machado, who once, in a noble moment, had been the youngest brigadier general of the Insurgency against the Spanish Empire (Vide Supra, Part I, Chapter 6).

In Cuabitas, there was an elegant railroad stop with a station and an adjacent quaint, grey-greenish brick and mortar building where a severe white and black sign said simply "Bacardi." Some of the help of the Cuabitas homes referred to this structure as the casino. I never learned why but I imagine that it had been used for gambling soirées under a full moon of warm, seductive nights. Don Emilio used the railroad to bring his entire entourage from the sweltering heat of Santiago de Cuba, six kilometers south, to spend long weekends and well-deserved vacations in his idyllic beautiful state.

In the spring of 1926, the road to San Luis from the capital city of

Modernity

Santiago de Cuba in the Province of Oriente meandered and followed curved crossings of the railroad track at several points. The beginning of Cuabitas was located at the second crossing and finished at the third, on the way to San Luis. To reach this agriculturally important city, the road climbed a range of beautiful mountains through dangerous narrow passages and hairpin curves. At the mountains' peak, passengers in precarious vehicles of all kinds crossed to the north by descending the Puerto Boniato ("Boniato's Gap"). This San Luis road was cut and leveled by teams of oxen with massive oxbows who pulled chained iron scoops of dirt that was used to pack the base of a future, more modern, two-lane road. In 1926 it was no more than an unfinished country road ("Camino Vecinal"), strewn with rocks of all sizes and occasional difficult holes and other defects that separated Chantilly from don Emilio's compound. The Chantilly house of the thirty-three-acre ("una caballeria") "finca" was on top of a gentle hill that was above the two Bacardi settlements, El Cocal and the Railroad Station. In the late nineteenth century and the early twentieth century the area comprised by don Enrique and don Emilio's compounds and Chantilly was known as "Los Cocos" to the weary travelers to San Luis, named after the many coconut trees that populated the entire spot. Around the southern border of Chantilly and meandering east, there was a horse trail which would take you to the village of "El Caney" just a few kilometers from "Cuba," a name Orientales liked to use to shoren the long and awkward Santiago de Cuba.

The order of French nuns who were Chantilly's original owners ran and operated some of the smaller charity hospitals and clinics in Cuba. They planted many species of mango, anones, tamarinds, cashew, royal palms, eucalyptus, and bayam trees. The cool house with its large windows and doors was a pleasant retreat. The house had a beautiful mural of the Virgin St. Eduviges of Poland in a chapel abutting a bedroom, a bathroom with a tub and a shower, separate living and dining rooms and an adjacent charcoal kitchen on the first floor. The second floor had four bedrooms and a bathroom. When the water pump worked, the bathroom was usable. Ample tiled corridors encircled both the first and second floors with French doors and shuttered windows.

The order of nuns was in decline when Chantilly was sold to Dr. Santos-Buch, my father. When Dr. Santos-Buch entered a partnership with his older brother Miguel, who was also an M.D., to start up a business to manufacture biomedications, they decided to buy it jointly to keep the livestock they needed to extract liver concentrates for the treatment of pernicious anemia with vitamin B12 extracts, and to obtain other derivative biological compounds, such as pneumococcus horse antiserum. After a few years of an uneasy partnership, Dr. Miguel Santos-Buch moved his side of this business to the remote western capital city of Habana and my father bought him out with a mortgage.

The giant roots of the Anacahuita tree. (Family heirloom photo)

He was enchanted by the French house, which had become his home. There were cement steps from the San Luis road that crossed a wrought iron gated fence with filigrees. Half way up to the house, a large round, whispering Mediterranean fountain stood at the center of a garden with Thailand's "arboles del viajero" and other species. The entire area was home to numerous native songbirds, mockingbirds, carpenters, wild doves, owls, and brightly plumed humming birds. On the southern side, there was another ascending pathway with a gentler and easier slope with fifty-foot-tall "Anacahuita" trees, with enormous canopies of brown-yellow scalloped leaves,

120

with trunks over a meter wide. My father believed these trees were from the primeval forest of Cuba, dating millions of years ago, after volcanic southern Oriente Province emerged from the deepest waters of the Caribbean Sea and plants and trees began to evolve and assume lasting, triumphant characteristics. The motor road entrance had a tall gate with "Chantilly" in large metal letters at the top. The road climbed the hill in a rounding curve, which was also bordered by "cañandonga" and "mamoncillo" trees, and then, near the top, there was a huge emerald green Ceiba with a more than meter-wide trunk and characteristic, rather large, trunk spines. Further along were two very tall eucalyptus trees and bamboo bushes which guarded a motor court. The garage, storage house and the help quarters were separate on the north side. A long horizontal water tank, like an enormous metal tube, stood ready to supply the house and the milking stalls with their water troughs.

At first light, the thirty-two-year-old bachelor and charismatic doctor, wearing a big appealing smile, was seen in his bouncing car just barely negotiating some dangerous curves and evading deep pot-holes and stones, on his way to his office and bustling clinical labo-ratory in the oldest, central area of Santiago in the corner of the very quaint San Basilio and Calvario streets, where he conducted his prac-tice. He had hired a family of peasants to care for the farm, a cook, and a teen-aged house servant of Jamaican origins, Celeste Favour, who would later be my African-Jamaican mom, whom I adored and called Makinkina. She soothed my troubled soul many, many times and to this day, I miss her dearly.

Shortly after Chantilly's purchase, my father's pastoral life took a sudden turn when he married nineteen-year-old Herminia Greig Cossío y de Céspedes, and Chantilly, full of wonderment and excitement, was to be my birthplace and our home for many years.

CHAPTER 2.

◊ Carol, "La Hija De La Americana," Is Brought-Up According To Strict Spanish Traditions.

◊ The Establishment of Spanish Enclaves: "Juntos Pero Separados."

Glossary

La hija de la Americana — The daughter of that American woman

El Dia Que Me Quieras by Amado Nervo —

(The Day You Are to Love Me)

Juntos Pero Separados — Together But Separate

The noisy pirouetting warhorse on the dirt outside his cabin woke him and it wasn't very long until Colonel Charles Lee caught his attention.

"Rise and shine boy! Our forces are cannonading Fort Sumter! You come with me boy. Get up! Get up! We ride to Charlotte sir! Right now! The war has started and we won't be late. Saddle up boy!"

He noted with envy the colonel's impeccable Confederate grey uniform, gold-braided epaulets, heavy cavalry saber, and his side arm, an 1860 U.S. Army Colt, showing just below the officer's yellow sash at the waist.

Captain of the Confederate States Army James Lovelace White, now all of twenty-two years of age, remembered that January, 1862, morning well. Events had moved quickly since that memorable beginning. He was sworn to join the 37th North Carolina Infantry Regiment in the square of Charlotte, North Carolina, and now, as fate would dictate after General Robert E. Lee's surrender at Appomattox, General Ulysses Grant's officers in the same square decommissioned him. He had witnessed the horrors of the Civil War from the relatively safe vantage of serving in the headquarters staff of the Adjutant General and Inspector General of the Confederate Army, West Point Graduate and Virginian, General Samuel Cooper, for almost the duration of the Civil War. He was recommended for service in General Cooper's headquarters by Colonel Lee.

The mission of the adjutant general – inspections, provisions, records, military chains of commands, creation of regiments, appointments, battalions, etc. – kept their headquarters physically close to the government of the Confederate States, President Jefferson Davis and his Cabinet in Richmond, Virginia. With Grant's successes, the confederate government had to move to Charlotte, North Carolina, from its original venue in Virginia. Captain White's jobs ranged from messenger to different Confederate Army units to that of yeoman's servitude as a cleric, which he hated.

He shuddered lightly as his bright blue eyes under a mop of black hair looked upon the weary, defeated rebel soldiers, some barefooted, others with bandaged dried blood on their limbs, sweating profusely under the bright North Carolina sun.

He had to survive this no matter what, he said to himself.

For now, the Blue Coats had treated him well; they did not disarm him and he kept his sidearm and sword. He kept his horse and they sent him home, a broken soldier with a few Yankee dollars in his pocket. The first thing he did was to sell his cavalry sword to a slimy carpetbagger on his way home. He needed cash badly.

Captain White's ancestors were of the English stock that sought refuge from the religious conflicts that afflicted the homeland for decades in the 18th century. Shortly after their arrival in Charleston, South Carolina, the Crown sold them twenty acres of farmland near Salisbury, North Carolina, for eighty pounds and set out to build a wood frame cabin and plant tobacco and other vegetables.[33]

Captain White was the principal of the original frame house at the end of the Civil War. With the few Yankee dollars he had, he bought a mule and a covered two-wheeled wagon. On the sides he painted in an arch "Captain James Lovelace White Patent Medicines" and set out to sell snake oil, Carter Little Liver Pills, whalebone corsets for low back pain, and many other medical sundries of his era. He made a fairly decent living until his death in the 1890s. He is buried in the National Cemetery at Arlington, Virginia, in honor of his duties in the Confederate Army.

But he needed a wife in this post-war South. In his travels, he handpicked a handsome and healthy girl about four years his junior from a penurious tenant family. Although born in Scotland, she was also of English ancestry like him. He asked for her hand and married her shortly thereafter in an all-white Charlotte Baptist Church. I could not confirm her first name, which may have been Harriet or Hattie, but her family name was Bringle and the couple settled in Salisbury. She managed the little farm and in a period of about twelve years she gave Jim six children, and died during childbirth of the last. The oldest child, born in 1894 and twelve years old, was Hattie Irene White, who was told to take care of her siblings and manage the small plot of tobacco planted dirt and house. He brought food and money, from time to time, at the end of the vagaries in his travels of his patent medicine business run from his horse and wagon-cart. There was

33. Paul Johnson, the brilliant British historian, describes in his book, "A History of the American Peoples," how this single edict by the Crown of England that redistributed royal land, 20 acres for 80 pounds, led to the creation of the early wealth of the American colonies enjoyed in sharp contrast of the Encomienda system used by the Spanish Crown in its colonies.

some schooling at the nearby Baptist Church where Hattie and her siblings enjoyed the poignant Christian hymnals on Sundays.

Hattie was a beautiful strawberry-blonde girl with alert, piercing blue eyes and a powerful voice. Her friends and neighbors noted how clearly she vocalized country ballads of the day and men noted with lecherous comments her magnificent full figure even at this early age. She was very poor and swore to God as her witness that she would never live in the isolation of poverty and she devoutly yearned for the freedom that, she sensed, only money could bring.

On a bright sunny weekend, Hattie, with her brothers and sisters, were taken to visit Captain White's friends, also veterans of the Civil War, in Roanoke, Virginia – some eighty miles away. It was the first time away at some distance from the little farmhouse. She was seventeen and a fully developed attractive girl with a commanding voice. In Roanoke, she met George Carter Friend who was beguiled by her beauty and sharp personality. On the first instance, she decided that she would marry Mr. Friend at a drop of a hat. She was done with her siblings and her tyrannical father, Captain White.

The Friends hailed from East Anglia and immigrated to South Carolina early in the eighteenth century. One branch of this family moved to Massachusetts and then to Mount Etna, Maine, to found the town and produce successful businesses, state senators, and administrators, and did well through the years. The remainder of the family immediately took part in the Crown's farming program in the South and bought several twenty-acre farm plots near Roanoke, Virginia and prospered, always subject to the unpredictability of the cotton and tobacco market. They prospered sufficiently enough to own African slaves, as documented in the town's records. George Carter Friend in the 1910s, however, did not want to be a farmer although he recognized, with regret, that his principal source of income was his ancient family's lands. George was able to learn the photographic techniques made popular by daguerreotypes when northern newspapers documented the participants and the horrors of the Civil War, and later, of World War I. His enthusiasm for photography convinced him to invest in a studio in Roanoke itself, which supplemented his income and challenged his intellectual curiosity. Among his photographic achievements was winning a third prize in a citywide competition and his subject was no other than Hattie White, in her youthful sensual splendor. It was not long after that Hattie and George married in 1913.

Hattie White Friend had a difficult marriage with George. She gave birth to an attractive red-haired girl, Shirley Irene, on October 17, 1914, and two years later delivered a handsome boy, Edwin Hugo. In spite of the growing family, she disliked George. George was self-centered, morose and quick-tempered, not an easy man to get close to. He was five feet four inches tall, a trick pistol shooter, and collected guns. He was athletic and agile but reminded her too much of her father's irascible and intemperate disposition. Hattie was not to be subdued by multiple marriages, as we shall learn later in this narrative.

Despite having her young family, Hattie dreamed of the newly distributed movies and fantasized about the silent screen's stars. She obsessed about the legitimate theatre. She took short singing lessons and had diction classes she clearly could not afford. The local newspapers had publicized Lowe's Theater of Atlanta. She began to think about a career in the theater or movies. Ever so slowly, she connived to divorce George and take her children with her to Atlanta. After some correspondence, she was greatly encouraged by Lowe to join the theatre company.

The divorce happened when Shirley and Ed were four and two years old. After the papers were legalized, she had the opportunity to change her name to Harriet Carter Farnsworth, a resounding and extravagant play on her family initials. Indeed, she hoped to see her name shine on theater marquees. She kept this name until her death in her 90s.

On arrival in Atlanta she was able to find employment in the local Western Union office and, at nights, she joined the company of

Harriett Carter Farnsworth with her two children, Shirley and Edwin, in Atlanta

entertainers of the Lowe's Theater. She solved the problem of raising her kids by placing them in the care of an orphanage for a fee. The orphanage lasted through the years of a high school education, such as it were those days in Fulton County, Georgia. After a brief encounter, she married again, a Dr. Calloway, who was unable to keep his practice, so she quickly divorced him within the year. With the little money she received in alimony and what she could scrape up from different day jobs, she was able to buy a two-floor frame house, which she converted into a guest home. Most of the tenants were theater people. Shirley and Ed were constantly exposed to many different types of artists and experienced the enjoyable development of their multitalented mother who belted out the high Cs in many of the operetta and semi-classics of the day, such as "Indian Love Call" and "Roses of Picardy" that Jeanette McDonald and Nelson Eddy popularized when sound was introduced in films. In the course of time, she tap-danced and played the violin at Lowe's. Her running ambition was to be discovered and become another Pola Negri, Theda Bara, or Gloria Swanson.

It was not to be.

Harriett stayed at Lowe's for more than ten long years. Undiscovered and losing some her attractiveness as she aged, she found that she had a natural gift for writing and began to publish short articles in the *Atlanta Constitution*. Later, when her children found a large measure of independence, she struck out to scout California, Arizona and Death Valley. This grand scale adventure also led to two other marriages; she, of course, survived her frontier husbands. She managed to travel the western frontier of the United States with or without her men. She "boldly explored where others would not go." It was the kind of adventurous life that satisfied her intellectual and now literary longings. By the end of her incredible life she had published four historical novels, all on the travails of the pioneers of the western frontier, which told stories she had previously documented in local magazine and newspaper articles of the time.

A member of the National Writer's Club wrote in the "The Pioneers of the Western Frontier" that "'Too late tomorrow'" might well be Harriett Farnsworth's motto. Thanks to her diligent scouting, you relive the roaring days of placer mining in California; you meet the vigorous characters who prospected the Mother Lode; the ghost towns of Death Valley teeming with ore-loaded burros again; ghost railroads thread the mountain passes."

In "Remnants of the Old West" there is an excellent photograph of this attractive lady. Born and bred in the Old South, she became an active collector of western Americana for more than three decades. She was a member of the National Writer's Club, an honorary life member of the "Manuscripters" of Los Angeles and winner of its Award of Merit. Her working base was Prescott, Arizona, and in the last years of her life, her son, "Uncle Ed," moved her to Atlanta to be near her surviving family.

During the early period, Shirley and Ed struggled much on their own. Flying fascinated Ed and at age sixteen, he lied about his age and joined the United States Army Air Force to become a pilot before the beginning of the Second World War and he was out of Harriett's life for a long while. Shirley, at nearly eighteen, was finishing high school and taking typing lessons to find work at night. It was in this academy that she met a young man who bore a striking resemblance to Rudolf Valentino, the movie star. He was about her age, spoke broken English, and said he was from Cuba. She had never heard of the island, had a very vague idea of its whereabouts, and knew nothing of its violent history. She fell hopelessly in love with the charming youngster. Her spark, bright eyes and arousing sexuality smote him. His name was Eusebio Valle Gómez of Vista Alegre, the high-end suburb of Santiago de Cuba.

Euskadi

The Basque Country straddles the northeastern region of the Iberian Peninsula and a smaller area of the southwestern frontier of France. Anthropologists believe that the Basque people are descendants of the original European peoples and lived there for 40,000 years. Basques speak Euskera, a language that has no connections with any other and they have some genetic markers that are unique to their race. Blood groups like Group A Rh negative determinants are significantly higher among the Basque, for example. The mountainous region, which encompasses the Pyrenees, has protected the Basque for many centuries and it is true that neither the Visigoths nor other northern or eastern invasions conquered the Basques. Their isolation favored the retention of their original European genetic character. When Spain was under the boot of Islam for nearly 800 years, the Basque Country was never under the Moorish yoke. The Basque Country was conquered only by the Fascists under Generalissimo Francisco Franco near the end of the Spanish Civil War in 1936. To this day, the Basque people yearn for their complete independence from Spain and France.

In the Middle Ages, the Basque tribes, some say numbering twelve or sixteen, gathered under an oak tree in the village of Guernica to discuss the "fueros," a chart that respected the rights of the landed barons and agreed to select a relatively effete king who ruled a loosely connected confederation to assure common military protection from foreign invaders. The site of this government was Guernica. The Basque Country is rich in iron ore and today has the largest arms factories of Spain. It is rich in timber and has a large fishing industry.

While Bilbao, the capital city of the Basque Region in Spain, developed into an industrial and cultural powerhouse, Guernica is the iconic soul of the Basque people. The Nazi Luftwaffe recognized the organic importance of Guernica and the civil population was bombed during the Civil War and the government had to move somewhere else. The air attack was the first rehearsal of the technique of bombing civilian populations to submission in World War II. Picasso marked the event in his famous painting hanging in the Museum of Modern Art in New York City.

In the Guernica Museum, the heraldic crests of the original barons of the first enclave of the "fueros" are displayed. There the visitor can find the Valle crest.

In the autumn of 1895, Eusebio Valle Espiga, fourteen years old, stood in the busy quay of the port of Antillas, in the Bay of Nipe of the northern coast of Oriente Province, besides his meager possessions in a small cloth bag with wooden handles. Six feet tall with strong features and dark blue eyes under a mop of black hair, he was disconcerted by the strong Afro-Cuban stevedores toiling mightily with the ship stores that accompanied him from Santander in northern Spain. He waited impatiently under the biting sun, cooled his heels and marveled at the strength and stamina of the Africans who seemed completely oblivious to the shiny sweat on their black skin and the burning cobblestones beneath their bare feet. He had not seen any Africans in his entire life in Castro Urdiales or Bilbao or anywhere in Cantabria.

He was told to wait for Don Antonio Gómez Cianca, his father's close friend, to pick him up to take him to the small port city of Sagua de Tanamo. Don Antonio had met his father, Marcelo, by chance, some years back, and they struck a liking to each other that had been genuine and lasting.

When he looked south, he saw Don Antonio. You could not miss him. Rotund, dressed in white with a Panama hat, with a pleasant face, a modest moustache and balding, he was the very stamp of a prosperous Catalan merchant. With a big smile and a stretched hand, Don Antonio welcomed him warmly and explained that the road from Sagua to Antillas by coach normally took six to seven hours. He was late by two hours because the heavy rains had made the roads impassable in some parts and his coach and horses had to be pulled out by a powerful oxbow of bulls.

Eusebio, suddenly with watery eyes, feared for his uncertain future in this strange land and silently questioned the reasons he had been ordered to go to the Antilles, away from his beloved Castro Urdiales, his mother, and his three sisters.

What will become of them? Why was the family dispersed? Why Cuba for him?

A Fateful Sea Storm

Eusebio Valle Espiga's father, Marcelo Valle, who was born in Castro Urdiales of Cantabria barely forty kilometers from Bilbao, worked to become a professional fleet fisherman early in his youth, and later married Josefa Espiga of Castilian roots. Castro Urdiales always was a prominent fishing port since the beginning of the Roman Occupation and the fishing fleet was large and well known. The ninth century Santa María Catholic Church, as big and tall as a cathedral, and the Templar Fort at the head of the bay dominates the beautiful city to this day. It is very probable that Marcelo and his children were baptized in the ancient tenth century stone fount of the medieval Santa María Church.

Marcelo Valle and Antonia Espiga had five children. The boys were Marcelino, the eldest, and Eusebio the youngest. The girls were Josefa, Julia, and Victoria. In due course, Marcelino and later, on special trips, little Eusebio, worked the characteristic wooden, double-ended, sea-worthy, diesel powered boats and fished the treacherous waters of the Cantabrian Sea.

The boats of the Castro Urdiales fishing cooperative would leave the breakwater protected man-made basin ("darcena") early in the morning under blasts of the town's own horns for three- to five-week long fishing trips to work the Cantabrian Sea, teaming with an enormous bounty of fish. On their return, horns announced their arrival and their women, in all manner of dress and heels, with two-wheeled barrows and some with many employees with bigger transportation facilities, helped tie the boats, wash and tidy them, and transport the catch to the free market for the highest bidder. The fishermen would leave all of this commerce to their women and head for the nearest bar to have shots of cognac, served in small glasses to be gulped down with gusto.

On the last day of their lives, Marcelo and his eldest, Marcelino, missed little Eusebio who was sick with the gripe. By mid-week, their boat was swamped in a storm with thirty to forty-foot waves and it quickly sank in the turbid cold waters in a matter of minutes. None of the crew survived. Antonia Espiga was devastated and never recovered; she was assigned to her surviving family. The girls were distributed among three different Castro Urdiales families of distant uncles and aunts, and Eusebio was sent to Sagua de Tanamo, Cuba, under the wing of Don Antonio Gómez Cianca, the prosperous charitable Catalonian merchant and close friend.

During the trip back to Sagua de Tanamo, Don Antonio carefully explained the situation at home. His second wife, Luisa Sedano, and his three daughters, Manuela, Rosalina and Antonia, lived in a house near his large store of general merchandise. His daughter Manuela was the issue of his deceased first wife with the Catalonian surname of Gómez Serret. The store was a veritable bazaar. He said the store was doing well and that he was to learn his business and, naturally, he would start as a low-ranked store clerk principally responsible for the orderliness and cleanliness of the establishment. He would have a room in the store and sleep there but he would have dinner at his house every night. He explained that his youngest daughter, Manuela, was also his age, and he expected his best behavior at home.

In time, young Eusebio exceeded Don Antonio's expectations. Not only had he learned the store's business and accounting quickly, he also promptly married Don Antonio's daughter, Manuela. He expanded the business, bought his own store in town, invested in real estate, bought a large farm in southern Oriente Province, and moved to Santiago de Cuba, where he prospered even further and was, suddenly, very wealthy. With the capital he saved, he bought several lots in the newly developed Vista Alegre suburb, targeted for the well to do and the rich. In a short interval thereafter, the arriviste Eusebio Valle Espiga finished a veritable mansion, and while construction was progressing, he took his entire family on a trip to visit northern Spain that lasted nearly a year, replete with servants and their kitchen accouterments.

The first-born was a male, Eusebio Valle Gómez, on June 8, 1907. Three daughters followed him (Antonia, Josefa, and Manuela) but it was little Eusebio who was to be overindulged beyond any measure of prudence. His father favored him generously. Eusebio's home was essentially a center of Spanish nationalist pride; the boy learned Spain's national anthem long before he learned the Cuban National Anthem. When members of the pro-Spanish Roman Catholic Church clergy visited the Valle mansion, shouts of "Viva Viscaya!" were heard in the expansive corridors.

Spain in the late 1920s was deeply divided politically. The anarchists were the majority, liberal republicans were next, and the conservative fascists were a well-organized minority with close affiliation to the officer class of the armed forces and the all-powerful Catholic Church. The fascists were to initiate the Spanish Civil War in 1936 when they could no longer tolerate the liberal fiats of the republican government of the day. Eusebio's sisters and his aunts and uncles gravitated to the fascist factions and joined membership with them. Tia Julia, who had blue eyes, not given to idle talk, and of strong character, fought with the fascists in several skirmishers and was severely wounded by a grenade explosion as she aimed a faulty throw, but she escaped a violent death to live to her 80s.

As difficult as this period was in Spain at this time, when conversations turned to the politics of the young Cuban Republic and of its inept and corrupt Criollo leaders, both were severely criticized because the Cuban politicos were favoring leftist principles and ideals. When the American government intervened in Cuba's politics under the authority of the peace treaty, it was discussed with disdain and nationalist bias. There was resentment against Americans for the Spanish surrender to them after the 1898 Spanish War.

If you had to characterize the Valle family those days, you'd say that they were, foremost, a group that longed for their beloved Spain in a violent and restless Criollo country struggling mightily with the political ideas of the time. It is fair to say that had Eusebio been borne in the nineteenth century, he would have been seen by Criollos as a "gachupin," a well-to-do male borne of first generation Spanish immigrants who strongly supported Spain.

Over time, Eusebio, in his journey from adolescence to young adulthood, showed that he was prodigiously intelligent, selfish, a restless and penchant romantic, an intractable reader, a lover and collector of classical music, books and paintings, an expert of the poetry of Amado Nervo (author of the romance "El Dia Que Me Quieras"), a local champion tennis player, and a member of a photography club. He was sent to the Jesuit School Dolores in downtown Santiago de Cuba, where he received the attention of its very best teachers and he won their confidence and special treatment. As the years went by, he graduated with distinction and subsequently entered the School of Law of the National University in Habana, more than six hundred miles to the west. Much later, when he was a practicing lawyer and a

University of Oriente professor, he was elected a member of the prestigious Grupo Humboldt, a claque of naturalists and historians dedicated to the study of the rich history of his native province. In his last years in Cuba before he immigrated to the U.S., he was named dean of the University of Oriente.

However, early in his academic career and once he was on his own and free in the Habana University Law School far away from the provincial capital and his tyrannical father, his life-long troubles began to take shape. Predictably, Eusebio had a fondness for the "liberated" sensuous women of the capital city. His remarkable good looks and his facile erudition were very effective with them. These attributes, however, also made him vulnerable to the political forces at play in the young republic, particularly in the university. Antonio Guiteras' underground Marxist movement "La Joven Cuba" singularly attracted him, and even the prevailing violence of the university student political groups held a certain attractiveness that challenged his intellectual curiosity and his rebellious devil may care instincts.

His alarmed father took notice and he feared for his adventurous son. Before the university student groups declared a strike and the Law School was shut down indefinitely in 1930s, and before a populist sergeant named Batista had taken command of the armed forces, his father did not hesitate to deliver him from harm's way and sent him to Atlanta, Georgia, to learn business office techniques badly needed in Cuba those days. Batista and his noncommissioned officers would take military and political power from the young republic later.

In Atlanta, the mutual attraction between Shirley and Eusebio took an unexpected turn when they decided to marry, skewing his conservative Catholic upbringing and without first seeking permission from his father and mother in Vista Alegre. On the other hand, the couple had the strong support of her mother, Harriet Farnsworth. The inopportune marriage was a civil ceremony on December 7, 1931. The couple settled in Harriet's guest home and they continued their studies in the business academy. Eusebio wrote a long and elaborate letter home announcing and explaining his marriage to an American girl of indistinct family background, religion, and questionable or non-existent dowry. To them, his betrayal of ancient beloved Spanish procedural customs was beyond the pale.

When the news was read to all members, the Valle family was angered, bitter, and disappointed. Devastated, Eusebio Valle Espiga announced in an explosive letter to his son that he and his family could not and would not accept the marriage and declared, in no uncertain terms, that he was legally "disowned," that he was no longer his recognized son, and he was no longer responsible for any costs generated by him, by Shirley, or her family. On receipt of this response, Eusebio and Shirley did not grasp the depth of the emotions on display by his family. Both actually believed that the emotional outbursts would be temporary and that retractions would be soon forthcoming. Harriet said she was not worried; she lied to them when she said she believed his father would change his mind shortly.

Both sides made irresponsible miscalculations.

Shirley and Eusebio looked for temporary jobs during Hoover's Great Depression and Roosevelt's New Deal. It was a very difficult and desperate time. None of his letters home were answered and he was totally cut off from Cuba for two long years. Their lives were made more difficult when Harriet Farnsworth announced her plans to go west within the year.

By March 1933, Harriett had sold the Guest House and was gone and Shirley was in the family way. As desperate as the situation was for the young married couple, Eusebio unexpectedly received a letter of rapprochement from his father announcing he no longer was disowned and that he was sending money via Western Union for their return trip to Santiago de Cuba. He explained that his friend, the statesman Don Cosme de la Torriente y Peraza, the distinguished lawyer, politician and diplomat, had convinced him to take these actions.

The young couple was received in the Valle mansion in August

1933 amidst deep mutual misgivings, tears, and seemingly warm embraces. Shirley was at the end of the last trimester of her pregnancy. On September 2, a baby girl with large, clear green eyes, large mouth, and alert features was delivered with ease in the family mansion. She was strikingly beautiful and was baptized Carol Marie Calixta Valle Friend.

When Carol was just about two years old and her brother, Tony, about eight months old, Shirley and Eusebio broke up and were divorced. The cultural clash between the two was too much to bear and the dominance of the male culture wore heavily on Shirley's mind. Eusebio's wandering eyes for other young women was added to the confounding mix. Several witnesses also testified that Shirley was unfaithful. It was a bitter and shrewdly contested divorce between an American and a Cuban pro-Spanish father. Eusebio's divorce was finalized in Cuba's Supreme Court. Shirley lost adjudication on the grounds of "abandonment" and Eusebio retained his children legally. The grandparents and aunts were to raise Shirley's two children with a lot of financial difficulty.

Later, much later, Carol was disdainfully called by some in Vista Alegre, the pro-Spanish enclave, "la hija de la Americana." She was the first in her class to read and to develop an extensive knowledge of the Spanish language. She attended the Sacred Heart School in Vista Alegre for girls for more than ten years and distinguished herself more for her rebellious comportment and lack of study interest of subjects other than literature and music, which her father avidly nurtured from his extensive library. The Catholic Church hierarchy had banned many of her readings in Boston and the Sacred Heart School for Girls in Vista Alegre.

At school, she befriended another rebellious student, Vilma Espin Gallois. Both girls published an informative school newspaper, "Eco" distributed widely among their friends.

While her brother Antonio (a.k.a. Tony) was the apple of his grandfather's eye and doing remarkably well at the Dolores Jesuit

School for Boys, Carol was under the diktats of a tyrannical father who made it nearly impossible for her to develop her mind and amazing athletic prowess in basketball, softball, and tennis. On her last visit to her children in Vista Alegre, Shirley requested permission to play basketball for her.

She was selected to the Cuban National Olympic Basketball Team to play in the Helsinki Olympiads after her record that year showed she was the highest center scorer of the island nation at age eighteen. True to his beliefs, Eusebio prohibited her from going to the Olympics, on the grounds that a young lady of her class should not be allowed to go with the Cuban Olympic Team and represent Oriente Province and Santiago de Cuba at the Olympiads.

She was to have many other bitter confrontations with her father particularly when she began to date many young Santiago men.

When I met her the first time, I was taken by her extraordinary beauty and bright mind, and determined to pursue her. My guest at Santiago the summer after my graduation from Harvard College was Peter Gunderson, son of Harvard's clinical professor of ophthalmology at Massachusetts General Hospital in Boston. Peter, ever the dry humorist, said she was "triple A, Charles, triple A."

Carol, la hija de la Americana

For me to freely court Carol, I climbed the short hill to their summer place in Santiago's Bay and formally petitioned Eusebio's pemission eye-to-eye. Eusebio, somewhat speechless, granted it to the

139

brazen young man.

We fell in love and in due course, I married her at a very young age, despite the muted objections of both of our families. I was twenty-four and she was twenty-two years old. I was a Criollo of an ancient Cuban family, a fourth year medical student at the Cornell University Medical College, and penniless. She was irreparably pro-Spanish and "the two will clash," or so conventional wisdom dictated.

It turned out quite differently.

CHAPTER 3.

◊ The Difficult End of Criollo Ways
◊ The Greig Family Dissolves and Dr. Santos-Buch Marries an Impoverished Herminia Greig Cossio and Starts An Unusual Family In Chantilly, His Country Retreat.

After my grandmother, Adolfina Cossío y de Céspedes, was widowed, she received no help whatsoever from the more successful de Céspedes who had all moved to the immune and dynamic republic's capital, Habana. Importantly, much needed help and guidance was received from the Scot, Richard Beattie, and his brother.

She had virtually to fend for herself and her five children alone. The oldest was a fourteen-year-old teenager who became heavily burdened with raising his younger siblings. She was happy that her older brother, Randolfo, and his family was nearby but she also longed for Pedro, her other sibling, who was away in Habana and did not keep in touch with her. She was pleased that her youngest, Herminia, had formed a bond with her bright first cousin, Adolfina Cossío Esturo, Randolph's youngest. They were inseparable and competed with grace academically. [34]

The ever-faithful Richard Beattie helped not only with occasional

---

34. Later, much later, Adolfina Cossío Esturo, a.k.a. Cucha, received the highest civil honor awarded by the Soviet Union, the Lenin Medal, for her achievements in abolishing illiteracy in Castro-Communist Cuba.

monetary gifts but also as a reassuring companion and close friend. For this, she was appropriately grateful. A glimpse of her state of mind was revealed after many years when she confided with my sister that after an adequate period of one or two years of mourning, dressed severely in black as was the custom, she should have warmed to the advances of Richard Beattie and accepted his marriage proposals. With tears streaming on her cheeks, she averred, "A young woman in my precarious situation has to be more realistic, and although I would have continued to love Charles for the rest of my life, I and my children would have had a much better life if I had accepted Richard. My loving granddaughter Enid, you must never make the same mistake I made." My sister, a faithful observer of Adolfina's social and wealth decline across the years, never forgot her advice.

Adolfina's situation worsened as time rapidly went by. The farm was difficult to manage for her; it was even more difficult to deal with the legal claims of lost property, and she did not know what to do when she tried to get advice from the budding corrupt politicians who paid little attention to her. Her family became progressively more dysfunctional as her younger boys rebelled and bucked the system. George, Richard, and Lizzie all wanted out.

The first to go was the rebellious and handsome cur, George Greig, who at age eighteen announced he had saved enough money for passage to England, that he was not a farmer, that life in Media Luna was limited and boring, that he felt trapped, and that he deserved better. He wanted to travel and see the world and find a new and more prosperous future. No one was able to convince him otherwise and he left promising to keep in touch by post. He never did but he did come back unannounced with disastrous results as you will learn later in this narrative.

Next in the exodus from Media Luna was Richard, who had become something of a gambler. He was very lucky to marry a very bright, hard-working and attractive young lady, María Teresa Fernández León, who was employed by the telephone company and had been promoted to a job in their headquarters in Habana. Richard followed her to the capital city to live with her family when she discovered she was pregnant. She named the boy after his father, Richard Greig Fernández. Richard and María Teresa did not get along, however. His gambling worsened and he was unable to make it financially, preferring menial jobs with no future. Soon they were divorced and he parted to New York where he married again and had a disastrous impoverished future.

Little Richard, when he reached his twenties and married, left Cuba with his mother and daughter for Buenos Aires, Argentina, following his capture and torture in the hands of General Batista's agents for suspicion of abetting and aiding the Insurgents of the twenty-sixth of July Movement during the Cuban Revolution.

Elizabeth, the red-headed intemperate beauty, was courted by a young man of French descent, Luis Rosell Castelnau, from an ancient propertied Santiago family. The family managed a farm, Fleur de Lis, which was situated in the hills north of Santiago. Charles' uncle Luis loved life and he was a carefree and happy man. His guitar, voice, and conversational agility and good humor easily conquered the fickle and very feminine Lizzie. They married within a year of courting and Lizzie left the family nest of Media Luna. She produced three attractive girls, Georgina, Rose Mary, and Flavia who survived to old age. Eventually, many years later, Luis was the director of the Coca-Cola bottling plant of Santiago de Cuba.

As Adolfina's nest was diminished, the responsibilities to carry on and make an adequate living were made worse by the uncertainty created by the travails of the young republic. Her situation, she realized, had become unsustainable and increasingly burdensome. During this period, the oldest and handsome son, Charles, fell in love and married a wonderful and gentle young woman, Lirio, a.k.a. Lilly, Fernández, who turned out to be barren.

In the course of time, Charles Greig Cossio and Luis Rosell agreed to start a new business in the Fleur de Lis farm. Together they convinced Adolfinita and his brothers and sisters that this was a good move. They needed seed capital to start the enterprise. In time, Adolfina was convinced and the Media Luna bungalow and the Macaca farm property were sold. With the money she made on the sale, new, albeit modest homes, were rented in Santiago de Cuba, and Fleur de Lis was prepared for the new projects.

It was doomed from the start.

The Great Depression, personality conflicts among the principals and their lack of business experience finally collapsed the project. To make matters worse, the very handsome George Greig Cossio showed up unannounced with Lady Marjorie, his London socialite lover. Their affair had been amply announced in the London society pages. The very attractive Marjorie used her feminine wiles and it did not take long for her to seduce the men who had not known that they had fallen in a trap that turned them against each other. The project and Adolfinita's dreams quickly darkened. After the breakup, the disgusted Charles and Lilly left for Habana to open a dental distributing franchise. Family members chastened Luis for a while and the never-do-well George and Lady Marjorie hurriedly departed for London in disgrace.

With the scarcity of what was left of her savings, the ill-advised and bewildered Adolfina and her youngest daughter, Herminia settled in a small house near San Basilio and the Santos-Buch Laboratory in Santiago de Cuba. Home schooling had slowly, and with difficulty, taken Herminia to a grade level that prepared her for the pursuit of a bachelor's degree and she made plans to register in the Instituto de Segunda Enseñanza de Oriente in Santiago de Cuba, housed in what was once Don Andrés Duany's ancient and expansive mansion in Marina Alta.

Herminia was seventeen with a splendid figure and spectacularly beautiful, blonde with blue eyes and classic Scottish features and tall, at five feet nine inches. She would take the trolley car in Calvario Street or walk to the Instituto some ten blocks away.

Modernity

Santiagueros were fascinated and awed.

One early morning in the fall of 1926, as he was looking out his office window, Dr. Santos-Buch saw Herminia's majestic figure climb the steps of a trolley car, and right there and then, he decided she was the woman he was going to marry. He thought: She is tall, blonde, intelligent, with careful, impeccable speech and social grace, and she is everything I admire. The fact that she was from an ancient criollo family that opened up the land centuries before perked his curiosity and he knew that would help his reputation and social standing.

He soon courted her, and the well-to-do and gentle doctor won the day with his worldly charm and his overflowing confidence that made up for his lack of physical attractiveness. Even though he was the son of a Spaniard, Adolfina, the aristocratic mambí, liked what she saw and encouraged the relationship, despite the age differences between the two. The doctor was thirty-two and she was eighteen.

The first wedding took place March 8, 1927, in the Iglesia de la Purísima Concepción in Manzanillo. After a short honeymoon in the mambí city of Bayamo, and true to his penchant for the grand style, he chose to reintroduce his young bride to Santiago society with a reaffirmation wedding ceremony in the 18th century chapel of San Basilio Magno, which housed the ancient Las Siervas de María Order and a seminary known for astrophysics and other sciences. The members of Las Siervas de María Order were his pro bono patients. The 18th century edifice was not far from his laboratory.

To this beautiful and small chapel came Don Tomas Beattie and family and his brother Richard, as well as almost all members of the Buch and Santos clans and his Chantilly neighbors, Radames Covani and Marina Bacardi, don Enrique Schueg and their respective families. These guests dazzled the impoverished de Céspedes family members. The affirmation ceremony was headlined in the major newspapers of the ancient provincial capital. After the ceremony, the couple and Adolfina settled in their country home, Chantilly.

The couple left for a honeymoon car trip in the United States that took them from the southeastern seaboard to Niagara Falls in upper New York State. It was a grand educational trip as Dr. Santos-Buch showed off his beautiful bride to his Manhattan, Washington and Baltimore friends and acquaintances. A photo was taken of her on the rock in the center of Central Park Pond, which he kept in his gold watch fastened to a chain, for the rest of his life.

Herminia, now far away from the violent labyrinths of her heritage, fell in love with New York City and her splendid theater, opera, and art museums, which was to last for the rest of her life. She was a million miles away from the uncouth travails of her youth and looked on her husband with admiration, love, and the knowledge she had found a close, kindred spirit. Time was to prove she was right in marrying him.

On their arrival home with a newly bought Desoto car, Herminia announced she was pregnant. On January 3, 1928, she delivered a blue-eyed blonde girl, Enid María, my strong willed, sharp-as-a-tack sister, who is four years my senior. My father was beside himself with joy – she was beautiful, alert, attentive, and playful. What else mattered?

The joy was to end abruptly.

When she had come to term and a midwife had delivered Enid María on the dinner table of the Chantilly house, the baby and the delivery had occurred in good order. However, she had retained parts of the placenta, which had to be removed by hand to prevent continued bleeding. As it was, she had lost some blood. Nevertheless, everything looked and felt right. Makinkina had taken the baby and her mother, Adolfina, was now in charge.

She felt weak, however, and the next day developed an unrelenting fever. Angel, her husband, was agitated and worried. He used a speculum to take cultures for a cervical bacterial infection and he was able to confirm she had puerperal fever. He cursed himself and then the midwife (the morphine-addicted mistress of a prominent Santiago doctor). She had never heard him curse so violently, and then

146

he immediately called his cousin, Dr. Jesús Buch. It was an emergency situation and she was to be treated at home.

Dr. Jesús Buch measured her thready pulse for the second time, Tardus et Parvus, he determined. He was now looking at the thermometer. The fever was read at 38.7 degrees Celsius. It climbed rapidly to 40 degrees by eleven p.m. Her husband took large samples of blood for bacterial cultures in his laboratory.

Herminia was staring, and in a firm voice, asked him. "Is it endometritis?"

"Yes," he answered. She lay back on her propped-up pillows and looked at his piercing eyes directly. In a steady, clear voice she said, "I know both of you will do your very best to keep me alive, I am sure of it. Let's get going with it." They set up a saline intravenous infusion.

Angel María explained that she had a severe intrauterine infection refractory from the medications of the day. He wanted to treat her with an intravenous mercurochrome-saline solution to cut the raging sepsis she clearly was developing. The blood cultures were positive of a streptococcus bacterium. Sepsis was almost always the fatal result of "puerperal fever." Then he told her of the risk of mercury kidney toxicity. Dr. Buch agreed and they were already getting ready. First, Angel had to prepare the sterile isotonic Mercurochrome sterile solution in his laboratory.

She said she understood that there were no other known clinical options. Makinkina and Adolfina remained silent and deeply fearful as the two doctors set up the intravenous infusion (January 6, 1928). Dr. Buch made himself as comfortable as possible in the bedside chair and gently took her hand and held it for a long time, looking for convulsions. From time to time in the late night he took her pulse and with his stethoscope in his signature professional style that was both reassuring and informative to so many of his Santiago patients, he listened to her breathing and heart beats. She was now at ease.

By mid-morning the next day, Dr. Buch found that her pulse was firmer. She had had a peaceful night. Her fever had dropped to 38.1 Celsius. Her chest was clear and the heart sounds were astoundingly strong. She was no longer sweating.

That night her fever was normal.

She steadily improved the following days and the two University of Maryland graduates had good reason to sport their contagious broad smiles.

There was another woman who had been delivered by a midwife in Santiago who had not been heroically treated with intravenous Mercurochrome. She had died about three to four days after the onset of the sepsis. Herminia tolerated the heroic treatment devised by the two University of Maryland Medical graduates and she survived. Her urinary output was normal and did not change. Her blood urea nitrogen remained normal. There was no detectable kidney damage.

Herminia convalesced in bed for three months or so. Because of this, she developed phlebitis and had to elevate her legs until the thrombi in her veins dissolved. In time, very slowly, Herminia resumed her life and enjoyed her beautiful daughter, the delight of her young doctor husband.

She was told not to have more pregnancies for a long while because of her varicose veins, perhaps for three to four years.

But there were other more important developments that required the postponement of further pregnancies. This was a time of Keynesian easy money lending practices and a false prosperity, based on huge amounts of printed money, and it was unsustainable. The collapse of the United States economy brought on a depression the likes of which would not happen again in Cuba until the advent of World War II and the isolation of the island by German submarines. The survival of the family members fell almost entirely on the young doctor's shoulders and his brother, Miguel, and his sisters. But, defying her youthfulness, it was Herminia's indomitable character and almost icy logic and ability to see the panorama in a realistic perspective that held the family together for decades.

For now, after several keen conversations with themselves, sometimes deep into the night, Ángel and Herminia outlined their future. In sharp contrast to the custom of the day, Herminia was to finish her secondary education to get a bachelor's degree and enter the National University of Habana to study pharmacy. She would become an active working partner of the Laboratory, which was now producing patent medicines. The child would be under the care of Adolfina and Makinkina while she attended Habana University for four years. For now, Herminia would go to the Instituto de Segunda Ensenanza about six miles away to finish the required subjects to enter the University in Habana. To do this, she had to leave by car early in the morning with her content and enterprising husband. She hated getting up so early in the morning.

They waited three years to try another pregnancy. This time it was an uneventful episode. I was born on the dining room table of the Chantilly home on March 20, 1932. An earthquake and a tsunami that destroyed the fishing village of Santa Cruz del Sur in Camaguey had preceded me. But in Chantilly, there was happiness and love all around.

For a period of years, until I was about nine years old, my grandmother Adolfina and my Jamaican nanny, Makinkina, brought me up.

Well, not entirely, you see. My loving mom, when on university leave, did keep a vigilant eye from time to time, whenever she could. It wasn't my fault, she thought. She just had too much on her plate. She would be absent for a long time in the fabled capital city of Habana to finish her studies while she was housed with her brother, Charles, and his wife, Lilly.

As for me, I really did not care. Why? Makinkina and Abuelita were there for me. Pop came to me from time to time to hug and kiss me. And my sister and her Angora cats were great. I did not need anyone else and I was having a ball, horsing around in Chantilly with my close friend, Manuel Jorge Cutillas and others from the house of Don Emilio Bacardi, as the years rapidly went by.

Four Cuabitas friends
(Family heirloom photo)

I never really missed my mom those early years of discovery and wonderment. I was becoming increasingly self-sufficient and a little bit of a nerd. Makinkina taught me Jamaican English and I learned to say "Our Father" with a Jamaican singsong by myself. I dressed and ate by myself and my grandmother, María Buch, taught me how to tie my shoelaces.

I was not getting satisfactory answers to my incessant questions. I questioned the meaning of the painted figure of St. Eduviges in the wall mural of the small chapel on the side room, next to my bedroom. No one answered and I decided I liked her a lot.

Secretly, under her kind and loving eyes, I dislodged a loose floor tile and created a hiding place for my red scorpion I had desiccated in alcohol. I noticed that the alcohol on desiccation extracted the red pigment.

Across from Chantilly in Villa Retazos with its tennis court, another young boy was rapidly developing. Manuel Jorge Cutillas was exactly my age and we became fast friends in a relationship that was to last more than eight decades. He was a true friend, a confidant and partner in exploring our fabulous Cuabitas surroundings. We stared at the five Anacahuita trees of the primeval forest in awe. We held a burning interest in observing and questioning the origins of the innate nature of life around us.

Later, much later, I became a Connecticut Yankee, a full tenured Professor of Pathology and a Harvard and Cornell scientist, while Manuel Jorge's success reached its zenith when he was named Chairman of the Board and Chief Executive Officer of the fabled International Bacardi Rum Company.

I believe that our early years in Cuabitas had a great deal to do with our success.

CHAPTER 4.

◊ I Am Introduced to Practical Economics, To The German Master Race And A Popular Oriente Province Populist.

Manuel Jorge Cutillas Covani, and I, Charles Augusto Santos-Buch, all of five years old, arrived on time that September 1937. The Echemendia matriarch had opened a kindergarten in her garage in the second rail crossing of the San Luis road near both Villa Elvira and Chantilly, and it had attracted many of the local children. Curiously, neither of us clung to our Jamaican nannies, Anita and Makinkina. We ran into the classroom in a second. The nannies placed small metal boxes with our lunch on our tiny desks as they eyed the teacher and the room suspiciously. They left worried, saying to us in Jamaican English that we would be picked up at three o'clock.

Many of our Cuabitas friends already sat in assigned desks. A brand-new chart of capital and lower-case letters of the Spanish alphabet hung prominently from the wall next to the large blackboard. They noted the "ñ" and the double l, the "ll." We questioned in our minds why there was a double l in the Spanish alphabet but said nothing. The "ñ" must be used for "coño," the curse word heard so frequently from the help. Several windows opened to an open meadow where youths had fabricated a baseball field – sort of. We looked to the open spaces longingly.

A Differing View of Cuba's History

On top of our desks were one-foot by eight-inch slates framed by hard wood and a chalk stick, which we students stared at suspiciously. After a warm welcome, the teacher read the list of names and we raised our hands when ours was called. Mrs. Echemendia taught us how to use the chalk and trace the first letter with a big capital A.

She said, "Aaahhh," and repeated with emphasis, "Aaahh."

We repeated loudly, "Aaahhh," several times. With difficulty, we traced an "A" on our small slate board.

On our way home our hands and blue uniforms were covered with chalk.

Manuel Jorge and I thought school was very boring and we lied to our parents when they asked how it was going.

Six months later we reached the letter G.

We never really learned the rest of the alphabet by rote and later, when we were eight, our studies took a sudden serious turn because we had to use our minds to figure out what came after G.

Chinese Farmer's Work Ethic

My father had indefinitely rented the small glen next to the river coursing the back of Chantilly to two Chinese families that had taken refuge from the Mao Communist revolution. They had built a dilapidated but sturdy home that housed the four adults and several small children. In a matter of three short months, I marveled at the greenery of the farmed land. Cabbages, tomatoes, lettuces, eggplants, peppers, and others that I did not know how to identify stood in multiple rows which were irrigated by river water propelled by an ingenious artifact made out of bamboo cut from Chantilly's riverside! It was extraordinary to watch the Chinese peasants ever so carefully weed, cultivate, and protect their produce with rudimentary but effective farm tools.

Modernity

Later, I talked to my father about my observations and I was told that every first of the month at six a.m., the peasants waited in the front door of the main house to pay their rent. "They have never missed a payment Charles," my father said.

"But what do they do with their money, Pop?"

"They use it to better themselves, but I believe most of it is saved underneath their mattresses for a rainy day," my father told me.

Why a rainy day? I asked.

The learning spiral really began when our families moved to the provincial capital, Santiago de Cuba. My new home was a large, colonial house, three centuries old, with a large patio, a cistern for rainwater and fruit trees, about two blocks away from my school.[35] The home was also modified to become Dr. Santos-Buch's clinical laboratory. In the back, patent medicines were prepared and marketed.

I asked my father, "What about the Chinese farmers?"

"Well, they came early this morning to make their final payment because they bought a parcel of land in nearby Boniato and they do not need to pay rent to us anymore. What do you think about that Charles?"

I looked my father in the eye and said, "I will miss them, Pop."

"You are right, son. We have learned a lesson how savings appropriately used brings freedom and prosperity to those who work hard and efficiently."

What did he mean by that? I asked myself.

35. The patio had a cistern to collect rain water and was a veritable botanic garden with two mango trees (biscochuelos), one guava, one guanabana, bananas, flower bushes, cacti and incredible leafy arecas. There was in the center a running Spanish colonial water fountain with Japanese fish and Thailand water lilies with their buddings. The adjacent high ceiling living room supported an ancient roof sustained by massive tree trunks shaped by axes. The walls were about three feet deep of meshed guasima branches covered by cement. A colonial gallery ran more than fifty feet to the back where my father ran a pharmaceutical laboratory. The wood was severe, thick and elegant. A lining mural by a local painter with filigrees of crimson and purple-blue flowering bougainvillea decorated the separate dining room. It had stood without damage by the severe earthquakes that occurred in this volcanic area of the island for over three centuries.

A Differing View of Cuba's History

That very night, in the gallery of our new home in the colonial area of the ancient city, I heard an elegantly dressed doctor referencing the idea of redistributing wealth to the poor: "The more you give them, the more they will ask and become more dependent on government's handouts." I noted how different the Chinese had been in Chantilly. They are independent and free now, I thought with admiration.

Manuel Jorge, who moved to the high-end suburb of Vista Alegre, entered La Salle Catholic School in the colonial area of Santiago. For him, coming from a family of free thinkers and mambí patriots, the initiation of academics and the ritual of Catholic dogma and concepts was a very challenging experience indeed. La Salle School was in the ancient Roman Catholic complex of San Basilio Magno, well known for its scientific center and astrophysicists and higher mathematics. La Salle was a superior school managed largely by French priests.

The Juan Bautista Sagarra school complex, across the way in Marina Alta (Aguilera) Street about one mile away from La Salle, included Herbart School for Girls and Sagarra for boys.

For Manuel Jorge and I, these experiences were a mind expander. The Sagarra first grade was co-educational. On the other hand, the Salle first grade was strictly for boys who were almost all of Spanish origin. After first grade, there was separation of the sexes; the girls continued in the Herbart School for Girls in the subsequent grades and the boys continued across the street in the Sagarra facility.

For all students of both sexes, from second grade onwards, the day began with a congregation of all students in the open-air sports facility and with the raising of the Cuban flag by student monitors as the student body sang the national anthem and the recitation of a significant moment of Cuba's independence wars. In the magnificent La Salle school, on the other hand, every Friday began with High Mass and Orations to God and the Lord Jesus Christ in Latin. Swearing allegiance to the Cuban Flag several days a week in La Salle encouraged patriotic fervor as well.

156

Modernity

The flag was also raised in Sagarra as the Cuban National Anthem was chanted with gusto and pride by the entire student body every day before classes. The director of Sagarra, Don Francisco (a.k.a. Pancho) Ibarra, followed the flag ceremony with a short albeit emotional briefing on a noted event of the long and difficult Wars of Cuban Independence. Over the years, I was always impressed by the seriousness of the ceremony. I was to be selected a monitor much later when I was in the top 5 percent of my class.

I faced a questioning lay teacher who used the Socratic method, a truly terrifying moment for me. In the classroom of twenty or so students in separate desks, on my first day, I was given a list of books, rulers, pencils, pencil sharpeners, and erasers that had to be bought for the next day. This was followed with a list of homework assignments. I was not sure what "la tarea de la casa" meant. My teacher was Señorita America and I immediately liked her. She reminded me of St. Eduviges of the Chantilly Chapel. How could I go wrong? America proceeded to go through the early mechanics of reading, writing, arithmetic and Cuban history. I took it all in and scored very well in un-announced tests. I did well the next three years. Manuel Jorge did as well in La Salle.

To my surprise, my mom announced that I had to be baptized in Santa Lucia, a Catholic Church near my neighborhood. My mom explained I was not baptized when I was a newborn as customs dictated because she and my father had difficulty in selecting the two godparents-to-be. They finally came to a satisfactory agreement and I was baptized, fair and square. After the baptism I was told that I would be instructed in the Catholic faith and have my first Communion when I was satisfactorily tutored. These difficulties indicated to me that my parents were not as true to their faith as expected. I didn't quite understand why this was so.

It was a sunny Saturday morning that fall of 1940 when I learned my first political lesson from, of all unlikely people, Don Pepe, Pop's master bricklayer and stone mason. I idolized the strong, thin-as-a-rail old Catalan. He migrated to Santiago from Barcelona, Catalonia. His Spanish brogue was faulty; I thought it was slurred (I did not know the Catalan language). He had a thick, white moustache that was yellowed from his continued smoking of half-lit cigars. I admired his strength as Don Pepe laid heavy, three-inch-thick flag stones to cover the inner patio of our home. And yet Don Pepe was so thin – really scrawny. I marveled at Don Pepe's determination to conquer his physical impediments, and watched the magnificent artisan's labor in wonderment. In great concentration he easily decorated the flowerbeds with borders of cemented filigrees imitating green tree trunks that lined the long gallery and the large patio. It was a magnificent showpiece of artistic labor. I decided right there and then that I wanted to be like Don Pepe and I wished I could learn his trade.

A rising of crowd voices from the street immediately interrupted the moment. I could not believe the crowd noise. Don Pepe put down his tools and grabbed my hand and took me out the front door to see what was happening. There, in the Plaza de Dolores, half a block from the doctor's office, was a large, enthusiastic, and happy crowd of common folks of all races and dresses who loudly saluted the politician who stood up in an open car for all to see and to honor.

It was an electrifying event to see the crowd of Santiagueros celebrated the smiling hero.

"Who is he?" I said.

"A man of the people, a man who speaks to the people, a man who is admired by all common men, a man who cares for them and helps them," said Don Pepe.

I vaguely listened to the speech and was able to make out a man of color, perhaps with Asian features, or perhaps a light mulatto, I wasn't sure. He was a mix of different races. He had a broad smile and a confident look and was obviously enjoying the adoring crowd around him. There were no guards or policemen I could see.

Don Pepe, somewhat angered, puffed on the cigar stub and

looked at me, his protégé, and said, "Who is he, you ask? How can this be? Why, he is General Fulgencio Batista, who was recently elected President of Cuba, of course."

I was absolutely dumbfounded. How could that be? Pop and Mom had not once but many times said General Batista was abhorrent and evil. He had opposed freedom-loving folks like them. I had heard stories about Antonio Guiteras' assassination. He was hero to many Santiagans. What was happening? I had not been told of any presidential elections I could remember.

Embarrassed, I looked away and wanted to go home. What was going on? The people of Santiago looked happy. That was unreal. When I turned to look again, Don Pepe, my idol, was screaming, "Viva Batista!" repeatedly and as loud as he could.

Later, I asked my father why Don Pepe was a supporter of Batista. I learned that Don Pepe and his family had suffered during the Spanish Civil War when he supported the Republic and had briefly fought against the onslaught of the Fascist armed forces as they surrounded the outskirts of Barcelona to conquer it. The Fascists had executed his boys. He and his wife, Maria, escaped and sought refuge in the warm Catalonian enclave of Santiago de Cuba.

"A man of the people" lingered in my mind and I asked myself, "What does that mean, anyway?" I didn't give it further thought and slept soundly that night.

The Day of the U-Boat

It was a hot October day and the early morning was breaking with cloudless bright blue skies that eventful 1941. Leaving the massive antique front doors of my father's medical office, I squinted when I hit the corner of Calvario and Marina Alta on my way to Juan Bautista Sagarra School, already dreading Marañon, my fourth-grade teacher. I was sure that I would be called to answer pointed questions on my reading assignment. Marañon had kept me on my toes lately and I, all of nine years old, wanted to be sharp.

Santiagueros were on the way to work, walking ever so slowly, many carrying parasols to fight off the intense radiance of the day. As usual, the poor swarmed about me, begging for a portion of my lunch. Why there were so many poor? Pop had a curt answer: the war. I really didn't understand what Pop meant. We had just arrived from a car tour of the East Coast of the United States that June and I had not seen any beggars. When I returned home, the war had taken a turn for the worse for Churchill's allies while the U.S. remained neutral. One morning the banner headlines in the *Diario de Cuba* of Santiago de Cuba read that France had fallen and was in German hands.

As I rounded Reloj Street and crossed in front of the ancient Dolores Church, the bustle of the always-busy park suddenly stopped and a growing babble of curious voices made me turn. Exiting from Enramadas, the downtown business Main Street, never in groups of less than pairs, were sailors wearing bright white uniforms. I had never seen or imagined them before. They were remarkable for their similar size and fitness. They were blonde or had black hair and it seemed that all had deep blue eyes. They were a determined and militarized group.

In white ducks, they wore caps with a blue band that trailed in two ends neatly hugging the neck and upper back. I recognized the language they spoke – German! And I gathered from a passerby that they had disembarked from a U-boat anchored just off the quay.

In class, after the obligatory singing of the Cuban National Anthem, I asked Marañon how was it that German sailors were visiting Santiago? What he told the attentive class was more than I expected. After all, President Roosevelt had recently provided a number of destroyers to Great Britain at war with Germany. Furthermore, after the Fall of France, it was headlined in the local papers that the Luftwaffe was bombing London to the ground. British Spitfires and Hurricanes were giving the German air onslaught fits and had bloodied Herman Goering's (Commander of the German Air Force) and Adolph Hitler's noses.

It was difficult for us to understand how a German U-boat had evaded the British Navy and entered Santiago Bay to refuel and provision, far from their bases in Kiel and Hamburg. After all, Jamaica, a British Naval Station, was a mere forty miles south of Santiago. Perhaps they had refueled from a mother ship in the dark of night. Was Germany bringing the war to us?

At home, my father had spread a map of the world on a wall of the main corridor and had placed small little German flags with swastikas to show the success of the blitzkrieg. We listened to the British Broadcasting System every night and Mom and Pop kept my sister Enid well informed. U-boats, in wolf-packs, had sunken a dreadful tonnage of British ships in convoys protected by corvettes and destroyers, many obtained with Roosevelt's Lend/Lease Program. Nevertheless, the swastikas that decorated Pop's map had alarmingly grown in number lately and curiously, there were very few St. George flags. All of this seemed so far away to me.

Marañon, as usual, answered directly and clearly. No one ever dared to challenge his information. The all male class of ten-year-olds admired this great teacher. We knew that no one else was smarter.

He described how the captain of the U-Boat had refused the Cuban harbor pilot and entered the bay without any help. He told us that the German captain had maneuvered the U-boat without incidence smartly avoiding the reefs of the Morro Castle canal and the dreaded Las Mucaras. The sleek black submarine was this morning anchored near the Michelsen quay flying the black ensign of the Third Reich's Navy with the white cross of the Black Knights.

After the mandatory boarding by Santiago Customs authorities, permission had been granted to the crew to disembark in rubber auxiliaries and visit Santiago and its surrounding parks and beaches. The crew had been briefed by her officers to comport like gentlemen of the Third Reich and to be respectful of all Cubans. Marañon did not expect any troublemakers or embarrassing incidents between Santiagueros and the German Navy, widely regarded as an elite unit. He explained that Cuba was a neutral country and that refueling and provisioning was necessary for the U-boat.

After a few questions, the issue was not broached in class again. Predictably, Marañon questioned me on my home study assignments and I forgot two answers. But I managed to survive the school day somehow, and my mind raced on the submarine and the German sailors.

Out of breath, I ran into my father's front office, almost staggering into his awaiting patients, excited to bring in the news. But I noticed my father's secretary's alarmed face as she held her finger to her mouth. I meekly entered the interior patio of our home.

My father was busy with his patients and I ran into Mom's arms and kissed her excitedly, describing the arrival of the German mariners. She was not happy and barely smiled at me. I quieted down. As she only could do, my mother icily described that England and Scotland were at war with Nazi Germany. She reminded me that her father, Charles, was from Aberdeenshire, Scotland. She said that Germany was evil and that she suspected that the war would touch us in Cuba as well. The good-looking disciplined sailors I had admired were our enemies.

Father will be different, I thought. He had joined in family discussions of the war and friends and several of them spoke eloquently – I believed – and argued in favor of Hitler's success; Mom had steadfastly defended Churchill and England. Pop had been sort of neutral – sort of, mind you. He had said that if the United States entered the war, he would support President Franklin Roosevelt to the end. And Dr. Santos-Buch was a man of his word.

My sister wandered to the gallery and she listened as my mother broke the unexpected news to them. The German captain had seen our father's Germanic name in the bronze plaque in the front door and had come in and requested a moment of conversation with him.

Modernity

He said the German surname, Buch, alerted him and that he wished to visit and get to know our family. My father invited the captain to a formal dinner that night at seven sharp. We children were to dine with them and we had to be in our best behavior. My grandmother, Adolfina, the Scot's widow, excused herself in anger. She was to visit her other daughter, Lizzie, that night.

What is going on? I thought. Why did my father invite Mom's enemy to dinner?

I didn't understand much of this and I couldn't put two and two together. Maybe after dinner when we were excused and sent to our rooms to study, we could put two and two together, I thought. Anyway, Enid was wiser and she would straighten me out with explanations. There was a lot of excitement among the help as dinner was prepared.

It was a memorable dinner for us children and an awkward situation for Herminia Greig, daughter of a McGregor. The civilized captain of the U-boat, polite and perhaps somewhat arrogant and pedantic, in full white dress uniform with the Iron Cross around his neck, brought the conversation to the responsibility of persons of Germanic origins like ours to take over the political leadership during the coming of the Third Reich's World Order. He spoke with daring certainty, and if he had not impressed my mother and father with his message of world domination, he left his mark on us children, who never forgot this event. I noted the controlled anger in my mother's face, but no one else seemed to care. My father was impassive and seriously listened to the spokesman of the "Master Race." We children were excused and sent to bed.

What is a "Master Race" anyway?

I did not sleep at all that night. I had Marañon tomorrow and I was not ready for his probing questioning. I had noticed the hardly repressed anger in my mother's voice. On her return, my abuelita Adolfina was doing a slow burn. Mom or Pop did not raise the subject of the Master Race again.

A Differing View of Cuba's History

The now rapidly waning Criollo Civilization allowed the progressive populist movement of the early 1940s to prosper virtually unopposed. It had a rich and vibrant substrate in the immense Spanish immigration that happened during the bitter wars' historical developments. It was not recognized as a threat and it was not given the importance they deserved by historians of the day or by political analysts who seemed to be anchored in the vibrant capital city of Habana and knew little of the uncouth "interior." They were "desk bound" analysts and did little if any travel. It was not widely taught in schools or publicized in the radio or in newspapers. Cuban history was explained in simplistic, romantic, nationalistic formulas with many dates, statistics, sacrifices, and much blood and martyrdom.

On their own cognizance, small circles of the intelligentsia and the well-educated meaningfully broached the political whys in depth. For the rest, there was little generally said about economics, economic imperialism, and the expansion neither of powers nor of the adoption of political doctrines by the participants of the wars. There were significant critiques of the socialist movement by notable Ten Years War Patriots. For example, Major General Ignacio Agramonte in 1865 and, later, Jose Marti in 1885 who, prior to the War of Independence of 1895, both discussed Socialism and Karl Marx. Agramonte essentially attacked the tyranny of collectivism and defended the free will of the individual in his oral public defense of his thesis on graduation from the Habana University Law School. Jose Marti, on the other hand, greatly praised Karl Marx's achievements on the occasion of his death in the Buenos Aires newspaper "La Nacion" (See Appendix). These expositions were generally ignored in pre-Castro Cuban public education facilities, conservative Catholic Schools and progressive secular schools, like Juan Bautista Sagarra.

It was easier, more acceptable, and politically correct to bash the United States of America's expansionist policies and gringos in general.

These subjects were raised principally as clichés and their crowd-pleasing and motivational importance were not usually stressed. Capitalism, socialism and communism were not critically taught. The educated upper classes, although they recognized the disparate economic chasm between the have-nots and the haves, thought they were immune to its potentially explosive nature, something that would compel the masses to violent protests or insurgent activities against tyranny.

They felt that they were not in any danger or that they were facing a socio-political "reckoning."

The passion of the don Pepes or the disfranchisement of the poor and agricultural laborers in Cuba was sorely missing from intelligent discussions. By simply saying "Cubans are not racist" or "They have their social clubs and our Santiago Mayor is Afro-Cuban," magically dismissed the idea of "raging racism or the dismal poverty of the have-nots."

Literature Nobel Prize winner Gabriel García Márquez would have defined this phenomenon correctly as an excellent example of "Magic Realism" he popularized.

Hunting Trip to El Turquino Mountain by Sea

To my delight, I was invited by my father to go with him on a hunting trip for wild doves ("torcazas") in the foothills of Cuba's tallest mountain, El Turquino. This was an elaborate journey because hunters had to cruise by sea to reach and spend an overnight in a little cay about half way to the Turquino River, Cayo Dama (Lady Key) owned by the Bacardi family.

The final leg of the trip was to the river entrance on the southern shores. Once the sand bar at the entrance of the river was passed, the thirty-six-foot cruiser anchored and a base camp was set on shore with hammocks and with a neatly constructed fire to do the cooking. Our guides explained to my father that the hammocks were necessary because wild pigs loose in the underbrush were ferocious and dangerous.

My keen ears heard what I thought were the sound of French horns in the distance. The guide explained that it was a conch trumpet used by the natives to communicate across the mountains and that they were announcing our arrival. The crew and hunters met them at first light next morning.

My father and I did not go hunting with the Turquino guides. My father stayed behind with his little black doctor's bag and other medical accouterments to service many of the local natives: old ladies, mothers, children, old and young men, everyone, all day. It was a pro-bono service that he had rendered previously. I noted how friendly and grateful his patients were.

The five days of hunting was incredibly productive as more than a thousand birds were killed and packed in ice for the return trip and the redistribution of the prizes among the participants. Just before departing, the fishermen among the crew caught two bull sharks in the river basin that measured well over six feet. I did not know that bull sharks ventured into river waters from time to time.

I had long forgotten this adventure with Dad when, on one clear day in Chantilly, I recognized one of the leaders of the Turquino natives talking to my father extensively with a great big smile as he looked on his surprised and yet pleased face. Dad explained that the guajiros were going to repay his pro bono services by building a beam-and-post "guano" roof (a peasant thatch roof) for a two-bedroom, one bath, and living room house in Chantilly.

The experience overwhelmed me. A large crew built it in less than three weeks and my father added the walls, doors, windows, floors, and the plumbing for what became a delightful work of criollo architecture enjoyed by our family on many weekend retreats without telephone service. It became known as the Santos-Buch "Bohio" (peasant ranch) retreat.

Modernity
Unexploded Yankee Cannon Rounds In Ciudamar

The weekend was cloudless, and terribly hot. Manuel Jorge and I climbed the hill just above La Estrella, where the old Spanish fort was out-gunned and destroyed by the American Navy in July 1898. Now we faced a deep crevasse and the crumbling sandstone and dirt clung to our sweat, our shirts, and shoes. We stopped and looked south to the Morro Castle and marveled at the beautiful entrance of the deep Bay of Santiago de Cuba.

We had a notion that we might find evidence of the battle in the scarred façade of the steep hill. We tried to avoid the prickly "guao" bushes and with some success entered another crevasse where we distinguished a black shiny object buried loosely in the sandstone dirt. Not far from this one, we detected three other metallic intruders. With a flatter stone the size of our hands we dug the first object and pulled it out of the hillside. It was an unexploded four-inch cannon projectile. We deduced that the American fleet preferred four-inch rounds and we had found four of them. The unexploded rounds were very heavy and we realized we could not bring them up to the nearby road by ourselves.

Satisfied and proud of our findings, we ran home and reported them to Manuel Jorge's father, Captain Cutillas, who was retired from the Spanish Navy. He immediately disposed of the four rounds with the help of Cuban Navy authorities. After a stern ten-minute lecture from him about the danger of handling unexploded rounds, we were summarily dismissed to swim at the Ciudamar Yacht Club below. We nonetheless wore broad smiles as we jumped into the sea. Later on that day, calmly, I practiced free-style and Manuel Jorge, diving, for the club's swimming team.

A Differing View of Cuba's History
Graduation at Sagarra

Upon graduation from the Juan Bautista Sagarra School, I was ranked at the top of my class and was awarded the school's highest prize for academic achievements, the Don Luis Buch Gold Medal in great ceremony. I was embarrassed and mortified that my good friend, Fermin Sarabia, who scored second from the top, could not share this prize with me.

Immediately after graduation, my father announced to me and the rest of the family that I would be sent to study in the United States at the Augusta Military Academy in Fort Defiance, Virginia. My cousin, Jorge, son of Dr. Jesus Buch, would attend Augusta Military Academy as well. I received the news with mixed feelings and apprehension.

A military academy for me? Why?

The blow was lessened after I learned that my sister, Enid, was also destined to enter the Junior College of The Visitation Convent of Georgetown University, a Catholic enclave, dedicated to "finishing" well-to-do and aristocratic young Catholic ladies. All of these decisions and the timing were a mystery to me.

All thinking Santiagueros closely followed the raging events of World War II. The radio shortwave BBC was a reliable source of information. On one hand, the Santiago Left and Communists watched Soviet movies and applauded Stalin, the Man of Steel,

My father and mother, on the other hand, went to the movies to learn the triumphs of our western allies and consumed their war propaganda. As time passed they developed enormous respect and an almost sycophantic admiration of President Franklin Delano Roosevelt and Winston Churchill. All but forgotten were the maneuvers made by President Roosevelt to consolidate the support of the Latino dictatorial republics. During his tenure, he supported statist regimes in Brazil, Venezuela, Colombia, Santo Domingo, Nicaragua, Cuba, and

Haiti through a program euphemistically called "The Good Neighbor Policy."

As far as I was concerned, it was a form of commercial tyranny because the price of sugar sold to the U.S. had dropped so low that hunger and political malaise had gripped the violent island, particularly in the eastern lands of Cuba. To make the mix worse, the rate of inflation was dangerously high and rising and a black market was growing faster than was anticipated. In a telling episode, my father had bought four contraband tires just outside the U.S. Naval Base in Guantanamo with an American Naval officer for (U.S.)$1,000 in 1945. I was with him as a cover when the transaction and transfer to my father's car trunk was done in the dead of night.

The victory in Europe was received with relief that summer and the Cuban newspapers covered the reactions in Manhattan, London, and Paris. As the summer progressed into August, General Douglas MacArthur's island-hopping plans in the Pacific War were successful, and as we waited with fearful trepidation for allied landings of the Japanese islands, an incredibly powerful atomic bomb was dropped in Hiroshima, and a little later, another in Nagasaki just outside the bay. The mysteries of the atom had been unraveled and had been used in the war against Japanese civilians.

The Santos-Buch family was greatly troubled by the dawn of the nuclear age but was content that World War II had finally ended.

CHAPTER 5.

◊ Abrogation of Cuba's Scheduled Free Electoral Process following a Fated Suicide.
◊ A Foretold Batista Coup.
◊ An Academic Career In Medicine Under a Dictatorship.

"Enter To Grow in Wisdom."

Frieze above the Massachusetts Avenue arched entrance to the Harvard College Yard in Cambridge, Massachusetts

In September 1945, at the end of the Pacific War against Japan, my father drove me, at age 13, across the Shenandoah Valley to Fort Defiance, Virginia, to register me in the eighth grade of the Augusta Military Academy under the direction of Major Charles Roller and his staff, which had recently increased by a large number of American soldiers who had just returned home from WWII. I was accompanied by my sister Enid and of course, our mother Herminia. After registration, my father planned to take my sister, Enid, to the Visitation Convent Junior College of Georgetown University in Washington, D.C., and intern her there.

Enid had to give much thought about her beaus as well as the academic and religious rigors of the Catholic Junior College. She made friends easily and one of her closest was Ana Chamorro, a member of the ancient and politically important Nicaraguan family. Her suitors were a problem. One was Archibald Rogers (a.k.a. Archie), a WWII Navy veteran, architect and member of a prominent and old Maryland family, and the other was Andres J. Duany (a.k.a. Andrew), offspring of the powerful ancient Santiago family. I had the distinct impression she was favoring Andrew.

It was very difficult to adapt to military school. The upper class hazing of the entering students was initially brutal and I could not make any sense of it. The violent discipline exacted by the upper class cadets was frequent and did not need to be explained or justified to anyone. I understood for the first time what racism meant in real time: I was a "spic" and a "worthless piece of shit" from a "shoeless insignificant Negro nation." Here were enrolled a few Jews and a larger group of Catholic cadets who were also discriminated against. There were no AMA African American cadets although there was a small number of Chinese. Interestingly, appeasing their own demons, the spics, Catholics, kikes and Asians helped each other to survive the fury of the abuse of the racially biased, upper-class Gringos.

I found relief with my assigned upper classmate mentor and WASP, Jimmy Ragsdale, who became a close friend,[36] and also by secluding myself in the comfort of the library and my studies. I was very good in all of my subjects, but the German and Reserve Officer Training Corps classes attracted my attention more because they piqued my curiosity. I was awarded a medal for being the best student in German but I only received a curious glance from my U.S. Calvary Full Colonel teacher, who could not quite understand why a "spic" was first in his classes and not a southerner. Major Hoover, my geometry and advanced trigonometry teacher and Captain McCue, my physics teacher, were among my best mentors and I flourished. I was ranked

36. My roommate, James Ragsdale of Florence, South Carolina, and my close friend and mentor, was awarded the Silver Star for heroism in the Korean War.

third in the nation after a competitive national test in advanced trigonometry. The first year at AMA was significant because I was only thirteen and I began an incredibly fast growth spurt that resulted in added height, strength, quickness, and interests in football, swimming and wrestling.

I developed friends from Cuba; among them were Mario Garcia, Otto, Pelayo Cuervo and their oldest brother, Orlando Cuervo. The Cuervos were the sons of Senator Cuervo Rubio Navarro of the Cuban Congress. He was a gifted oppositionist of Santo Domingo's dictator General Rafael Trujillo, who had been a U.S. Marine veteran.

Senator Cuervo had presented certifiable evidence of Trujillo's massacre of over 10,000 Haitians who had dared to cross the Haitian frontier to Santo Domingo to the United Nations. He had also announced and presented evidence that strongly suggested that more than 20,000 Cubans had been killed for political reasons since 1933 and some of these deaths may have implicated General Fulgencio Batista. Senator Cuervo had sent his three sons to AMA to protect them from possible government violence.

My classmates who were in the varsity football team were much older and most of them were hardened World War II veterans. AMA's football team excelled and played like national champions. I was determined to grow quick and fast enough to play in the varsity team, but I was a puny youngster in a sport I did not quite understand how to play. The varsity team liked me, with the exception of Cadet Doucy, an arrogant second-string quarterback and racist southerner, who made sure I was punished for any infraction. The older war veterans, on the other hand, befriended me.

A major relief from my duress was during Christmas vacation in the Darien, Connecticut, home of Mrs. Frances Schneider von Kreuter and her husband, Loys, my father's long-time close friend. I was joined by Enid. The von Kreuters treated us like our American parents and instructed us to address them as "Madia" and "Padio," a cross of aunt/uncle and mother/father. Our relationship with them and their children lasted a lifetime.

In the course of the AMA years, I rapidly developed into a physically powerful young man who was shy of his looks and of his academic success. I was an introverted loner, albeit a distinguished cadet. I was a starter in the junior varsity football team and a third-string player of the varsity team. AMA's varsity team did not lose a single preparatory school game my last year and it won a preparatory school championship in a well-advertised bowl game. My dedication to excel led to my selection by peer cadets to the Roller Rifles, an elite squad of riflemen who performed with ultimate precision in funeral memorial ceremonies and public parades and used athletic close-order drills in front of a large audience.

Enid and Andrew finally were engaged and celebrated their marriage of the two ancient families in the grand manner. The wedding was in Santiago de Cuba's 1514 Cathedral that faces the old "plaza mayor" — "el Parque de Céspedes." The guests came from far and near lands that evening of January 3, 1948. There was a palpable warmth and awe among the people outside the stately centuries-old cathedral.

Marriage history was being made on a scale never to be seen again in the venerable provincial capital city. I played a minor role as an usher and was very happy by the turn of events.

In time, I developed a very close relationship with my brother-in-law, Andres J. Duany. Andres was center-right on politics, but surprisingly, he supported prime-pump Keynesian economic maneuvers.

I graduated in third place from AMA in a record time of three years. I was awarded accelerated extra courses to have sufficient credits to graduate early. But I was an emotionally immature sixteen-year-old youngster who was not ready for the freedoms and social challenges prevalent in colleges of the day.

Although Cornell University accepted me on graduation, other colleges denied me admission and on further inquiry, they advised my parents to send me for a fourth postgraduate year to improve my English and my maturity before reapplying. I did all that at the famed Taft School of Watertown, Connecticut, where I did well in all courses with the exception of "Beany" Weld's English class. The courses I liked best were advanced algebra under Professor Douglas, the biology classes where I dissected a frog, and modern history with Professor Reardon, whose students had to read *The New York Times* daily. I frequented the Taft library to read many books not assigned in my courses.

After taking the college admissions tests, I felt very comfortable with my performance. I had made a number of friends at Taft and among them were Clifford Schroeder, who graduated at the top of his class, and Peter Hathaway, who introduced me to the wrestling team.

Despite Beany Weld's grades in English, Taft's college advisor Mr. Fenton nonchalantly dropped Harvard College application forms by my side at lunch and curtly said, "I want you to fill these out and please have them on my desk day after tomorrow by five o'clock." I thought he was joking. I looked up quizzically and Mr. Fenton, who taught Latin at Taft, was not smiling. The thought of applying to Harvard was very far from what I had in mind and I was sure it was to be wasted time and effort. There was no way I would be accepted at Harvard College, the elitist and oldest college of New England.

To my great surprise, I was admitted with the entering class of Harvard College in Cambridge, Massachusetts (Class of 1953). After graduation, a Taft record total of five of my classmates, including Clifford Schroeder and Peter Hathaway, were also going to Harvard with me. Peter and I decided to room together at the college.

That 1949 summer, my very close friend, Alan von Kreuter, who had recently graduated with a business administration degree from Fordham University, and Peter Hathaway came with me for a memorable vacation to Santiago de Cuba. It was a wonderful experience for everyone. Santiago's populace welcomed the two Americans warmly. There was only one anti-American episode when all four tires of our car were punctured one night while it was parked in the Spanish-Cuban enclave of Vista Alegre. On pursuit I was able to identify the leader who later became a Castro-Communist, Toto Cuervo.

Remembering Drs. Thorne and Gray

The following September 7, 1949, Enid delivered her first son, Andres Martin Duany, who was to become a world leading American architect. I also learned that Manuel Jorge Cutillas was accepted by the Taft School for a postgraduate year. Later, he was graduated from the Rensselaer Polytechnic Institute of Troy, N.Y. with a chemical engineering degree and joined the Bacardi Company at the bottom of the salary scale of young executives.

My first visit at Harvard was to the Widener Library, the largest of its kind in the world, and I was impressed to find all of Jose Marti's first edition publications on display in the entrance hall to celebrate his birthday. I was to spend many hours in Widener, studying the works of the classics, including the works of St. Thomas Aquinas in Latin with an adjacent English translation.

The tradition at Harvard College is that it only awards bachelor of arts degrees. I learned quickly that many in the entering class chose to major in Soviet Union studies and in the Russian language. The Cold War had gained momentum in those heady years. The CIA later recruited these graduates.

My immaturity played a significant role my initial two years in college. My major fault was in enjoying the company of Cambridge Irish girls more than devoting more time to my studies and my grades suffered for the first time in my life. I developed acute abdominal pain due to a bout of pancreatitis secondary to severe dehydration and loss of weight to one hundred and fifty-five pounds from my normal one hundred and sixty-eight pounds before a wrestling match I won. I was admitted to Harvard's Peter Bent Brigham Hospital for treatment. The medical school hospital opened up horizons that I had not imagined before.

There, I was exposed to brilliant research ventures of the Harvard Medical School faculty. I immediately formed a close relationship with my doctor, professor of medicine and gastroenterologist, Dr. Seymour Gray. Dr. Gray was indeed a "renaissance man." His clinical prowess was only exceeded by his broad scientific knowledge. I was to learn from Dr. Gray's recent publications which had to do with the fate of circulating red blood cells labeled with Chromium 51 isotopes. His observations determined the natural half-life of red blood cells in normal human volunteers. I was to appreciate that an M.D. could be a great physician at the bedside as well as a basic scientist. Today, Dr. Gray's discovery governs the techniques used for blood transfusions. Dr. Gray was to write a letter of recommendation for my medical school applications later.

During the week of my hospitalization, I was observed to determine if I was bleeding from the upper gastro-intestinal track. The working diagnosis was that I had had a limited episode of acute pancreatitis. I regained my health rapidly and was able to follow Dr. George W. Thorne's rounds every day, from one bed to another. He was the professor and chairman of the Department of Medicine of the Peter Bent Brigham Hospital.

Not only did an intern or a resident detail the patient illness to Dr. Thorne every morning, but also the experimental treatments were discussed at length in a language that I knew was incomprehensible to the patient. It was a battle of wits and knowledge of medical science.

Thus, Thorne's Socratic teaching rounds introduced me to a substance called adrenocorticotropic hormone (ACTH) and another, cortisone, recently synthesized by the chemists of the college. I saw patients with renal failure treated for the first time by an enormous apparatus known as a "kidney dialysis machine," designed and built in the hospital machine shop. I saw patients with primary rheumatoid arthritis treated with these compounds and the beneficial results that were obtained, as well as the significant secondary effects that attended the treatments. I learned the importance of regulating electrolyte imbalances of sodium and potassium in blood caused by the hormone treatment. It was an uplifting and challenging experience and I decided right there and then to make my major "biochemistry" and to enter a medical school on graduation. Secretly, I wanted to be like George Thorne and Seymour Gray.

My decision also introduced me to two important college professors and their courses. Biologist Carroll Williams' stylish and brilliant methodology that discovered the hormonal control of metamorphosis of silk worms opened up a huge field of study to me because the concept of plasma membrane receptors was initially introduced. A student of Nobel Otto Warburg, biochemist George Wald, offered excellent lectures and laboratory exercises, which included the polymerization of actinomyosin, the contractile protein of rabbit skeletal muscle. Dr. Wald later won the Nobel Prize in Medicine for his work that elucidated the biochemistry of vision. Williams and Wald, in particular, were keen to stress in their lectures the intrinsic necessity to use the "scientific method" in experimental designs and forced their college students to consult in the library peer-reviewed scientific papers of prestigious journals.

My Peter Bent Brigham Hospital nurse, Miss Beach, introduced me to an attractive and vivacious student nurse, Eugenie Cordelia Faitoute, and we both fell in love, although the romance was ill-fated from the start. I was irreparably enrolled in career goals that would take many years to complete before I could make a decent living. Gennie would not wait and abruptly left me and married a Harvard trained urologist. It took a long while to repair my ego and broken heart.

Modernity

A Foretold Coup D'état is Kept Secret

During my Cuba summer vacation of 1951, Eddie Chibas, the Santiago-born politician whose Habana radio Sunday programs called for a new political effort to rid the nation's widespread corruption, introduced me to his hypnotic spell. In the thatched roofed ranch of the Chantilly Sunday retreat with my family glued to the TV screen, I saw how a large number of peasants had silently broached the windows to watch and hear the program undetected by our family. It was a speech with significant populist and nationalist appeal.

Subsequent political discussions with my family and friends convinced me that Chibas' own party, the Orthodox Party, was popular enough to win the coming national presidential elections. To impress his followers of the truthfulness of his promises and revelations, Chibas attempted to dramatize his ideas and drew a revolver on the television stage. A shot was fired and he was mortally wounded. He died of his self-inflicted wound after a ten-day frightful fight for his life in August 1951. Despite this tragic event, the Orthodox Party became even more powerful and flouted a serious left-of-center reformist program with the certainty that it would enforce the provisions spelled-out in the progressive 1940 Constitution.

On my return to Cambridge, Massachusetts, I invited my close friend, Ana Mari Ganivet, to spend a November weekend with me and attend the Harvard-Princeton football game, college parties and enjoy time with my friends and classmates. To my pleasant surprise, Ana Mari did accept my invitation and came with her mother, Marina Fernandez of the powerful Oriente Province cattle landowners, as the chaperone. The visitors stayed at the stately Copley Plaza Hotel in Boston. We had a lot of fun. It was an opportunity to get to know each other better and talk politics.

She gave me a contrarian revelation after I told her that I believed the Orthodox Party stood to win the coming Cuba national presidential elections. She said that it was not going to happen because the cattle ranchers and the large landowners were "supporting and financing a General Batista takeover of the Cuban government, scheduled for the Spring of 1952." This was, indeed, very serious because she was well positioned to know of this conspiracy. I did tell her I could not believe that would happen because the Orthodox Party was strongly organized and very popular. Her riposte pointed to the socialist left-leaning platform of the Orthodox Party that clearly endangered the landed gentry. I listened with care to this very attractive and intelligent young woman, a good friend. I promised not to betray her confidentiality to anyone else. Despite it all, Ana Mari and I had a great time together that weekend and, as time went by, I forgot her political forecast.

It turned out I was very much mistaken. The following spring, on March 10, 1952, as Ana Mari had prophesied, General Batista did take over the government of Cuba in a bloodless coup without effective opposition. President Prio Socarras fled to the safety of the United States and Batista moved quickly to name a cabinet for his new government. Shortly after the coup, a young lawyer named Fidel Castro Ruz, a member of the Orthodox Party, submitted a fruitless stay to the Supreme Court denouncing Batista's illegal coup d'etat. The Supreme Court did not take up Castro's stay.

By the end of my Harvard years, I had matured. I was further educated by participating in the bull sessions covering many topics with my classmates and roomies who comprised a compendium of a great many personalities and backgrounds: Peter Hathaway, Wallace Campbell, Horton Reed, Francis Russell, Louie Laudani, Aram Mardirosian, Daniel Moulton, Donald Barrengos, Clifford Schroeder, Bobby Curran, and Peter Curran. It was a magnificent group.

Wally and I shared a room in a fourth-floor suite in Adams House with Peter, Franie, and Horton. Peter Curran, the captain of the varsity track team, was a specially gifted student. Suffice to say that he was the lonely grade blip on the right side of the bell-shaped grade curves of all the advanced scientific courses in which he had enrolled, including Wald's biochemistry and Kistiakovski's physical chemistry. I never missed an opportunity to study with him.

It was the organic chemistry course by Professor Louis Fisher that propelled me to the upper 10 percent of my class and the Dean's List, despite my poor record in my freshman and sophomore years.

F. R. N. Gurd, my major advisor and expert on the biochemistry of human lipoproteins under the directorship of Dr. Cohen and his group, was delighted with my progress. Wally Campbell and I applied to several schools of medicine, but after our interviews at the Cornell University Medical College in Manhattan, we agreed that the elitist New York Hospital-Cornell Medical Center offered what we considered a better-organized venue that suited us best for our graduate studies. We needed a change of academic challenges. Both of us were admitted to enter the College of Medicine in September, 1953.

On March 5, 1953, Wally and I were invited by an assistant professor of history and two other faculty members to watch the televised news of Stalin's death. The discussion by the faculty members and some of the more vocal students was whether Stalin's death would lead to the fall of the Communist Stalinist state and the Soviet Union. The majority of the faculty and students strongly believed his death would rapidly lead to a popular uprising and that we were witnessing the dawn of a democratic government. Nothing happened.

Stalin's death was followed by a succession of strong upper echelon communist dictators and the Soviet Union did not fall until the Berlin Wall was torn down on April 9, 1989, thirty-six years later. The lesson learned was that ingrained Stalinist type of Communism was very hard to defeat, even after many internal convulsive upper echelon movements largely supported by the system's "nomenclature."

The U.S. Army drafted higher mathematics majors Peter Hathaway, who became a captain of the artillery, and Aram Mardirosian, who had a U.S. Navy contract for his studies, enrolled as a fighter pilot to fight in the skies of the Korean War. Both survived with distinction. All of the other Harvard friends were spared the draft because they had attained very high grades and were exempted by recent Congressional law. Later, Peter Hathaway was admitted to the Albany School of Medicine and entered a career in academia by way of Johns Hopkins and the Osler Institute, attaining a professorship of genetics of the Kansas University School of Medicine. Aram Mardirosian was admitted to the Harvard School of Architecture, was a very effective Yard freshmen advisor and a distinguished architect. Clifford Schroeder graduated summa cum laude as expected and graduated from Harvard's School of Business to become a successful director of his father's corrugated paper box businesses.

The M26-7 Moncada Attack, Orders, Repression and a Fated Congressional Amnesty

When my father left Cuba to go to my Harvard graduation, he announced he was going blind. He had an appointment with Dr. Gunderson, professor of ophthalmology of Massachusetts General Hospital, and the date of the cataract operation was scheduled for June 1953. Cataract operations those days often had questionable results. He asked me to chauffeur him and my mother to tour the United States before the surgery to remember America's wonderments. The car tour visited the Atlantic, Middle and the far west and southwest states and returned to Boston where our family had rented a home on Massachusetts Avenue for his long convalescence.

The subsequent surgery was successful. My father was so grateful that he invited Dr. Gunderson's son, Peter, to a vacation in Santiago de Cuba for almost two months. I drove from Boston to Santiago de Cuba and Peter and I got along famously. When we arrived in Santiago the night of July 25 we slept soundly. The next night at home, we woke up startled by repeated gunshots that Peter had mistaken for fireworks.

Modernity

The commander of the Moncada Barracks, Colonel Alberto del Rio Chaviano, defeated Fidel Castro's insurgent Moncada barracks attack, planned a violent repression condemned by all sides, and immediately ordered the arrest of the "usual suspects." A similar but smaller attack was also repressed successfully in Bayamo.

It was fairly apparent to the public that the government's repression was fierce and many of the insurgents had been killed suspiciously after surrendering. Torture may have been used on interrogation of the captured rebels. The Catholic Church bishop interceded for the safety of Fidel Castro's and his close compatriots' surrender. I learned that my close childhood friend, Renato Guitart, had been shot dead in the firefight.

My brother-in-law was on the list of suspects and jailed. His cellmate was the leader of Santiago's Communist Party. Both were released two days later because they had tight alibis before and during the Moncada Barracks attack. On his release, the on-duty guard said in full voice for all prisoners to hear: "Count Duany! Report to the front desk!" I deduced that Batista's secret police's peculiar bias had incarcerated two socio-economic extremes – Andres J. Duany, a well-known conservative millionaire, and the local Communist Party leader (name unknown). Interestingly, when I asked Andres how he got along with his cellmate, he said, "Swimmingly, because we occupied ourselves talking economics and FDR's New Deal. We learned a lot from each other."

Later, the insurgents were tried, convicted of sedition and imprisoned in La Isla De Pinos penal facility. A liberal judge, Manuel Urrutia Lleo, wrote a lone dissent that argued that the 1940 Constitution permitted an armed rebellion against a dictatorship that had violated it in the first place. At the end of his trial, Fidel Castro announced in a well-publicized speech that "history would absolve him." The speech became a rallying rebel propaganda piece.

Incredibly, within two years, all insurgents were released by what was a popular Congressional amnesty that received the reluctant approval of General Batista. Castro and his compatriots used the opportunity to travel to the United States, Bogota, Colombia, and finally Mexico, where retired President Lazaro Cardenas and deposed Cuban President Carlos Prio Socarras sponsored his revolutionary efforts to fight another day. After a poorly planned participation in the short-lived "Bogotazo" coup that failed, a few Latin-American leftists revolutionaries joined him, including Ernesto, el Che, Guevara. Other important contacts were also made with the Directorio of University Students in Habana and with a little-known charismatic rebel, Frank Pais, of Santiago de Cuba. Pais was most impressive because he offered realistic plans to take the Revolution to the fatherland.

For Wally and I, the Cornell University Medical College years were extraordinary, replete with significant scientific discoveries before our graduation. In addition, reputations were rising of the Cornell medical scientists specializing in cardiovascular pathology under the heady supervision of brilliant George E. Murphy, Professor of Pathology, and a specialist in rheumatic fever and rheumatic heart disease. It was the years of the meteoric rise of modern immunology. Actually, as George Wald had pointed out, when we looked at the stack of scientific volumes in the library, there was an enormous increase in the numbers of publications from 1938 on. The volumes of the earlier years were dwarfed by an incredible output of seminal discoveries. Later, these scientific discoveries spiked even higher after Watson and Crick's double helix structure of DNA discovery published in Nature (1953).

There were medical science giants walking the halls of the Medical College. They were genuinely interested in medical students. They were very friendly and constantly pointed out to us that the most important thing of our Medical College years was to learn how to teach ourselves independently of the curriculum, its lectures or laboratory exercises. They told us that by the time we bought our textbooks they were out of date. We had to keep up with the recently published journals received by the library and that these were there to be used by all of us. We understood and did what they said.

It was tough going. We were informed that it was "normal" to lose a few classmates by the end of the first three months when they realized that medicine was not for them. Indeed, we lost three.

I was surprised when the Professor of Gross Anatomy came and asked one of us from the podium to stand up and answer a question like "Describe to us, doctor, the course of the arterial blood supply of the thyroid gland?" It was scary but a learning moment for all of us.

The study load was immense and filled all the hours, 24/7. Wally Campbell, my roommate, was incredibly helpful and we did well. The professor of biochemistry was Professor Vincent duVigneaud, who was to be awarded the chemistry Nobel Prize for first-time laboratory synthesis of a hormone polypeptide of the human pituitary in 1955, and he was attentive of his well-managed course. Both Wally and I had majored in biochemistry at Harvard and did very well. Then there was Robert Pitts, professor of physiology and world-renowned for deciphering the control of respiration in the central nervous system and the functions of the glomerulus and tubules of the kidney. In pathology, the longest course of the second year, Chairman Dr. John G. Kidd, had just been awarded the highest pathology prize by his peers, and was renowned for his studies of the development of experimental lymphoma in mice.

The pathology course required writing a paper on a disease process or doing an experiment with living animals that may explain a disease process by the end of the course. Wally and I decided to do experiments on living laboratory animals and skewed the pathology essay. The experiment we designed was based on specifying the morphological changes that attend immune deposits in blood vessels and how they differed from the small artery lesions induced in rabbits with experimental hypertension. Dr. George E. Murphy was our mentor. The results were extraordinary and later led to numerous scientific papers that gained international recognition over a period of decades.

A Differing View of Cuba's History

The Cornell faculty was challenging and accessible. Dean Dr. Joseph Hinsey memorized the full names of all newcomers and their photos; he would stop you in the halls and enthusiastically recite your biography, your success, failures and triumphs, and ask about your parents, all within five minutes or so in the public halls of the Medical Center. It was a command performance for the entire medical center. The head of the first-year course was introduced and explained that the Medical College did not post grades, that the class was to be divided in thirds from the highest to the lower performances which was provided to you by letter at the end of each trimester, and that medicine required knowledge of everything. Doctors did not have much time to consult the library or look for an expert in emergency situations. All of us learned this dictum.

The classes were divided into small groups of four students and were assigned studies we performed on ourselves in biochemistry and physiology. It was an extraordinary group. Glen Koenig and Tom London, our partners, formed a long lasting close friendship. Glen Koenig and I, on the invitation of Professor of Medicine David Rogers, head of the Infectious Disease Unit, studied the treatment of subacute bacterial endocarditis in living patients with oral Penicillin V. To do that we had to devise a technique to determine blood levels attained with the oral antibiotic first in ourselves and later in our patients. It was our first published investigation in the New England Journal of Medicine. It was a privilege to work with David Rogers and learn internal medicine and how to design a clinical study following classical science without falling into the pitfall of a "self-fulfilling prophesy." The editors of the NEJM were very much aware how good our study was.

After finishing the third-year clinical rotations successfully, I had a month's summer vacation in Santiago de Cuba in July, 1955. When I arrived my sister, Enid, had already arranged a blind date with Carol Valle Friend, who accepted my dinner invitation in Rancho Club. The popular club overlooked the splendid view of the city from its heights.

Somehow, she was able to go on the date without the ubiquitous chaperone required by local social customs. It was an incredible moment for both of us. We were attracted to each other instantly and by the end of the evening we both realized that the relationship we had formed was serious and promising. Despite worrisome objections raised by both sides of our families, we were engaged and married to honeymoon in the medical student quarters of Olin Hall of the Medical College in June, 1956. I was in the fourth year of the medical curriculum and was to graduate with honors the following July. Wally Campbell and I had moved forward on our experimental models of immune complex injury of rabbit coronary arteries and also in injury of small arterioles and small arteries in experimental hypertensive disease. We received offers from three sources: surgery, medicine, and pathology departments. In practical terms, the New York Hospital Department of Pathology offered the best opportunities to us and we applied for internship and residency.

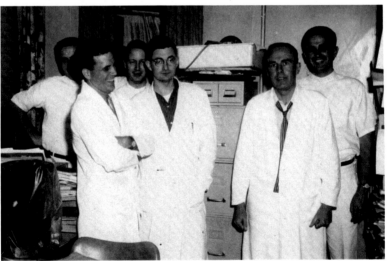

Dr. George Murphy in his laboratory.

It was an extraordinary and productive experience. Wally and Noreen Keating, his Radcliffe College muse, married during our Medical College years. As a result of our publications of our experimental findings we both received United States Department of Health Fellowships that enriched our curricula. We both passed the Anatomic Pathology Boards without any difficulty.

I was a Cuban citizen and the draft board did not bother me. It was different for Wally – the Army drafted him. I had another unexpected issue: The Cuban Revolution.

Carol and I followed the news of the insurgency's successes since November 30, 1956, in Santiago de Cuba. One early evening in March 1957 I was confronted by five M26-7 operatives led by Commander Lester Rodriguez. Rodriguez produced a letter of introduction. My father asked for my cooperation with Rodriguez who was in a special mission to unify New York City Cuban immigrants against General Batista's dictatorship. He asked me to organize a branch of the Cuban Civic Resistance Movement in the New York area. Rodriguez and his operatives left and I began the difficult task of recruitment among the heterogeneous Cuban immigrant groups. I was extraordinarily lucky because I was able to find a group of five diverse but very intelligent and resourceful, hard-working Cubans who were enthusiastic and dedicated to run Resistencia Civica. All were center or center-left politically who wanted the return of a representative democracy in Cuba. My liaison with the M26-7 was Haydee Santamaria, Armando Hart's wife and veteran of the Moncada Barracks attack. My parents also were very helpful. Dark clouds, however, were rising on the horizon.

CHAPTER 6.

◇ The Story of Frank Pais.

◇ The Establishment of a Safe Sierra Maestra Insurgent Stronghold.

◇ A Foiled Presidential Palace Assault.

◇ Defeat of Urban Guerrilla Tactics and the Military Resurgence of Fidel Castro in the Battlefields of the Eastern Interior.

The critical year of 1933 marked an engrossing change in Cuba when the "bubble" finally busted. Revolutionaries of the day became knowledgeable of the economics of the Left on the rise by the historical moment. Notably, Cuban progressives like Levy Marrero and Martinez Saenz, and Communists like Tony Guiteras, Blas Roca and Lazaro Peña, and many others, were gradually widely understood and carefully discussed by the power elite, today's "establishment." Free enterprise and the landed gentry of the Criollo Civilization, many of them now absentee landlords in immense luxurious Habana mansions, were placed under the microscope by the middle class and by their own intelligentsia.

Collectivist ideas and land reforms to break up the immense

agricultural empires were put in plain words. They discussed the wonderful results of land reform imposed on the defeated Japanese by America's pro-consul, General Douglas McArthur. The Cuban Communist Party became larger, politically more influential, and a force to be reckoned with. Left-of-center newspapers sprouted across the breath and depth of the violent island. And the radio became an effective tool of leftist demagoguery. It was the "intelligent and progressive" chic thing to do and discuss.

What was more difficult to visualize was how existing political parties had changed and how they had adopted politically convenient agendas. By the first years of the 1930s, the Conservative Party, greatly diminished by the backlash caused by the Racial Wars, was reorganized and renamed to obscure its core agenda, but other larger parties were newly formed, all with populist, politically attractive, left-of-center up-graded agendas. The importance of the Liberal party was greatly diminished as the new "revolutionary" parties were organized by many of its members.

Once in power, their actions sometimes betrayed their conservative positions but when push came to shove, their policies were by and large left of center. Certainly, when one reviews the presidencies of Gerardo Machado, Fulgencio Batista and Grau San Martin's it is obviously apparent that their political positions shifted to the right somewhat, some more than the others, as they accumulated more wealth and power.

All of these governments, with exception of Machado's, made important concessions to labor and their unions and to the Communist Party. Grau and even Batista named Communists to their Cabinets or other lesser positions to appease them. The rampant corruption and the over-use of the taxpayer public wealth to construct around the magnificent city of Habana rankled further the forgotten taxpayers of the "interior," the middle class and the peasantry generally, further alienating the have-nots.

When economists spoke of the Cuban economy, more often than

not they were actually referring to the booming post-World War II economy of the nation's capital – dismissing outright what was going in the obscure political sanctuary of the eastern lands.

In fact, it is a glaring mistake that they did not have an accurate census of the population of the distant eastern lands on which to base their per capita calculations. "Educated guesses" were somehow translated as "factual." The government did not register most of the Cuban peasants that populated Cuba's inaccessible areas at birth. Peasant families did not have birth or death certificates. The census takers in the eastern lands were mostly sinecures who did not do the tedious ground work in the difficult terrains. They stared at the enormous spacious mountains and discouraged, guessed at what the population might be.

Under the Castro-Communist dictatorship, on the other hand, an accurate census of the population density of the island was achieved with the obvious intent of using this powerful tool to suppress the rise of a possible "counterrevolution." After the Castro-Communist take-over of Cuba, all of the sudden the general population "grew" to over twelve million people from ten million, overnight. It is important to understand that "statistically based studies" prior to Castro are skewed to Habana and its adjacent provinces.

Since the powerful of the day viewed politicians as corruptible, the rich and the well to do thought they had "a default maneuver of last resort" to survive if an assault on their way of life took place. Furthermore, the intelligentsia and upper classes believed that Cuban class inequality was generally accepted by all economic and social classes, and stubbornly, did not believe an explosive reckoning would happen.

Importantly, upward mobility of recent university graduates was slow and stuck on neutral while the number of high salaried employees was insignificant compared to the booming economy of the very rich and their faithful acolytes. Many, if not the majority, of the leaders of the M26-7 in Santiago de Cuba were later rapidly recruited from the sidelined, out of the loop, discontent university graduate group.

A modern psychiatrist would have named the generalized angst of the Cuban "establishment" toward the less fortunate as "la belle indifference."

They were also wrong in believing that they had, at the end of the day, ultimate political control. Besides, they strongly believed that their sturdiest ally, the United States, would never allow a Communist state ninety miles from their shores and were certain that Americans would never abandon their promising $80 billion investments dispersed through out the island.

Unfortunately, a social class reckoning did happen later, and a weak-kneed USA abandoned them because its leaders misinterpreted history's lessons and misused its flawed derivatives and premises regarded as "truths" that resulted in disastrous consequences to Cuba, as you will learn in this narrative.

Importantly, the word "movement" had been cast in the minds of Santiagans with a real understanding of its meaning by the time the "M-26-7" graffiti was painted on the walls of the Santiago Catholic and conservative school for the wealthy, "Colegio de Dolores," when Carol and I married in June 1956. The Castro brothers attended the elite school, as well as many other prominent Cubans. I remember well staring at the daring graffiti in my short vacation from medical school, well aware of its impact. By that time, Batista's military intelligence suspected that a violent event was about to happen in Santiago de Cuba. Carol and I married literally under the vigilance of army patrols bearing Thompson submachine guns.[37]

---

37. When Carol and I, with a chaperone, drove to the Santiago airport to pick up some wedding gifts from Habana friends we were stopped and searched under a Sergeant Thompson. I noticed with apprehension that the safety was off. New York Times reporter Herbert Mathews was famously impressed by the wide rebel support that crossed social and economic classes in Santiago at this time. The rise of Cuban leftist populism as a political tool did not take long to develop after the debacle of the Racial Wars and the election of President Zayas y Alfonso of the Liberal Party. Violent Liberal thought spread like a stubborn wildfire from the western most provinces to the eastern recesses of the embattled island. Even in the "safe" suburb of Vista Alegre, just east of the venerable city of Santiago de Cuba, the intellectual and well to do elite regularly socialized in soirees, which invariably broached the heady issues of the New Deal, and the economics of pump priming and Keynesian ideas on deficit spending. The scholarly left of center Professor Jorge Mañach, a champion of José Martí, the progressive hero of the War of Independence of 1895 and

Modernity

There was an unexplained excitement among the politically and economically sidelined Santiago youngsters, recent graduates and social institutions. There was a general agreement to watch out for "chivatos," the government informers, even though the participants in the Movement were unknown and relatively small in number.

The apprehension was diminished by the anticipation that something inevitable was about to happen to change the political landscape of the Batista dictatorship. The majority of Santiagans, the well to do and the middle class, believed in their hearts that this time around, "the good guys" had a real chance of winning. They seemed not to critically question who "the bad guys" might be among the revolutionaries. Many of the cynical among the well to do believed that they would be as easily corruptible as the reigning politicians had always been.

It was in this "politically confounding" environment that a great revolutionary hero stepped up with alluring and specific goals to join the revolutionary cauldron that Santiago de Cuba was and he is Frank Pais. To understand his compelling character is to understand today's opposition to Cuba's Castro-Communist iron rule.

In Winston Churchill's worldview of English speaking heroes, Frank Pais would compare favorably with the Irish revolutionary Michael Collins of the Oglaigh na hEireann (Gaelic: The Irish Republican Army). Collins was twenty-six when he fought for Ireland's independence from Great Britain in the Irish Easter Rising, mostly in Dublin, on April 24, 1926. Pais was twenty-three years old when he organized and staged the successful M26-7 insurrection in Santiago de Cuba on November 30, 1956. Both men were brilliant, passionate, principled, and unquestioned natural-born leaders. Both men's fathers were older when they were born, devoutly religious middle class, well-educated, dedicated patriots and self-made.

Don Joaquín Martínez Sáenz, the progressive leader of the underground ABC movement, attended these meetings. Dr. A. M. Santos-Buch and his wife, Don Luis Augusto Mestre and his wife, Nena Mascaro, and the president of the Rotary Club, Gerardo Abascal and his wife, admirer of President Franklin Roosevelt New Deal with others of the intellectual elite frequently met in their respective homes.

A Differing View of Cuba's History

Collins' father "instilled in his son a love of Irish poetry and ballads." Frank's mother taught him the piano and he wrote moving and passionate poems. Both revolutionary leaders were acutely aware of the "have-nots" and firmly believed in "inviolable" tenets of a representative republican government for their respective countries. Frank was helped greatly by his able brothers, Josué and Agustín, who enjoined the dangerous revolutionary tasks with great courage. Similarly, Michael Collins' family also contributed to his revolutionary partnerships.

Veterans of the insurrection say that Pais' sang-froid under withering fire and inspiring leadership was outstanding. Collins climbed forth to the top command where a vacuum was created when the British executed the entire Irish leadership. Collins, today, is acknowledged as "the father of modern urban guerrilla warfare."

What possible motivations drive people of the stature of Collins and Pais to enjoin an insurrection in a tyrannical environment where they had to plan and deliver violent deaths? Was nationalistic patriotic fervor enough to steer them to confront the lethal odds they faced? Or was it a call to arms by their God, as it was to Isaiah, the Prophet?[38]

Certainly, Christianity and heroic deeds were deeply ingrained in Cuba's youth. There are many examples of this. Many Cuban patriots who faced Castro-Communist firing squads during the reign of terror after Fidel Castro took over the government roared at the top of their lungs, "Viva Cristo Rey," as the volley of rifles blighted their lives. Then again, the heroic cavalry assault on the impregnable Spanish defenses of the 1895 battle of "El Desmayo" in Camaguey is another example of what lengths Cuban patriots would go to live and die for a higher cause than themselves (*The Battle of El Desmayo image, page 50*). The battle of El Desmayo is compared by military historians to the fated cavalry assault of the British light brigade at Balaclava.[39]

---

38. Isaiah 6:8. "Then I heard the voice of the Lord, saying, "Whom shall I send, and who will go for Us?" Then I said, "Here am I. Send me."

39. The Battle of Balaclava, fought on 25 October 1854 during the Crimean War, was part of Siege of Sevastopol (1854–1855) to capture the port and fortress of Sevastopol, Russia's principal naval base on the

194

Modernity

Given that devoted Christian fathers raised both patriots, it is reasonable to ask if their rationale to put their lives on the line for a daunting cause was not just "patriotic fervor." In the case of Frank Pais, his father was a devoted and successful Baptist missionary in a largely Catholic city. In the case of Michael Collins his strict Catholic upbringing also laid the foundation of his passion to fight for independence of Catholic Ireland from foreign Protestant English occupiers. It is interesting to reflect if Collins or Pais believed, deep in their hearts, perhaps secretly, that their God placed them on Earth for a higher and noble purpose, revealed to them by their remarkable leadership qualities, their successes in urban guerrilla warfare and their courageous actions under fire.

We have not found any plausible evidence of this rationale in biographies of Michael Collins, the Irish Revolutionary. Importantly in this regard, the only Pais brother who survived the Batista suppression of the Santiago insurgency, Agustin Pais, a devout Christian and student of the Bible, said to me that Frank Pais' role in it was not significantly motivated by Christian mysticism. On the other hand, he believes Pais was profoundly moved by the nationalist fervor of the heroes of Cuba's Wars of Independence.

Pais became the de facto leader of the anti-Batista insurrection when Fidel Castro and many of his followers were imprisoned by General Batista's dictatorial government after his failed assault on the Santiago Moncada Barracks on July 26, 1953, and also when Castro reached the safety of the Sierra Maestra mountain range in December 1956. After a disastrous landing he was late to what was initially planned as a coordinated event in the shores of the Gulf of Guacanayabo with the M26-7 urban insurrection in Santiago de Cuba, the provincial capital itself.

Both Collins and Pais initially directed their rebellions with previously tested urban guerrilla strategies designed to gain, firstly, the trust of the deep-seated nationalist sentiments of the civil non-

---

Black Sea. Lord Tennyson, the poet laureate, made the charge of the Light Brigade famous.

combatant population; secondly, to direct lethal violence to military patrols and guards only, and thirdly, to discredit the political and economic advantages of the iron rule that gripped their respective countries. Once the civil population gained their trust and sympathy, their plan was that a sizable guerrilla could then proceed to occupy significant territories that would discredit their tyrannical regimes and their respective international supporters and allies. For the Batista dictatorship, its principal supporter was the United States of America, and for Ireland, it was the British Government. When the time was ripe, the final phase of the revolution was to be an organized crippling general strike that would topple both tyrannies by joining the insurrection.

Pais was accountable for delivering reinforcements from his Santiago de Cuba organization to the minuscule force in the safety of the Sierra Maestra Mountains successfully. Collins organized Ireland's successful civil war from top to bottom; his plans triumphed with frontal confrontations of British troopers in city streets with "underground action groups" that were previously organized by him nationally.

When veterans of the Pais-led underground of the M26-7 movement organization were interviewed and questioned about the start of the Cuban Revolution on November 30, 1956, in Santiago de Cuba, what deeply impressed observers of widely different political stripes was how disciplined the action groups were and how well the insurrection was planned and executed. A command and control center was created in the colonial home of well-known, high-end anti-Batista non-combatant patriots at great risks.[40] Pais' action groups responded to his orders without hesitation or ineffective delays; otherwise, they would be subjected to severe revolutionary peer review, and if found guilty, severely sanctioned, sometimes lethally. Some unfortunates did pay with their lives for their treacherous actions and strict revolutionary discipline was restored.

---

40. Don Santiago Rousseau and his wife, Suzette Bueno of the Santiago elite.

Only military targets were attacked; no innocent civil members of the Santiago population were killed or wounded or imprisoned. Wounded guerrillas were removed and relocated to have their wounds treated by local doctors in predesigned and equipped safe houses. The guerrillas wore distinctive olive-green uniforms with black boots, black berets and an armband with M26-7 in red lettering on a black background.

The insurgents' targets had been studied carefully. The most important and valuable attack was the assault of the National Navy garrison under the command of Jorge Sotus. The firefight was intense, room-to-room, and bloody for both sides. But the Navy garrison was killed and Sotus and his companions captured thirty rifles and many Thompson machine guns that were rapidly stowed away safely.

Importantly, when it was all over and Pais' command and control center found out that Fidel Castro's force had not landed in a coordinated operation, they were recalled by Pais and faded away to become part of the everyday working civil population. The number of rebel fatalities was small but significant because a few of the leadership close to Pais paid with their lives.

On the other hand, the number of police, soldiers and navy Batista personnel killed was significantly higher. Their wounded were transported to military hospitals and kept away from the press. These data were censored to the public at large by the government and likely under counted. In the public mind, the rebels had held the second largest city of Cuba in their hands for almost an entire day and they were not a "rabble in arms." The news, however, was heard nationally by word of mouth, fast and unforgiving. *The New York Times'* Ruby Phillips in Habana reported extensively on the insurrection success.

This, clearly, was not a repetition of Fidel Castro's failed wild and loose efforts of July 26, 1953, the desperate rebel attacks in Bayamo, and the Moncada Barracks of Santiago de Cuba. This time Batista government's nose was bloodied and out maneuvered by a disciplined and intelligent, dangerous foe. The foreign press, including *The New*

York Times, picked up on the striking differences between the failed 1953 Castro event and Pais' successful 1956 urban strike.

The government was unpleasantly surprised and tried to brush off Pais' strike against the dictatorship in the media as insignificant, run by "malcontents and gangster types," but it knew better. Their intelligence apparatus had learned and concluded that this was clearly a very dangerous underground urban guerrilla group that had to be suppressed by cutting-off its head, Frank Pais. Their calculation was that a well-disciplined and well-supplied militarily organized guerrilla could not be allowed to operate effectively in the provincial capital.

Batista's government was somewhat redeemed of its Santiago anti-insurrectionist failures when Fidel Castro landed at the foot of the Sierra Maestra Mountains. The guerrilla force under the command of Fidel Castro was late, of course. To many critical observers, this was his way, always, to the end of his days to lead an undisciplined, poorly organized force. The landing force was almost totally wiped-out by pre-alerted air, naval, and ground forces of the dictatorship, which struck hard at the discovered landing guerrillas. Their boat was captured. Of the eighty-plus combatants, only a dozen or so were able to leave the beaches and hide in the manigua and proceed to meet the peasant guide who led them to the safety of the Sierra Maestra mountain range hideouts. The disgusted rebel peasant guide of the moment could not believe the disastrous loses.

The Pais underground urban guerrilla received news of Castro's failure with little sympathy because the failed landing was blamed on the lack of discipline of the would-be mountain insurrects. The Santiago rebels were bitterly disappointed that Fidel Castro and his staff had not followed the letter of the orders of a planned coordinated landing on the shores of the Guacanayabo Gulf with that of their urban insurrection in the provincial capital of Oriente Province, Santiago de Cuba.

The element of surprise was key for the planned strategy of the urban revolutionaries and the Santiago insurrection had been successful for it, whereas the lack of surprise of the Castro insurgents' landing operation resulted in the loss of many arms and lives. No excuses were accepted and the rancorous animosity between Castro and Pais was evident to both sides. Doubts of the mountain guerrillas' capacity to effectively fight in the mountains was raised among Pais' urban staff.

Eventually, both sides agreed to put their rancor and doubts aside for "the sake of a larger cause than themselves." It was not easy to achieve. It was generally acknowledged that the better-known insurrectionist leader with name recognition, nationally and abroad, was Fidel Castro. All agreed that he was the designated leader of the M26-7 because of this. His lack of military prowess was not discussed. His life had to be preserved at all cost and it was agreed that it was best defended in the safety of the Sierra Maestra Mountains.

Pais agreed to this narrative because of the strength of his character and his confidence in his plans and actions. He could point to his successful military operations and his obvious command of an extensive underground organization that had spread nationally. (Castro's charisma and military leadership qualities were to grow and be recognized later.)

Pais let it be known that he assessed that the other unaffiliated, underground revolutionary groups with the significant exception of the University Student Directory were weak and ineffective and that these groups, including Communists, must be excluded from the united urban M26-7 revolutionary action cells. It was agreed that accusations of alleged Communist infiltrators of the M26-7 were to be emphatically denied to the media, to the Santiago reinforcements and to the supporters of the Resistencia Civica movement. Both "El Che" Guevara and Raul Castro chafed and frowned on this important strategy but remained silent.

Pais emphasized that it was most important to portray that M26-7 was a "nationalistic movement that was free of Communist sympathizers or ties" to better recruit the people of Oriente, as well as the rest of the Cuban population that largely distrusted "ñangaras."

Importantly, it was suggested that the outward public face of the revolutionary movement was of an honorable and noble fighting force, which spared lives rather than wantonly take them. Revolutionary tribunal lethal sanctions of informers and traitors were to be kept secret from the press to maintain the compassionate heroic persona the revolutionary movement had gained from the supportive urban populace. [41]

Recruitment of Action Groups

Carlos Iglesias, a.k.a. "Nicaragua," a young teller of a local Santiago de Cuba Bank, chafed worriedly as he stared at the bare wall of the room. Frank Pais had come to cash a check and recruited him for the action groups of the 26 of July Movement right there and then. He had agreed to wait for him at a safe house not far from home. He thought that the meeting was to talk in secrecy about the organization of the Movement and its goals and how it was going to be operating under Pais. What role would be assigned to him exactly?

He looked at his watch and Frank was already twenty minutes late. The knock on the door startled him as a clear-eyed, young white man opened the door. The stranger said he was Juan Nuiry and he was a friend of Jorge Manduley, a common acquaintance, and he lived with his parents near The Placita, not far from his bank. Iglesias had seen him walking pleasurably in Enramadas, flirting with a few girls. Or was it in the church of San Francisco, also close to the Placita? He could not remember well. Nuiry fretted as he explained Frank had

---

41. The execution of informers and traitors did take place, principally under El Che Guevara's and Raúl Castro's commands, and reached the cameras of reporters and the free press published them but did not receive the attention they deserved at the time until much later after Fidel Castro took over the government. The press disregard was based on the prevalent belief that these were part and parcel of all revolutions. Some observers believe these executions served as paradigm of the reign of terror after the M26-7 ousted Batista.

asked for a meeting in this safe house, more to calm himself than anything else. Both men took a pause to measure each other. They were almost exact opposites. Iglesias was dark, thin, muscular with angular looks and an easy smile, whereas Nuiry was very fair, taller and heftier, more powerful but not quicker, and had attended Juan Bautista Sagarra School with Juanito Escalona, another common friend and his schoolmate. Nuiry's parents were Europeans and Iglesias was a Criollo orphan who had never met his parents and had been raised by Catholic foster parents in Santiago. Iglesias played basketball and frequently was seen in the company of other players in several of the social clubs in town. Both men showed their surprise that the other had been recruited for the action groups of the Pais insurrection. They didn't dwell on this because the door suddenly opened with Pais carrying books, wearing dark glasses, a lit smoking pipe and a friendly smile. He looked like an effete nerdy student of the Bachillerato Institute in the Sueño district, not far from the safe house. Without a moment to lose, Pais produced four different handguns to teach them how to disassemble and arm in complete darkness. Their first trial by fire was announced the evening after the meeting.

Fidel Castro agreed to Pais' initiatives with a straight face. Even though Pais knew that some of the mountain insurgents held Communist sympathies – if not outright strong Communist ties – he did not dwell further on these issues because there were many other pressing matters that greatly occupied his mind. Pais needed the relatively feckless guerrilla incursions on the outskirts of the Sierra Maestra as "diversionary maneuvers" and believed that victory for the insurrection was via the urban guerrilla underground forces and a general strike and not via frontal confrontations with Batista's army groups in the Sierra Maestra escarpments.

Castro's failed landing had postponed Pais' strategies and underground revolutionary plans. He laid out new, decisive plans to reinforce the mountain guerillas as soon as possible. If one regards the November 30 urban insurrection as a masterful military plan, Pais' reorganization of the failed Fidel Castro mountain effort is, without a doubt, the most intelligent and ambitious plan of the early phase of the Cuban Revolution, because he was able to bond the civil oppositionist population with the urban action groups of Santiago and, reinforce the mountain fighters now in the safety of the Sierra Maestra successfully. In the urban struggle, the increased government security forces in Santiago were constantly challenged by the "action groups" who targeted the secret police and patrolling army soldiers and kept the population on its toes with the use of pipe bombs, placed widely in city corners with a low risk of causing innocent civilian casualties.

The very existence of the mountain insurgents served as a "romantic" but effective national and worldwide propaganda platform that, much later, used its own mobile radio plant that had the call "Aqui, la radio rebelde, en La Sierra Maestra, territorio libre de America" by a famously recognized female artist. The mountain platform successfully used underground links to *The New York Times*, CBS, Life, and *Time* magazines and to many other freelance correspondents of excellent reputation, as well as reliable links with the popular Cuban magazine, *Bohemia*, in the capital city of Habana. Recognizable names like *The New York Times'* Herbert Mathews, CBS' Robert Taber, *Time* magazine's Jay Mallin, *Chicago Sun-Times* Ray Brennan and freelancer Andrew St. George were able to reach the mountain hideout of the M26-7 through their contacts with Resistencia Civica and Frank Pais' underground urban action groups in the early phase of the Cuban Revolution.

In order to achieve all of these goals, Pais had to get Fidel Castro and his compatriots into the safety of the Sierra Maestra to agree. There were no other realistic alternative options offered to Pais when he confronted the group of desperados deep in the Sierra Maestra, not even from the sulking and contrarian Ernesto Guevara, "el Che," who did not appreciate Frank Pais' in-your-face presentations and favored an unrealistic Mao "Marxist peasant rebellion." Guevaras' Communist sympathies were kept secret. Pais, for all practical matters, took over the command of all the underground revolutionary programs.

In the underground effort, Pais worked closely with Armando Hart and his friend, Dr. Antonio Buch, to approach his uncle, Dr. A. M. Santos-Buch and Manuel Ray, an accomplished engineer and close sympathizer of the cause, to create "La Resistencia Civica" nationwide and abroad. Hart's wife, Haydee Santamaria, a veteran of the Moncada attack of 1953, played a major role in recruitment of Resistencia. La Resistencia Civica was to be a non-action branch principally working parallel to the M26-7 urban guerrillas under the rare input and guidance of Pais.

Resistencia Civica Directors — my parents
(Family heirloom photo)

Their ambitious goals were simple: 1) to organize the infrastructure to supply the mountain fighters with food, medicine, uniforms, and intelligence, 2) to collect contributions worldwide and deposit these monies with the M26-7 treasurer, Enrique Canto, to be used with the urban and mountain fighting echelons, and 3) to establish

Resistencia Civic cells nationally and abroad for propaganda purposes by establishing links with the national and international news media.

This was done in an astonishingly rapid time. Manolo Ray was soon heading the underground national network later because Dr. Santos-Buch became too hot and had to go abroad. Dr. Santos-Buch then established cells in Miami and New York City. I was named "Asesor" (Adviser) when I finished organizing a highly effective and hard-working Resistencia group in New York City. Armando Hart's wife, Haydee Santamaria, nome de guerre "Maria," regularly communicated instructions with Resistencia in New York City from time to time. Additionally, New York's Resistencia legally created the non-profit "Cuban Relief Fund" in New York City administered by M26-7 Commander Pedro Miret's sister with the mission of receivership of contributions to use for the benefit of unfortunate civilian losses caught in the violent revolutionary vortex of the eastern lands.[42] Both Resistencia members and M26-7 operatives developed a network of "safe houses" for the urban insurgents to use. One such safe house was the Santos-Buch Clinical Laboratory in Santiago de Cuba.

The New York Times Films

The modern Santos-Buch Clinical Laboratory was located at the entrance of Siboney Beach Road as part of the extensive Terrazas de Vista Alegre development of Andres J. Duany. The architectural plans, initially drawn by an enterprising undergraduate Harvard classmate of mine, called for two levels that were fairly independent of each other. The lower level was for the entry of patients and other professionals and had an airy vestibule and waiting room with a receptionist desk

---

42. The New York Resistencia Cívica branch created a very well-read newspaper, Resistencia, often with photos from the battlefronts that were distributed widely in New York City and the local press. A ship load of clothes, food stores and other items from Cuban Relief Foundation for the victims of the fighting was delivered to Santiago de Cuba and distributed by Dr. A. M. Santos-Buch after the triumph of the M26-7 Movement early in 1959.

and phone. A long room with a bathroom at the end housed the clinical laboratory apparatuses and the technicians that worked them. The family living areas were designed for the upper level. Frank Pais, Carlos Iglesias (a.k.a. Nicaragua), Armando Hart, Haydée Santamaría, and other notable urban revolutionaries had safely stayed in the upper level for varying periods of time because the doctor's children had grown up and moved away.

The building stood out for its understated elegance and the beautiful landscaping of royal palms, bougainvillea, and other exquisite plantings. To the northeast was the imposing suburban conservative enclave of the original development of Vista Alegre with its mansions, its Central Avenue and parks.

The doctor routinely opened the doors of the Laboratory early in the morning at six-thirty a.m.

On a clear Monday morning, Vilma Espin called Dr. Santos-Buch and informed him that she had to see him privately to give him four rolls of film to process by the Civic Resistance Movement. Lolita Juantorena, his receptionist and secretary, had received a brisk telephone call from Vilma Espin saying she was in need of several routine blood tests ordered by her internist. Her appointment was at eight a.m. sharp.

Her father, Mr. Espin, was very proficient in French and was secretary to Don Enrique Schueg, vice-president of the Bacardi Company and head of International Sales. Don Enrique, deficient in Spanish, preferred to conduct his business affairs in French, his primary language. Vilma was an honors student at the Sacred Heart School for Girls in Vista Alegre and she had been a ballet student of the Pro-Arte Society of Oriente Province, headed by the doctor's wife, Herminia Greig Cossio. She was not a stranger. All of them were collaborators of the Santiago underground to different degrees and Vilma had just returned from the mountain hideouts of the M26-7 guerrillas.

The good doctor, my father, was intuitively alerted that something was afoot. He had been kept in the dark about Vilma's role in the insurrection but she told him she had some 35mm camera films to bring him. Vilma showed up about ten minutes early of her appointment; she was dressed in the usual attire of many pretty Vista Alegre women. Her stressed eyes were very alert. She had not let him know that she was a suspect and under surveillance by SIM agents (Batista's Servicio de Inteligencia Militar).

As soon as she entered the Laboratory and Lolita started to enter demographics in her file, two young men abruptly stepped into the waiting room. They had the demeanor and dress typical of agents of SIM. They were carrying concealed 45-caliber Colt pistols under their "guayaberas" and both had a "gotcha" kind of smile.

Soon afterwards, two other younger men, bearing a large laundry packet, stepped in as well. One was Tony Valle Friend and the other was Toto Cuervo, both of Vista Alegre. Unknown to the doctor, they were hiding some of Frank Pais' arms and uniforms in their parked car outside. One agent sported a knowing and sarcastic smile and said, "Hey Toto, I didn't know you were delivering laundry for a living nowadays. Who is your friend? Oh, yeah, the shortstop, I know . . . Tony Valle, right? How are you and what is going on?"

"Listen Jose, the drycleaner asked me to do him a favor and these are the uniforms of the laboratory and Tony had a car and offered to drive me," Toto answered with a disarming smile. Lolita moved to accept the laundry packet that was opened in front of the agents to show the white uniforms.

The doctor, hearing the commotion, was out of his office, and moved quickly to the waiting room.

"What is going on officers?" the doctor asked, looking right into the agents' eyes.

With a smile, the tallest of them said, "I am SIM agent Jose Prado and this is agent Soler, my partner." (Both names are fictitious; the events are real.) Both showed their service photo IDs to the doctor.

Modernity

"We are under orders from our superiors to stop and search Miss Espin who is under suspicion of aiding the Communist insurrection. We want to search Vilma Espin's purse. You are Vilma Espin, aren't you?" one of the officers said, looking at her with piercing eyes. Looking at the doctor, he added, "If there is nothing in her purse that can compromise her, she is free to go, doctor." All of the Santiagans immediately understood that the agents' staccato speech identified them as Habanians.

"I am Vilma Espin, yes, but I'm not about to let you do that. You don't have any right to stop or touch me and search my purse, on a whim. The Cuban Constitution protects me and I have rights. What is it that you really want to do, officer? I am a free and peaceful Santiaguera! I have not done anything wrong, believe me. You have no right to search me, without a court order," she added firmly.

The doctor explained to the officers that Miss Espin had called earlier in the morning for an appointment to do some blood tests ordered by Dr. Jesus Buch, her famous internist.

The doctor, now in command of the situation, purposely moved to stand between her and the two agents and firmly and loudly enough for everyone in the room to hear it, said, "Vilma, there is nothing to fear. Look, the good officer is just doing his job and obeying orders from his superior. Let me see what you have in your purse, please, there is nothing to fear girl." He gently opened her purse and slipped four black plastic cylinders with Kodak films into his white coat's pocket. The purloined films were hidden safely in his pocket with a stethoscope and small notebooks. No one noticed the sleight of hand as he turned around and handed the purse to the surprised Batista officer who looked at it with keen interest.

At that precise moment, his cook, Clotilde, appeared with six small Cuban coffee cups and crackers on an elegant silver tray. The aroma was catching and friendly and drew the attention of everyone in the room.

The uniformed Clotilde, wearing a big attentive smile, handed

207

out the coffees and all appeared relaxed by the doctor's reassuring conversation saying with his easy engaging laughter, "We will bring more coffee, don't despair," signaling the entire company to sit in comfortable seats.

Prado handed the purse to Soler who also inspected Vilma's purse and nodded a negative affirmation with obvious disappointment. Prado apologized to the doctor for their visit that disrupted his morning and thanked him for the coffee and his cooperation. He said goodbye to Toto Cuervo and turned to Tony Valle, giving him a long look all the while thinking, "He is a good short stop with a possible future in a professional team. And Vilma Espin? She is a cold, two-faced bitch, la puta de mierda."

Prado turned and closely faced the immutable Vilma, now showing calm relief. In a steady and firm voice all could hear, he warned her, "Young lady you come from a very distinguished and well-known family. Don't get involved with the Communist insurrection and their intrigues. We are sure your father would not approve if you were. He would give you holy hell. Look here, they will lose this struggle and they will pay dearly for their mistakes and violence to the public order. Come to your senses, Miss! Good-bye and be good."

Vilma Espin Gallois in uniform. (Family heirloom photo)

After a silent and meaningful short period, the company filed out in unhurried steps, in single and small groups, with the certainty that all of them were now watched and their names permanently in

SIM's files.

One week later, Herbert Mathews published his award-winning front page New York Times article, confirmed with photos, that the Fidel Castro guerrilla insurgency was alive and well armed in the Sierra Maestra mountains of Oriente Province and ready to fight to the death to the dismay of the Batista dictatorship and his followers, who believed they had been successfully diminished and disbanded.

Simultaneously, Pais recruited and trained many more urban volunteers for the immediate reinforcement of the mountain guerrilla group. To do this, Pais created an un-detectable system of transportation that evaded Batista's intelligence and the army encirclement of the Sierra Maestra. It was very efficient and combatants reached their destination promptly without significant loss of either soldiers or military supplies. Jorge Sotus, the hero of the successful National Navy garrison attack, was the first to command a group of over eighty armed insurgent soldiers to reach the Sierra Maestra hideout. Many more came. Significantly, three revolutionary women joined the mountain insurgents: Celia Sanchez, who later became the constant companion and girl-Friday of Fidel Castro, Haydee Santamaria, who played an important role in recruitment in the urban areas, and Vilma Espin, who later married Raul Castro, Fidel's brother. Vilma Espin bravely transported foreign correspondents' films and other items from the mountain hideouts to trusted contacts of the urban underground for safe delivery to their destinations abroad.

After an onsite inspection, Commander Sotus, an avowed anti-Communist Santiago recruit of Catalonian origins, was not impressed with Fidel Castro's command and on his return to the underground headquarters he reported to Pais that "they are disorganized and doing nothing and it appears to me that they are not going to do anything that is important militarily anytime soon." Commander Sotus' animus, his best and most daring combatant, led Pais to recall and order him abroad to organize an important rebel expedition to bring needed suppplies for the insurgency out of Houston, Texas, which failed. Sotus remained absent from the rapidly developing revolutionary activities and combat for a long time, as you will learn later in this narrative.

In an abortive initiative that he did not share with the mountain guerrilla headquarters and kept secret, Pais attempted to create a second front in the northeast mountains of Oriente Province. It failed principally because most of the Santiago urban warriors and arms and munitions had been depleted when they were moved to strengthen the Sierra Maestra guerrillas. In a relatively short time thereafter the number of mountain guerrillas increased significantly by recruits from Pinar del Rio and Habana. The guerrillas were rapidly redeployed, and in a very short time had become a disciplined, highly enthusiastic, and motivated fighting force which excelled in hit and run tactics, baffling the poorly trained and underpaid Batista soldiers of questionable morale and motivation. The commanders of each insurgent "column" had developed an efficient system of getting military intelligence at a moment's notice from the recruitment of the native peasant population. They were rapid runners, who knew well the intricate geography of the anticipated putative skirmishers with a description of critical impediments like rivers, streams, dense manigua, rocks, trees, or simple open spaces. It appeared that the military maps used by Batista's army lacked this type of organic information. It is to Fidel Castro's credit that all of his commanders and critical underlings had learned this geography to their great advantage in a firefight. They could move rapidly in the dark without any misgivings to their preplanned destinations to ambush hapless army units.

As he travelled incognito the length and breadth of the island, Pais observed an auspicious but worrisome rise in outbreaks or "brotes" of M26-7 cells that selected unknown and unverifiable leaders of their "armed action" groups. He worried greatly these "brotes" were unpredictable and lacked effective communication between themselves and the urban umbrella of the national headquarters of the M26-7 movement. He knew little of their political beliefs. He discussed this particular problem with his confidant, Rene Ramos Latour, a member of the Movement's leadership. These types of "brotes" rose to staggering numbers. They were to play an important role later.

There were dark forebodings arising from developing situations out of his control. He was not aware of them but intuitively had a feeling of impending doom. His poems that reached Herminia Greig, Dr. Santos-Buch's devoted wife, suggested that the worse was about to happen to him and his two brothers. There was no question that the hunt to cut off the head of the urban guerrilla M26-7 movement had greatly increased and now greatly endangered his movements. He was no longer safe in Santiago de Cuba.

In the interim, the underground Habana opposition had been secretly organized and did not keep the urban headquarters of the M26-7 informed of their plans. The Habana conspirators also kept the headquarters at La Plata in la Sierra Maestra in the dark. They had a very loose relationship previously when Fidel Castro and his combatants were quartered in Mexico before their landing in Oriente Province. Significantly, they had now plotted a daring and heroic plan that surprised everyone.

On March 13, 1957, a group of twelve to sixteen well-armed insurgents attacked the Presidential Palace to assassinate General Fulgencio Batista in the center of the capital, the seat of all governmental power. An additional group of four university students were assigned to secure the Radio Reloj radio station to announce in the airwaves what turned-out to be premature news of the success of the assassination squads. The arms had been obtained from private sources and Aureliano Sanchez Arango's Triple A (sic) underground action groups that were possibly partly financed by deposed President Prio Socarras.

The key to their plan was the realization that the palace entrance guards and nearby posted police had to be rapidly overwhelmed first before a second wave of rebels advanced in a dead run to the elevators and stairs to the second floor, the site of President Batista's office. Carlos Gutierrez Menoyo, a Spaniard and a veteran of the Republican Army against the Fascists in the Spanish Civil War, secured the Presidential Palace entrance for the second wave. Menoyo was successful, but paid with his life in the intense barrage as the second wave rushed the first-floor interior access.

The rebels were cut down from above by a 30-caliber machine gun overlooking the yard from the tower of the nearby Church of Santo Angel and from the deadly crossfire of another 30-caliber machine gun placed across the yard itself. Of the twelve to sixteen attackers, only four reached the second floor, but they were unable to find President Batista, who had taken the elevator and stopped it for safety between the floors. There was only one survivor, Luis Goicochea, who lived to fight another day among the Escambray Mountains guerrillas later.[43]

During the intense Palace attack, Jose Antonio Echevarria, the president of the Federation of University Students (FEU) and leader of the offshoot Directorio Revolucionario, successfully announced over the radio waves that President Batista had been killed and that a new government was in the making. Three students that occupied the radio station were able to escape but Jose Antonio Echevarria was left behind and killed in the street by the police. The remaining students, Jose Machado, Juan Pedro Carbo and Fructuoso Rodriguez, were joined by Jose Westbrook Rosales in a "safe" apartment 201, number 7, of Humboldt Street in the old Habana district. Within a couple of days, their hiding places were found by an informer and they were subsequently killed by the police.

Later, when the Castro Revolutionary Government investigated the Humboldt 7 episode further, it indicted Marco Rodriguez Alfonso,

43. Robert Taber describes the Palace attack in exciting detail in his memorable book "Biography of a Revolution."

a card-carrying member of the Cuban Communist Party and who had been named to the Cuban revolutionary diplomatic corps. He was found guilty of informing the location of the Palace conspirators to Batista's police and summarily executed by firing squad.

The persecution of the student rebels continued with terrible consequences because it is estimated that seventy-five to eighty more were hunted down and killed by the police in a short period of time.

Shortly after the Humboldt 7 Episode, Senator Pelayo Cuervo Navarro was shot and killed on the grounds of the Country Club of Habana. All evidence suggested that the order to kill the senator came from President Batista's office. The senator had been a severe critic of President Grau, who was denounced by him and accused of appropriating over $174 million from the government treasures. Federico L. Justiniani y de los Santos was named a Special Judge to investigate it in "La Causa 82" and ended up indicting Grau and several members of his cabinet. The senator had also published a study submitted to the United Nations that showed that more than 20,000 lives had been mysteriously killed since the fall of President Gerardo Machado in 1933. Although this was not a direct accusation of General Batista, many believed that he was responsible for the deaths. There is no doubt that Senator Cuervo Navarro was a formidable impediment to President Batista and his policies.

Fidel Castro criticized the news of the Presidential Palace attack in the safety of la Sierra Maestra with the simplistic explanation that he would have preferred to have the people more involved for the success of the effort. To him, the effort smacked of an ordinary coup d'etat.

The fact was that, for the first time since the Hotel Nacional massacre of the Constitutional Army Officers by the Sergeants' Revolt in 1933, Habana had been dramatically introduced to what a bloody revolution was all about, close and personal, right in the center of the island nation's capital. It was a very sobering experience for Habana, whose population lived in relative peace. The rich and famous, the military, and the well to do now seriously discussed the view that General Batista's government was vulnerable. American investors were shaken by the event. All of this helped the M26-7 Movement and, of course, Fidel Castro became a household name.

Following the Presidential Palace attack the insurrectionists' leaders moved to the Escambray Mountains in Las Villas, principally under the leadership of Carlos' brother, Eloy Gutierrez Menoyo, to initiate guerrilla warfare against the Batista dictatorship. Others joined the M26-7 rebels in Oriente Province. A few others called it quits and exiled themselves abroad.

We have thoroughly reviewed Professor Jose Alvarez's contributions backed by eyewitnesses of the events that led to Frank Pais' ambush by General Batista's special agents and police, as he stepped out onto the street of a "safe" house in Santiago de Cuba, July 30, 1957. My son, Charles J. Santos-Buch, also had previously investigated these events in his Harvard graduation thesis. His findings and Alvarez's implicate Vilma Espin, wife to Raul Castro Ruz.

Frank Pais , commander of the
Urban M26-7
(Family heirloom photo)

Significantly, when you look at the timing of two significant events you come to the controversial conclusion that Vilma Espin may be culpable of treason.

Commander Pais had issued a strict order not to make telephone calls to his hideout, a "safe" house. She had to know what was at stake when she made the fatal telephone call. Very shortly, in a matter of minutes after the call was made, Batista's security agents surrounded the house for an ambush.

Modernity

Dr. Alvarez's telephone operator source also implicates Vilma Espin's telephone call. The specific telephone number of the home of Mr. Pujol, Frank's friend and host, was under continued surveillance by General Batista's secret service investigators at this time. It is very difficult to believe that Vilma Espin was not aware that secret Batista agents were tapping Pujol's telephone line and had the means and expertise to use established triangulation techniques to locate any suspicious call from any house in Santiago de Cuba. Vilma Espin was not captured and escaped to the safety of the Maestra.

Shortly after hanging up the phone and leaving Raul Pujol's home, he and Frank Pais were dead under a barrage of bullets before they hit the pavement. Was she ordered to call Pais by Castro or was this lethal call of her own initiative and plan? We don't know.

The news spread like wildfire through out the island and abroad. Santiago's populace was not to be denied. Batista agents and the police safely stayed home, some a distance way from the immense crowd that followed his cortege with the uniformed Pais wearing the highest rebel army rank at the time, that of full Colonel of the M26-7.

It was a severe setback to the cause of the M26-7 and demoralized its action groups and members of the Resistencia Civica.

Importantly, Frank's brother, Agustin Pais, was spirited to the safety of the United States by the revolutionary underground after his brothers, Josue and Frank, were killed in action by Batista's forces. To lose Agustin, the last of three brothers, was too much to bear for the Pais family. The leadership of the underground action groups of the M26-7 Movement ruled that the Pais family had suffered too many losses in the revolutionary effort and the surviving brother was spared from the risk of another violent death.

The undeniable result of all of these important episodes is that potential Batista oppositionists who could have successfully challenged Fidel Castro's political and military thrusts were sidelined, out of the loop, or dead. This pattern did not end there.

CHAPTER 7.

◇ M26-7 Military Victories That Mattered.
◇ Fidel Castro's Application of General Claus von Clausewitz's Precepts.
◇ The Last Man Standing.

The embattled Pais had continued to organize the urban action groups in the cities of the "interior" nationwide, as well as in the so-far relatively peaceful capital city of Habana. Pais' mobility in urban areas was helped by "safe houses" of trusted friends and committed revolutionaries. His contacts in Habana had been instructed in person to begin recruiting contacts with labor union leaders with the idea to call a general strike in a later phase of the revolution as the successes of M26-7 progressed.

He appointed Faustino Perez as his loyal point man to organize sympathizers among the members of the government labor syndicates. This was a difficult and dangerous assignment that initially appeared to progress advantageously but the adherence to plans of a general strike dimmed as the number of the recruits did not rise fast or widespread enough. Perez feared government sympathizers and informants infiltrated his new recruitments.

A Differing View of Cuba's History

Perez did find several reliable members of the Electrician Labor Syndicate who expressed great interest in organizing a general strike. A small group called "Direccion Nacional Obrera" was organized to provide specific plans, date of the strike, and the organization of an orientation/communications center for the strikers of each municipality. The National Directory failed miserably, principally because of in-house personal squabbles that severely questioned the leadership, offered uncontrolled discipline, and was unable to recruit reliable organizers and participants.

It was finally announced for April 9, 1958, but it was aborted almost immediately. It was doomed to fail from the start. As a result, the leadership stature of Faustino Perez, Frank Pais and their fallowers faltered in La Plata mountain guerrilla headquarters and elsewhere in the underground revolutionary cells.

On July 12, 1957, the "Sierra Maestra Manifesto" was announced from Radio Rebelde and widely publicized. It was co-signed by Felipe Pazos, a well-known economist and banker; Raul Chibas, brother of Eduardo, the deceased leader of the Orthodox Party; Roberto Agramonte, the presidential candidate of the Orthodox Party, and Fidel Castro. The manifesto listed the reforms the Insurgency would propose in the event of Batista's government ouster. The reforms almost paralleled those of the Constitution of 1940. There was no hint of a Socialist or a Communist take over and the only flagged alarm for landowners was a reform that would break up the huge properties. In no uncertain terms, it also stated that the courts would justly compensate landowners for their losses. It was a reassuring announcement to many sectors of Cuba's population that the insurgency was not a Socialist or a Communist revolution.

Another loss happened when Rene Ramos Latour, who was named the commander of the urban insurgents of Santiago de Cuba following Pais' death, was killed in battle under mysterious circumstances. The action groups of Santiago subsequently joined Raul's second front successfully, and for all practical purposes, urban guerrilla warfare was ended.

Lastly, Fidel Castro, on his own, had come to the conclusion that to depose the Batista dictatorship effectively, the political phase of the revolutionary war had to be won when his prestige – gained by military victories – attracted the sympathy and political support of "the majority of the people." Intuitively, he had come to embrace the precepts of General Claus von Clausewitz, explained in his famous book, *On War* (1832). The most famous thematic quote of General Clausewitz is "War is not an independent phenomenon, but the continuation of politics by different means." In my search, I have not found whether Castro had read von Clausewitz, but it is remarkable how Castro closely embraced his recommendations in the westward thrust of military operations toward the fabled capital city of Habana, the seat of Cuba's political, military and economic power.

What he had in mind next was to claim significant military victories that would be unequivocally attributed to his skills as a guerrilla war commander. Importantly, to achieve that goal, he had to take the war from the safety of the Sierra Maestra Mountains to Batista's surrounding army groups successfully, and simultaneously win the political phase by controlling the better organized Cuban Communist Party. It was a bold plan.

The Cuban Communist Party leaders were initially alarmed by the Manifesto, but did not announce their misgivings to the press or to their membership at large. They decided instead that a secret meeting with Fidel Castro was now in order to discuss exactly what, in their view, needed to be done to gain revolutionary power.

Following is their probable agenda:

1. to assure victory of the Insurgency by a significant participation of their card-bearing members, who were highly organized and disciplined;

2. to offer a plan to prepare for a counter-revolution that would certainly happen right after victory and was likely supported by the United States;

3. identify the role the Communists would have in the final stages

of the insurgency and in governance.

We know that Carlos Rafael Rodriguez, who was a director of the Communist Party and who General Batista had named to his Government Cabinet, reached La Plata Headquarters soon after the publicized Manifesto at an uncertain date. The date of the secret meeting and who attended the meeting has remained secret to this day. We know it was intense and thorough. It took more than a week to reach a secret accord.

What is certain to many observers is that right after the victorious Insurgency took over the Habana government quarters, the Communist Party played a major role nationally in sequestering the infrastructure of the government bureaucracy, controlling the mainstream media, and providing lists of potential dangerous counter-revolutionaries, as you will learn later in this narrative.

Later, many in those lists were arrested in their homes and executed by firing squads to disrupt their counter-revolutionary plans. We have not been able to document these observations further but the force of the events that happened immediately after Batista's ouster strongly suggests that the agenda Carlos Rafael Rodriguez discussed with the M26-7 general staff in 1957 was generally adopted and carried-out immediately after Batista's ouster.

Needless to point out here, the Manifesto was tabled. Meanwhile, Castro's facade to the public was to declare to the domestic and foreign press that his revolution "was as green as the palms".

M26-7 Military Victories That Really Mattered

In examining M26-7 military victories that really mattered, the conclusion is that there were at least six in the space of May 1957 to December of 1958 that preceded the Insurrection's final military victory.

That is not to acknowledge that there were many "outbreaks" that contributed to the understanding by U.S. State Department observers and President Eisenhower's military advisors that General Batista's government was now vulnerable, that citizenry unrest was now politically significant, and that the armed insurgency was winning. For example, Commander Higinio Diaz's (a.k.a. "Nino") attack on the Ramon de las Yaguas garrison (April 1958) was bitterly fought room to room and the insurgents emerged victorious. The wounded soldiers were treated well by the insurgents and they arranged their transport to Santiago de Cuba for treatment. Commander "Nino" Diaz captured arms and ammunition to sufficiently supply his rebel force principally made up of the loyal local peasant population he knew well. Similar outbreaks of armed insurgent combats flourished in the "interior" of all provinces and contributed to the view that the general insurgency was now taking the Batista armed forces to task successfully.

These uncoordinated outbreaks of firepower were distracting and confusing to Batista's Army general staff headed by General Francisco Tabernilla Palmero. The armed rebellion seemed bigger to the general staff than it really was in numbers and armaments.

Interestingly, America's spies in Cuba continued to believe something closer to the truth – the insurgency had not been coordinated and it was run by small numbers of insurgents.

However, they also understood that it could not be dismissed because, by the spring of 1957, it was a force with excellent intelligence in the field. They were very physically fit for combat and the rebels were accurate shooters because each rebel soldier had been ordered by Castro to conserve ammunition and had to manage combat carrying only thirty rounds each. They made them count.

The ability to move rapidly in a well-known terrain also rendered them a military force that was better motivated to win over the lost Tabernilla soldiers, who were better armed and supplied.

It is important to understand that the Cuban Air Force was active but very predictable. It bombed daily but rarely strafed the thick, dense mountain jungle or the plains. The old WWII B26 bombers only carried 500-pound bombs and they were delivered, punctually, at five-thirty in the afternoon, when the insurgents were safe in their anti-aircraft tunnels. Napalm was not used.

When I asked some of the combatants about this, they said that they were more fearful of the "avionetas" (slow single engine light airplanes) because they sometimes carried machine guns or sniper rifles and their attacks were better aimed and deadly. However, inexplicably, "avionetas" were not used very frequently.

The Castro offensive against Batista's armed forces was initiated when the Uvero Garrison at the foot of the Sierra Maestra Mountains was attacked and captured by Fidel Castro's column on May 28, 1957.

Even though the number of fatalities and wounded on both sides was approximately equal, the blow was taken very hard by General Tabernilla and his general staff. He announced to the mainstream media that this was a "Declaration of War" and that the army would initiate a significant offensive against the Sierra Maestra insurgents immediately. Tabernilla's directives were well publicized.

Indeed, he ordered his best field officer, the brave and resourceful Lieutenant Colonel Angel Sanchez Mosquera, commander of the three hundred soldier-strong Battalion 11, to prepare to battle the insurgents "in their hideouts" of the Sierra Maestra Mountains. Battalion 11 had been very well trained, its morale was high, it was well armed and it was instructed, over and over again, with the techniques used in an asymmetric skirmish.

But the government's offensive was delayed. Incredibly, it was scheduled for May 1958, one year later. The delay of the hailed "offensive" was an egregious mistake and was interpreted as cowardice or a failure to prepare it. Mosquera's troopers began to suspect that they would not be involved in serious combat in rebel occupied territory any time soon.

The reality check was that Mosquera was to face a cunning and enthusiastic enemy looking for a fight, who was well-informed of his deployments and movements on the hour, was very familiar with the battle terrain and now was capable to fight, toe to toe, with deadly accurate fire.

In the interim of the counter offensive delay, the political phase of the Insurrection was given a great impetus by Fidel Castro when he nominated Liberal Judge Manuel Urrutia Lleo as his candidate for the presidency of the Provisional Revolutionary Government. Urrutia was secretly shipped to New York City in January 1958 and given extensive American mainstream media coverage by Resistencia Civica and others. Charles provided pro bono medical assistance to his pregnant wife, Esperanza Urrutia. Cornell's Professor of Obstetrics, William Givens, delivered a healthy baby girl at the New York Hospital facility.

Furthermore, many politicos and civil leaders began to organize themselves with the advice and consent of Armando Hart, Manolo Ray and Dr. A. M. Santos-Buch of Resistencia Civica to enjoin the political phase of the revolution. These were new and alarming revelations to the dictatorship. Distrust among Batista's followers was spreading and it was difficult for them to know who was a friend and who was not. General Batista's leadership was waning and suspect.

In May 1958, Mosquera's troops penetrated deep into the Sierra Maestra and reached Minas de Bueycito, very close to the M26-7 headquarters in La Plata. His scouts did not know, however, how close they were to their primary target nor they were prepared to face a determined and elusive guerrilla. He occupied and camped in Las Mercedes, a little higher in the mountain range, and wisely prepared for a counterattack secured in the belief that headquarters would send troop and material support on request at a moments' notice. It was the deepest penetration of insurrect territory by General Tabernilla's officers and his soldiers.

Within the hour following his skilled plan, Fidel Castro's troopers, under the direction of Commanders Ernesto Guevara and Juan Almeida, out-flanked Mosquera's troopers on two sides, each from the south and the west. The savagery of the close ordered combat dealt a severe blow to Mosquera's valiant troopers and after more than a week of deadly combat and guerrilla harassment, he was running out of supplies and learned that his requests to headquarters for reinforcements were not forthcoming to relieve his command. He was forced to retire from the mountain range with the dead and wounded to bivouac in the relative safety of the rich valleys of Oriente Province, ostensibly to fight another day.

The significance of Fidel Castro's victory was far-reaching. When the news got to President Eisenhower's advisers, it was taken seriously. They viewed Castro's victory with newly gained respect.

General Tabernilla and his general staff had lost prestige, and importantly, Fidel Castro's stature grew now that he was seen as a battle-tested, well-versed and disciplined guerrilla commander who was winning the people's trust.

This view grew exponentially, nationally and abroad. Following the victory, the number of "armed rebel outbreak groups" rose with enthusiastic Cuban citizen volunteers. The members of the outbreak groups also understood the importance of the blessings of a winner, who was likely to take over the island's government reins. Contributions to the M26-7 Treasury increased two-fold.

The Civil Opposition was now in the safety of Venezuela and grew in significance because they were clearly not associated with far leftist politics or philosophy and Washington sympathized with their efforts. Secret CIA contacts with the M26-7 and Resistencia Civica increased and seemed sympathetic to their cause.

Importantly, Batista and his military appealed to the United States for arms and military supplies, but their pleas were denied.

Victory at Las Mercedes was followed by another significant operation in Pinos del Agua in June 1958. The rebels took their victorious offense to the Oriente plains for the first time. To do it, Commanders José Quevedo Perez, Camilo Cienfuegos, and Ernesto Guevara stopped another large counteroffensive effort by General Tabernilla, his staff, discouraged troopers, and noncommissioned officers.

On July 11, 1958, the last significant week-long battle of the rebel offense happened in "El Jigue" near the Oriente Province plains. This time, the rebels used 50-caliber machine guns, rocket propelled grenades and automatic rifles captured in prior battles. Armored vehicles were destroyed with Molotov cocktails and the army withdrew from the field of battle. Again, the insurgents were victorious. The International Press reported that more than 443 prisoners had been released to the Red Cross.

Standing on the tarmac of Machado's Central Highway facing west, the victorious and confident insurgents contemplated the vast plains of Camaguey Province to plan a nearly 500-mile march to the seat of power, Habana. In the planning interim, uncoordinated outbreaks of armed groups randomly attacked but did not capture small garrisons of the countryside villages.

After El Jigue, Commander Raul Castro and his troopers crossed the plains of Oriente Province to form the second front with headquarters in the Sierra Cristal Mountains with relative ease and safety.

Following Pais' death, Fidel Castro's general staff in La Plata had designed this very important maneuver in La Sierra Maestra. Commander Raul Castro and his warriors, including his wife-to-be Vilma Espin, successfully invaded the northeast mountainous region of Oriente Province and established a "second front" that closely surrounded all road and rail access to the second largest city of Cuba, Santiago de Cuba. It attracted many recruits from the peasant population as well as urban insurgents of the major cities and villages of the immediate region.

In time, the second front grew very large and it became a formidable, impregnable military bastion with an airport. Two of the famous officers of Raul Castro's rebel army, Commander Raul Menendez Tomasevich and Commander Huber Matos, excelled and rose in prestige for their disciplined and well-organized guerrillas that blockaded the surrounding hills of Santiago de Cuba. The second front held the attention of Washington when the Rebels occupied the Moa Bay Mining Company, owned by USA's Freeport Nickel Company, and held the principals hostage.

A Differing View of Cuba's History

The situation was solved with difficult negotiations with Commander Raul Castro. When the mainstream media reported that America's government officials had negotiated with rebel commanders under Raul Castro, it was interpreted as another victory nationally and abroad because it showed how strong the Insurgency had become and how weak Batista's government was for not protecting the Moa Bay Company principals.

On July 20, 1958, the Caracas Pact, organized by José Miro Cardona, was signed by a number of significant civil and political leaders who had joined in Venezuela's capital to discuss the role they would have after the expected military triumph of the M26-7 rebels (See Appendix).

Although the name of Fidel Castro appears prominently in the document, it is clear that he was not present in the Caracas discussions and that he did not sign it personally as the leader of the M26-7. The only revolutionary with a close alliance with the M26-7 was my father, Dr. A. M. Santos-Buch, the representative of the Civic Resistance Movement.

Other revolutionaries who signed the document were representatives of the Student Revolutionary Directory, the University Student Federation, army officers who had defected, and representatives of the Montecristi Group. All backed José Miro Cardona's initiatives for unity among the remnants of political parties and labor unions who opposed General Batista. The Provisional President of Cuba appointed by Fidel Castro, Manuel Urrutia Lleo, announced his support of the Caracas Pact from New York City.

Significantly, leaders of the Orthodox Party were not listed among them, like Raul Chibas and Roberto Agramonte.

The Caracas Pact agreed to five principles:

1. A call to arms to all citizens to join the insurrection

2. The formation of a post-Batista provisional government to usher the normalization of a "democratic and constitutional process" and the enforcement of "civil order"

3. A guarantee of the "delivery of Justice" which was vaguely defined

4. A general appeal to the armed forces to join the insurrection as soon as possible

5. An appeal to the United States to deny any help to the Batista government and its Armed Forces.

Miro Cardona's efforts were well received but it lacked detailed specifics. For example, it did not detail the formation of political parties, election dates or how and what type of justice was to be delivered. Despite that, the Pact of Caracas lended some credence to the sprouting idea that perhaps the post-Batista Revolutionary Government was not going to be bad in the long run.

Although the Caracas Pact lacked significant strong military or political "teeth" it was an international warning to Batista and his supporters in Washington that they were about to lose the political battle.

Some in Washington began to think that the next strategy was to cautiously approach the insurgency to gain some leverage among their possible winners. Others, however, thought that the insurrection was more likely to descend to the Far Left and vague plans began to erupt in the CIA and in the Pentagon to secretly create a Plan B with an elite counter revolutionary force to defeat the rise of the first Communist State of the Americas.

A Mission and A Narrow Escape

I stepped out the entrance of the Cornell University Medical College on York Avenue and for a moment I studied the steady cold rain and the puddles I had to avoid. I had had a long night at the bedside of an elderly gentleman struggling to live with metastatic esophageal adenocarcinoma in the G-5 ward of the New York Hospital. The G-5 Pavilion had five patients with the dreadful disease and I was determined to keep them alive. I had scarcely two hours of sleep in two nights. G-5 was understaffed because of an epidemic of infectious mononucleosis that hit the interns, residents, nurses and the chief resident of the medical ward. I received the call to substitute a G-5 intern even though I was only a fourth-year medical student. As I crossed York Avenue to reach the Lexington Avenue subway at a quick pace, I did not remember when I had been as tired as I was right then.

The call was from Dr. Antonio Buch, my cousin, who had a favor to ask. I was given the address. No questions were asked and I realized that it was certain that it had to do with the Cuban Revolution. After all, Tony was a partner of Armando Hart and both had just escaped imprisonment in Habana. The address was near the East River and Greenwich Village, an area I knew well. When I reached the warehouse, I realized it was closer to the quay and the merchant marine docks. It was night, rainy and cold.

Tony, a cardiologist, was brief of words and I immediately offered an envelope with two checks for the M26-7 treasurer totaling $30,000. "I'll take care of this," he said. "But I need you to do something for me you will not like. First, this is José a trustworthy M26-7 operative." José looked at me and determined I was a Gringo and immediately began a diatribe on the evil faults of Imperialism. I thought, "I don't need this crap now for God's sake!"

"Come on back, Charles, and sit down on this barrel head," Tony said with a smile.

We were alone and none heard us. Four or maybe five rebel activists stripped five Thompson machine guns and hid them in olive oil barrels to ship to a warehouse in Santiago de Cuba.

Tony looked at me hard and then asked, "Have you read about the news of the Cienfuegos Montecristi rebel outbreak who escaped in a merchant ship that is docked nearby?"

Modernity

I had read the news in the *New York Post* two days before. "Yes. But he was captured, the ship is Cuban territory, and he tried to commit suicide by cutting his arm veins rather than return to Habana. Is this right?"

Tony smiled and nodded. "I want you to go to the ship as an MD and try to reach him and find out if he is alright."

"I can try Tony but I doubt I can even get on board. I will let you know right away," I said. *Crap*, I said to myself.

The ship was not far away and it was easy to identify because an unruly mob of pro-Castro protesters on the opposite sidewalk with hurried signs was making traffic difficult. A couple of blue blood police officers were trying to moderate the crowd's outburst of bad English and Caribbean Spanish. I crossed the street, approached the ship's ladder and got on it to reach the top where I was stopped. I opened my London Fog raincoat to reach for my IDs, but to my great surprise, the officer of the day let me on board when he saw my white intern uniform overloaded with my stethoscope and other common doctor instruments. The officer said, "Get out of the rain, doctor, and the patient is inside that door. Thank you for coming to our help."

With brazen aplomb I did what he said and found many reporters but neither the patient nor his guards were there. I waited with the rest.

With no announcement, me, a civilian MD with my little black bag, the Montecristi rebel, and his guards were ushered into the ship's cabin. The unshackled prisoner was scared as he viewed the reporters and other visitors around and in front of him. He did not speak. The forearms showed deep cuts, but they were healing very well and no running blood was seen. I cleaned the forearms and bandaged him. I also gave him a tetanus shot before silently leaving the cabin, reaching the ship's ladder and walking into the street.

FBI agents were organizing the protesters rudely to control their outbursts. I closed my London Fog raincoat and calmly crossed the street. Two agents began to follow me.

"This is not good," I said to myself.

229

A Differing View of Cuba's History

I decided not to take the subway and cut to a side street. I sensed – more than saw – a lighted sign of a bar and the guard let me in easily. I walked to the bar and ordered tap beer. I began to calmly inspect the joint and realized that it was a stripper bar. A beautiful young woman in her early twenties finished her routine and received loud applause and many whistles.

"She is spectacularly beautiful," I muttered to myself.

I turned to the bar mirror and saw the quizzical smile of the bartender. He was sympathetic and he understood that I was in some kind of trouble and enjoined me in small talk.

To my surprise, the sultry stripper walked to my side and introduced herself with a stage name. Her smile was reassuring. I explained that I was a New York Hospital resident, that I had briefly seen the captured Cuban rebel in the ship, that two FBI agents were following me, and that I did not want to be arrested and interrogated by them.

She took my arm lovingly and said not to worry.

Her real name was Clara, she was from Habana, she understood what I wanted her to do, and we both engaged in a friendly conversation that held the attention of the bar.

She asked me, "Are they in similar suits and hats and very serious?" I nodded and she kissed me and we both laughed. In a moment, she said, "They are gone, Charles."

I asked for her telephone number and address. I left in a steady rain, positive that I was not to see my beautiful champion again.

I called Tony Buch with my observations. The prisoner was returned to Cuba, indicted and condemned for an unknown number of years of jail time.

But there were more prescient developments taking place in the island nation at this time that mesmerized the public at large because they showed the measure of the insurrection in realistic terms they could understand.

Using stealth provided by the moonless and rainy 1958 summer nights, two veteran rebel groups, respectively commanded by Camilo Cienfuegos and Ernesto, "el Che," Guevara, successfully crossed the dangerous open plains of Camaguey and reached the safer, mountainous strategic points to the west where well-armed local M26-7 guerrillas reinforced them.

When General Tabernilla and his general staff were informed that well-known Oriente Province mountain insurgent commanders were close to the capital, Habana, they were initially confused. They had been somewhat reassured by the knowledge that a forthcoming large shipment of NATO armaments with FAL rifles, machine guns, rocket-propelled grenades, C4 plastic explosives and ammunition, was forthcoming on the freighter La Coubre, sailing from Belgium and expected in Habana Harbor soon.

What confused them was that they were beginning to understand that a lack of political support in the general population was not just in the offing. It was now prevalent in the armed forces.

There was growing evidence of wavering loyalties among their troops. Furthermore, the insurrects' deployments were advancing to Habana at a credible speed they were not suspected to have.

They harbored dark premonitions of a rapid defeat. They were right.

When they received the intelligence that Commander Camilo Cienfuegos had captured the Yaguajay Garrison near the City of Sancti Espiritus in Las Villas Province, many developments began to rapidly escalate out of control.

The Escambray insurgents of Commander Eloy Gutierrez Menoyo joined the M26-7 campaign. Communists sporting new beards and clean M26-7 uniforms also joined the successful fray. Commanders Matos and Tomasevich slowly and carefully advanced toward Santiago de Cuba to occupy it without much resistance and no casualties.

Shortly thereafter, it was announced that Commander Guevara and his rebels had captured an armored train in Santa Clara Province that originally had been destined to stop the western insurgent advances on its track.

The sudden understanding of their vulnerable political and military positions led to the development of all manner of survival plans and their attention on the fields of battle rapidly waned. The officer class was well aware of what might happen to them and their families if they were captured in their quarters.

Many in the military, particularly soldiers of the line, were willing to strike a deal with the Insurrection and face the revolutionary vortex and unpredictable demons of the victors and surrendered without firing a shot.

The police, armed forces officers and their troopers tied M26-7 bandanas on their left arms and greeted rebel army soldiers as they surrendered en masse and were released home. The prisoners were welcomed but they represented a logistical problem for the highly mobile rebel forces.

Nevertheless, an all-out assault on the principal Army Camp of Columbia outside Habana was prepared, but it required the organization of armored vehicles, tanks and artillery the rebels had not yet learned to use effectively. Rebel operations in the interior provinces continued and all-important garrisons outside the Habana district were captured with little resistance.

The daunting tasks of capturing both the Columbia and Habana garrisons loomed darkly to rebel military planners because their calculations called for many casualties. As the Habana targets were surrounded the impending assault was delayed as successful rebel army operations against Batista army garrisons of the interior provinces continued.

A dark sense of impending doom spread to all sectors of the island's capital.

Fortunately, President Fulgencio Batista and his staff came to the understanding that prolonging military operations against the rebel army had reached "the point of diminishing returns" and some were deemed "unsustainable." A plan to fly government principals out of the country was constructed and executed.

Terms of surrender were drawn and approved. The non-specific general terms were as follows: 1) the government was to be transferred to a military junta of armed forces officers considered fair to the insurrection, 2) a cease fire was to be ordered, and 3) the cooperation with the M26-7 plan of a peaceful transition of power and the restoration of order and peace was necessary.

A petition for general amnesty of Batista combatants was considered but not submitted. The short-lived transitional junta understood that the terms of surrender would delay a rebel army all-out assault and facilitate the escape of government and armed forces principals.

When Commander Fidel Castro received the terms of surrender, he, in no uncertain terms, immediately dismissed them and promptly ordered all rebel army operations "to continue until all the military goals are completed as initially planned."

Fidel Castro initially declined going to Santiago de Cuba (now in rebel hands) to celebrate that victory. Instead, he first planned a slow march from Oriente Province toward Habana with a long column of veteran rebel soldiers with their captured armored vehicles and other splendid military booty. It was not a military operation per se, since it was to be in the safety of rebel-occupied territory.

The mainstream media picked up on this strategy nationally and abroad. Later TV news outlets in the U.S. covered the slow victory march and it resembled a very effective populist political rally, this time, celebrated by numerous bearded rebel soldiers.

Habana's final "Fall to the Insurrection" was on New Year's Day 1959 with little resistance. Commander Camilo Cienfuegos and his troopers occupied the Presidential Palace and ransacked it. Cienfuegos was photographed standing on the oil portrait of President General Batista as he read some of the printed communiqués of the former president. He and his family had been flown to Santo Domingo. General Tabernilla and his command were gone also.

The remains of the general staff surrendered and withdrew from the Colombia Military Base on the outskirts of the capital. In Santiago de Cuba, Commanders Raul Castro, Huber Matos and Tomasevich occupied the city's council building and the famed Céspedes Park in the center of the provincial capital. Batista's officers used the confusion of the moment to escape.

Smiles and relief accompanied the city's widespread exultation. Bacardi rum and Hatuey beers were sported by many. There was no more fighting. "A beginning with justice for all" was wildly proclaimed in the streets. A rebirth of democracy and a new beginning was predicted to happen very soon. There were tears and laughter.

Fidel Castro's scheduled Céspedes Park speech was late and it was somewhat ambiguous and confusing.

My mother telephoned and reached me and my young family in the home of Mr. Loys von Kreuter in Darien, Connecticut, late on the night of December 31. It was an emotional conversation. There were praises of Fidel, El Che, Cienfuegos, Matos, Raúl, and other well-known revolutionaries.

"Peace at last, Charles . . . at last."

I announced a planned visit in March with my wife and infant son, Charlie. There were promises of easier telephone communications now that "censorship" was gone and exiled families were to be reunited soon.

Importantly, my close friend, Alan von Kreuter, strongly warned me of Communist infiltrators in the ranks of the insurrection.

Manuel Jorge Cutillas was also celebrating the triumph of the Insurrection from the city's council balcony that faces Céspedes Park, which was completely filled by the joyous populace. Sitting next to him was the chief of police, who was wearing a M26-7 bandana on his left arm. They listened to several speakers praising the idea of conciliation and a possible "covenant" among Batista soldiers and rebel guerrillas to bring peace and prosperity to the embattled island nation.

On reading the newspaper the next day, El Diario de Cuba, Manuel learned that a revolutionary firing squad had executed the police chief in the early morning hours. Manuel was deeply moved; he became very agitated by the possible violent course the revolution might take and discussed his fears with José (Pepin) Bosch, Bacardi's CEO and executive officer. Both determined that all international and national legal papers that protected the Bacardi name and the marks used commercially had to be moved to a safe place outside Cuba itself. They recognized the potential danger the company faced if a sudden confiscation and takeover of their offices was serious and detailed.

Manuel agreed to secretly leave Santiago with the papers in a schooner bound for Miami, Florida. After pro-Castro customs officers inspected the boat moored in the Marítima Parreño, the schooner sailed away and eventually arrived at his destination without incident. The papers were safe.

Later, Pepín Bosch founded and organized a brand-new company, Bacardi International, in Nassau, Bahamas, and launched the highly successful phase of the family owned company that rapidly was to span the world today.

Many of the rich took measures to move their money to the United States, Switzerland, Spain, and elsewhere as quickly as possible. Others started to hoard American paper dollars; others withdrew dollars from their savings accounts. The middle class did not quite understand what was going on or what was to happen next.

A significant number of citizens were not fooled and understood what was happening. Cuban-Chinese, who had immigrated to Cuba during the Chinese Civil Wars and lost everything they owned to the Maoists, prepared in haste their departure from the host island. As early as when the Sierra Maestra Manifesto was first announced by the rebels, Cuban-Chinese families began to sell their properties and started a silent trek to the United States of America, moving decidedly to New York

City's "Chinatown." In a short time, more than 10,000 Cuban-Chinese restaurants opened in the five New York boroughs. No one cared to discover the whys of this en masse exodus.

When Carol and I visited Cuba in March 1959 with our infant son, the first order of business was to visit Provisional President Urrutia and his family in the Habana Presidential Palace. Bearded rebel soldiers heavily guarded the palace.

It was an awkward moment. President Urrutia was busy and was very careful with his words. His wife, Esperanza, ushered us to a more private room with comfortable furnishings and in small talk we described our difficult trip form New York City to Habana.

On the way out, I bumped into my relative, Luis Buch, the president's secretary, who briefly described how they intended to stop the flight of money and he was fearful of a counter- revolution. He made it very clear that President Urrutia and Fidel Castro and his closest followers were not on the same page with the president. He was confident that those differences were going to be ironed-out. He didn't mention how, and off he went.

We left the palace in less than an hour to prepare for the evening flight to Santiago de Cuba.

The Return

The beauty of Santiago Bay and surrounding mountains always surprised me. The pilot turned so that all passengers had a glimpse of the Morro Fortress at the entrance. There had been three long years of absence from home since 1956. Charles Jan, my one-year old son, had been a trooper all along the journey home from New York City. The reunion not only included my aging father and mother, but my sister, Enid and brother-in-law, Andrew Duany, who joined the boisterous welcome home. We slept soundly. Herminia, my mom, had employed a young nanny who was to care for my son. After breakfast, we dressed and planned to visit to my uncles and aunts and Carol's family. The visits were obligatory. The first was an easy step across a wide avenue to the home and doctor's office of my uncle, Jesus Buch, the famous internist.

As we stood on the sidewalk of the Siboney Road, two open army trucks blocked our way. About eighteen young men were packed like sardines in the back of each of two trucks. They looked thoughtful, not fearful, but saddened. Two of the heavily guarded prisoners sighted the Americans and yelled in a firm voice, "Please, please call our parents and tell them we are going to our executions right now." The trucks sped by. Surprised, Carol and I remained silent and it took us a moment or two to finally understand what was happening. It was a deeply disturbing and frightful episode. We turned, tried to alert the newspapers and found that they did not answer their phones. Thoughtful moments passed in sobering silence.

I deduced that the firing squad field must have been the San Juan Hill River Valley below, not far from home. The incident told us that in this post-insurrection period, no one knew who was a friend or a foe and that there were dangerous informers everywhere. "So much for peace and tranquility," I thought.

A man is readied for execution by a Castro-Communist firing squad.

A Differing View of Cuba's History

In the subsequent short vacation days in our hometown, Carol and I adopted a strategy of "listen and don't talk" to avoid difficult questioning. Our young house help had been recruited to serve in the militias and taught how to use Russian SKS automatic rifles. They were trained by local M26-7 officers to look to the night sky for American airplanes or worse.

M26-7 rebels guard the entrance of Santiago de Cuba Bay.

(Family heirloom photo)

On a visit to the city of Palma Soriano, we saw young peasants marching and performing close order drills supervised by a uniformed M26-7 rebel. When we visited the former military Moncada Barracks that had been converted in a school facility, an enthusiastic teacher described a curriculum to eradicate illiteracy of the grandparents of many of the enrolled students. The new history lessons for the young were heavy fawning exercises that praised the heroes of the insurrection and condemned the United States of America for its misdeeds.

Dr. Santos-Buch, my father, had been named director of the newly built and equipped Children's Hospital. President Batista had built the hospital during his tenure. There, I met a pediatric neurosurgeon who had been trained at Johns Hopkins Hospital and was a guest scheduled to operate on a young child with a lethal brain tumor. He volunteered that he was booked to return to his position in Baltimore, Maryland. He was not disposed to say what he knew of the course of the insurrection.

At home that afternoon the mainstream media, now occupied by sympathizers of revolutionary measures, announced that "Defense of the Revolution Committees" were to be organized by activists of the M26-7, who would recruit neighbors to spy on neighbors in every city block nationally. The Committees served subsequently as useful "informers" of any hint of counter-revolutionary activity in any home of any city block. Our immediate families gave significant signs of fear of expressing their opinions freely to their M26-7 compatriots and to us.

Carol and I returned home to New York with very dark premonitions.

CHAPTER 8.

"Revolution is like Saturn.
It devours its own children." [44]

The Resistencia Civica New York City branch was dissolved without incident and the Cuban Relief Foundation shipped a large load of clothes to Santiago de Cuba for the victims of the insurrection before closing its operations. In Cuba, the fight for ultimate power was over by Christmas 1959, as Fidel Castro defeated President Urrutia, Miro Cardona, his followers and others. The Rebel Army was tightly organized under the command of Raul, his brother. A reign of fear dawned over the island nation.

Professor Gibbs' "US Policy Towards Cuba Since the Cold War" is a scholarly, excellent source of pertinent information and timelines. I quote her extensively here:

Gibbs points out that America's deep preoccupation with Cuba was not new. Thomas Jefferson, James Madison and James Monroe wrote opinions that Cuba was not to be occupied or ruled by any other power

---

44. "The breath of an aristocrat is the death rattle of freedom. Revolution is like Saturn, it devours its own children. They say in the grave there is peace, and peace and the grave are one and the same. Government must be a transparent garment which tightly clings to the people's body." By Georg Büchner, 1813-1837. He was a dramatist and writer of poetry and prose, considered part of the Young Germany movement. He was also a revolutionary and the brother of physician and philosopher Ludwig Büchner. (Public Domain)

than Spain. The Founding Fathers favored "the ripe fruit thesis" which was loosely based on the notion that "a racially mixed slave owning Cuban society could not govern it." The other part of the thesis was founded on the belief that the poorer and less civilized island "would naturally be annexed for its own good and prosperity." They were also fearful of an exposed southern border that could easily endanger the trade sea-lanes of the Gulf of Mexico.

According to Gibbs, President Polk, and later President Pierce, offered Spain $100 and $130 million respectively to buy the island. As time passed by and the Lincoln and Civil War era was reached "the moment for territorial expansion in the Caribbean had passed." In sharp contrast, commercial links flourished, and by the 1890s, "the Foster-Canova's concessions and tariffs skyrocketed American investments in Cuba." These commercial links slowed considerably during both world wars but increased greatly afterwards and even during the Castro insurrection.

Gibbs points out that by 1958, American interests controlled "42% of Cuban sugar production, 83% of public rails, more than 90% of telephone and electrical services and Standard Oil and Texaco provided more than 70% of Cuba's petroleum requirements." The construction of the modern Mines of Moa in the north of Oriente Province had been finished by a crew of brilliant Cuban engineers and was providing nickel and other rare metals to enrich the arsenal of the United States of America. Some observers believe that the rising prosperity was vital to finance the insurrection against the Batista government.

The Eisenhower Administration was alerted by the rapidity of the radicalization of the revolutionary government. Professor Gibbs also indicates that President Eisenhower and Vice-President Nixon "were not so much influenced by the Soviet-Cuban Trade agreement of February 1960 or by the Soviet military alliance of May 1959 or by their concerns with the program of compensations of confiscated private lands by the newly enacted "Agrarian Reform Law."

According to Professor Gibbs, what really turned their heads was "the wholesale loss of individual property and human rights of the

242

Cuban people themselves." For the President of the United States this was self-evident when more than 26,000 of the best and brightest Cuban refugees reached American shores in the first six months of Fidel Castro's government. The Eisenhower Administration had not been advised that more than 10,000 hard-working Cuban-Chinese émigrés had already arrived in New York City by the previous year.

The freighter La Coubre, with seventy-six tons of munitions, arms and explosives bought during the Batista regime exploded twice, while moored to a Habana Harbor dock on March 4, 1960. The carnage accounted for more than one hundred dead and nearly two hundred wounded. Fidel Castro and his intelligence apparatus asserted that the United States government was responsible because it was the "work of those who do not wish us to receive arms for our defense" (Appendix and Phillips, R. Hart, 6 March, 1960. "Castro Links U.S. to Ship 'Sabotage'; Denial is Swift." *The New York Times*). The importance of this tragic event is that it convinced the Castro regime that the United States was seriously planning a counter-revolutionary armed process sooner than they had expected, and it alerted them to get ready for it.

By August 1960 the wholesale nationalization of private enterprises previously listed by the Cuban Communist Party had been completed. When push came to shove, Eisenhower and Nixon turned to the Central Intelligence Agency (CIA) to develop plans to solve the "Cuban problem" by military means if necessary. By June 1961, the USA ceased diplomatic relations with Cuba.

The outflow of Cuban families to the safety and freedom of America steadily increased. The Cuban refugee plan was encouraged by the Castro regime. To be permitted to leave their own country, they had to surrender their homes, savings accounts, cars, moneys, jewels, and art to the State. It was a bonanza of ready capital, in-hand cash, and properties that enriched the Communist State immediately. The distributive regime awarded their supporters richly. And it motivated the growing opposition to seek refuge and isolation in the United States.

By the mid 1970s, more than a million Cubans chose "immigration over a revolution with socialist reforms" and left the tragic island with a sense that they were never to return. Americans were generous by and large but many signs in Miami Beach residential buildings showed their displeasure by announcing: "No children, no dogs, no Cubans".

Despite these difficulties, the first wave of Cuban émigrés was probably one of the best ever for America. They learned English, they assimilated with the mainstream, ambitiously sought productive ventures, academic positions, and climbed the corporate, social and political ladders in record time. Miami, Florida, grew in importance and *expanded physically* with new skyscrapers and flourishing businesses because of it. Many returned the monetary help from American largesse they had received on landing. Their record will be very difficult to equal by any other immigrations of today that are creating ghettoes rather than assimilation by mainstream America.

Foretelling Georg Büchner's observation on revolution, a string of important fatalities among leaders of the M26-7 happened in the course of enforcements of socialist reforms. For example: Commander Pena, a "not guilty" adjudicator of the trial of Batista's air force pilots in Santiago de Cuba who was publically repudiated by Fidel Castro, committed suicide. Haydee Santamaría, a veteran of the 1953 Moncada Assault, Sierra Maestra combatant, and wife of Minister of Education Armando Hart, killed herself. Commander Manuel Piñeiro Losada, a graduate of Columbia University, better known as Barba Roja, and head of security and counter-intelligence, died in a unexplained motorcycle accident. Commander Camilo Cienfuegos, a successful military officer and conqueror of the Presidential Palace, was killed in an unexplained airplane "accident" on his return to Habana when he was ordered to arrest Commander Huber Matos, who was charged with treason. The plane was never found. Matos served many years of imprisonment. Commander Humberto Sori Marín, author of the more moderate version of an Agrarian Reform Law and a paraplegic veteran of the insurrection, was summarily executed with Rogelio González Corso, both of Castro's National Institute of Agrarian Reform. Corso was previously a member of the Habana University Agrupación Católica, and was the secret National Director of the underground MRR (Movimiento de Recuperación Revolucionaria) that numerous veterans of the Insurrection had joined. There are many other examples.

Confused and worried that we had been poorly informed, Carol, my wife, and I decided to visit Cuba in July of 1960. The purpose of our visit was to explore the breadth and length of the entire island by car to determine how deep the Communist control extended into the island's power infrastructure. Prior to our departure, I visited Herbert Mathews of *The New York Times* to inform him of the purpose of the Cuba visit. Mathews was friendly and encouraged me and asked me to report back to his office.

The trip took advantage of some of the connections Carol and I had with Resistencia Civica and the M26-7. The visit to all sites was by appointment and we were well received by their heads or subalterns of the local M26-7. It proved to be a very revealing experience.

In Oriente Province, we were shown the works in progress or activities of the tourist facilities in construction at La Gran Piedra Mountain and Mar Verde Beach. Manolo Ray had been appointed Minister of Public Works and he had gone to work without hesitation. A well-stocked Peoples Store was at these sites. The prices of the stores were set by the government and not by market forces. A visit to the Dos Rios Agricultural Cooperative showed a very busy farm and cattle organization still in progress. I noted a dearth of farmers and was not able to talk to them. On the way out we saw many crates of fresh tomatoes rotting in the sun near the border of Machado's Central Highway. Apparently, this loss happened because the cooperative had not arranged transport to the public central marketplace of Santiago de Cuba.

A Jeep was required to reach the San Lorenzo Agricultural Cooperative in La Sierra Maestra. After we were served coffees, about six peasants discussed their dissatisfaction with the planned centralized cooperative. They had expected to be free owners of parcels of the cultivable land and not indentured servants of the state. Carol and I were surprised at their candor in front of the M26-7 operative who was the acting boss of the Cooperative.

Our trip skipped Camaguey because we could not get an appointment. The next stop briefly took us to the city of Trinidad with an urban cooperative that specialized in making yarey hats and other items for the tourist industry. Carol and I observed that they were the only tourists who were visiting the ancient city. In the afternoon we headed to Santa Clara, the provincial capital of the province with the same name. We were the guests of our friends Lolita Pujol and her recent husband and our friend, Commander Carlos Iglesias, also known as "Nicaragua."

It was the highlight of our car trip. Nicaragua was the head of Santa Clara's Rebel Army forces and his home was the Governor's Mansion. Nicaragua was our personal guide and was forthcoming with much information related to security, training of women laborers and provincial peasants with the newly arrived Soviet arms and explosives, the appointment of Communists to head confiscated newspapers and radio/TV stations, and the construction of tourist sites in the Cienaga de Zapata and its beaches. He paid great attention to the organization of the women's militia more than the peasants'. He pointed out to me how the infrastructure of the government bureaucracy was replete with card bearing Communist party operatives. The next morning, Nicaragua and his labor organizer guided us through the swamp's roads to Playa Larga and the Bay of Pigs. The lagoon in the center was spectacularly beautiful with abundant fresh water fish, including trout. We were told that Commander Fidel Castro used it frequently for fishing with a light rod from Orvis. The tourist facilities were being constructed and the construction activity was spectacular and very busy with trucks and other motorized construction vehicles.

These previously "forgotten people" of the area were uniformly pro-Castro now and happy with the Revolutionary Government in Habana. Nicaragua and I had a three-hour conversation that night and I was lectured on the political, economic, and military advantages of Communism.

Modernity

The following morning after friendly good-byes, Carol and I headed to the Agricultural Cooperatives of northern Matanzas Province. The landless peasants there were organized according to their ingrained ancient customs. It turned out that polygamy is widely used in this region of Cuba. The Cooperative's homes were built to house the principal male surrounded closely by five to ten homes, each with a mother and his children. There was no question of the leadership authority of the Revolutionary officer in charge of the program. The local newspaper and the radio stations were all under Communist Party supervisors.

I continued my investigative trip to the easternmost Province of Pinar del Rio with similar findings.

In Varadero, we stayed with my sister Enid and Andres Duany and their children. I reviewed my findings with them and concluded that more than one half of the power infrastructure of Cuba that fateful July 1960 was completely controlled by Communist Party members and not by M26-7 operatives or other veterans of the successful insurrection. I had taken more than five hundred kodachrome photos to confirm my findings.

**The charges were all true
and I was facing several years
in jail if convicted.**

When Carol and I returned to our home in Santiago de Cuba, my father, Dr. Santos-Buch, called all members of the family to listen to me report my findings. It was a dreadful moment for all of us. The majority decided – right there and then – that Cuba would inexorably turn to Communist rule. Most of us realized that they had to choose between "immigration and revolution".

Carol decided to stay two months longer to help as much as she could. I had no choice but to return to the medical college as soon as possible.

Carol returned to New York City in September with our two infant boys, six-month old Kevin and a two-and-a-half year old Charlie, and with two of my sister's children, ten-year-old Andres Martin Duany and eight-year-old Enid del Carmen Duany. How Carol managed that successful trip with little help is an unexplained mystery.

The Duanys' close Long Island friends, Charlie and Coogie Powers, harbored Andres Martin and Enid del Carmen in their home for almost one year before their mother Enid and their youngest brother, Douglas Duany, were exiled to a rented house in Port Washington, Long Island, N.Y. After his Santiago construction and concrete company with five cement truck mixers was confiscated, it took almost two years for Andres J. Duany y de la Torre to safely abandon his confiscated savings, as well as ancient homes and lands to finally join his family in Port Washington.

The moment I arrived at my New York Hospital apartment on York Avenue, I was served a subpoena signed by the Attorney General of the United States, Robert Kennedy, the president's brother. I was charged with failing to register as an agent of a foreign power and of financing the publication of the Fair Play For Cuba Committee article in *The New York Times* with $5,000 provided to me by Raulito Roa, the son of Cuba's Minister of Foreign Affairs. The article had editorialized for a fair assessment of Castro's governance and a mutual resolution of grievances to achieve a peaceful relationship with America.

The charges were all true and I was facing several years in jail if convicted. I was ordered to testify in Washington D.C. at a public hearing of the United States Senate Committee of the Judiciary chaired by Mississippi's Senator James O. Eastland.

I tried to assume my busy New York Hospital schedules. I had been appointed Chief Resident of the Department of Pathology and my salary had been increased significantly. On my return from Cuba that summer, the first order of business was to report my trip findings to Herbert Mathews of *The New York Times* at his office on West 43rd Street. It was

248

not an acrimonious discussion, but Mathews was not convinced by my report.

Next, I managed to have a long conversation with my mentor and close friend, Professor George Murphy. I broached the possibility of leaving the United States to a neutral country like Mexico or Holland, sponsored by friends there to avoid my legal entanglements. Dr. Murphy convinced me that I should stay, that I would overcome my legal issues, and I should become a citizen of the United States. It was the right decision.

That night, my friend Maurice, a long time investigative FBI agent, visited me. We had formed a friendly bond over the years. I reported my Cuba trip findings and the conversation turned to my pending legal issues. Maurice was very helpful in the matter of my plans to defect from my ties to the Cuban Revolution. He advised that I should keep my plans secret until the Senate hearing scheduled for January 11, 1961. He also emphasized that a good lawyer was necessary.

The Duany lawyer in New York City was very helpful and on his recommendation, I contracted Paul Connelly, a brilliant and respected lawyer who was a partner in a well-known Washington law firm.

The hearing was in two parts. The first part was a secret hearing and the second was public. I confirmed that the Fair Play For Cuba Committee was not able to muster enough money to pay for its publication in The New York Times and that Raulito Roa had provided the money for it. I personally gave the money to Bob Taber, my friend, who arranged the publication with Times. The subcommittee completely exonerated me.

The news spread like wildfire in the mainstream media and in a matter of hours, I began to receive telephone death threats. The result of the hearing and the death threats was that my family and I found our home in New York City extremely "uncomfortable." Cuba's official newspaper, *Revolucion*, made our situation worse when it printed the news with front page banner headlines calling me a traitor to the revolution. The negative press greatly distressed my parents, who were still in their home in Santiago de Cuba.

On April 17, 1961, the Bay of Pigs fiasco commenced. That night Maurice and two other FBI agents sat with me, watching with great apprehension the development of the landings in Playa Larga and the surrounding sites of "la Bahia de Cochinos." I was worried. I remembered how the locals had been organized in enthusiastic militias and how the population of peasants and villages supported the Revolutionary Government. What mattered most in my mind were the swamps surrounding the only two access roads to the mainland that could be very easily defended by deployed artillery and armor.

When a single Castro airplane sank the "invaders'" ammunition supply ship offshore, the FBI agents and I knew that something was very wrong. It wasn't very long before the USA Ambassador to the United Nations, Adlai Stevenson, demanded that President Kennedy stop the use of the American Air Force that was scheduled to support the invasion and abandon the beached brigade of Cuban exiles. President Kennedy ordered the offshore armada not to rescue the Cuban exile brigade and it was "left behind." It ran out of ammunition and was forced to surrender to the Cuban rebel army.

The plans had been foiled very efficiently and it did not end there. Commander Higinio "Nino" Diaz, with his guerrilla force stationed off the Province of Oriente shores, refused to land. His scouts and intelligence staff warned him that the Castro rebel army had mustered their forces at the CIA assigned landing zone. On board, he was able to confirm this when he saw alerted enemy troop movements on shore with his binoculars. He averted a potential disaster. Diaz never was able to find out exactly why the landing zone was compromised so promptly.

Significantly, immediately after the first landing in Cochinos, the Castro security forces began an enormous round-up of the "usual suspects" that had been previously listed by the Communist Party. Many underground counter-revolutionary cells that had not been alerted of the invasion by the CIA were captured and arrested. Among them was my first cousin, Mario Santos-Buch, who was later convicted to serve twenty-two years in prison.

Carol's brother, Tony Valle-Friend, was able to escape and find his way into the U.S. Naval Base in Guantanamo. Tony had been a member of a secret counter-revolutionary cell of five armed combatants. The chief of the cell and Tony survived the ordeal, but the other three were captured and executed by firing squads.

I was able to convince Senator Eastland to arrange for Tony to fly out of the U.S. Naval Base of Guantanamo to the mainland. Tony was detained at the Florida Opa-Locka Detention Center for a year and a half until his underground CIA cell director, who was still stuck in hiding in Cuba, finally escaped by way of Spain and was able to vouch for Tony in person. Tony was subsequently freed to his family in Atlanta, Georgia.

Following his triumph at Cochinos, Fidel Castro announced he had been a Communist revolutionary all along. No one was surprised. Cuba's Revolutionary Government was reassured by the victory that it had won a secured place in the Caribbean and began to consider exporting its Revolution to its neighbors at risk.

The Soviet Union's Premier, Nikita Khrushchev, was delighted by the news and promised help. He immediately sent his Vice Premier Anastas Mikoyan with a negotiating retinue to Habana shortly after the Bay of Pigs fiasco and a deal was struck to buy "Cuban Sugar for Soviet Oil." The close Cuba/Soviet protectionist relationship was to increase and last a long time thereafter but that is another, albeit, familiar story.

Our opportunity to leave our "uncomfortable" situation in New York City came when Dr. John T. Ellis, Professor of Pathology, was offered the Pathology Chair at the Emory University School of Medicine in Atlanta, Georgia. I had been offered an Assistant Professorship at Cornell but declined it with regret and accepted Dr. Ellis' similar position at Emory. This time, I sought peace and tranquility and vowed to stick my nose into the new faculty job to raise the Department of Pathology to Cornell's standards of excellence. At Emory I applied for a National Institutes of

Health (NIH) Research Grant, which was awarded. I was selected by Dr. Ellis to compete for the prestigious "Markel Scholar of Academic Medicine" national award and I won it. [45]

For me it wasn't soon enough to receive my mother's phone call that they had arrived in Miami, Florida, in exile.

I am second from left, with my fellow professors in the Department of Pathology of Cornell University Medical College (1968)

A Farewell To The Fatherland

Dr. A. M. Santos-Buch retrieved the two medium-sized suitcases with their last possessions from the Miami International Airport baggage claim, and with difficulty, dragged them to the nearest public telephone booth. The despondent man in the booth hung up and briskly left with tears. He searched his pants pockets and his small briefcase. He did not have dollars or silver coins. Herminia looked in her bag and did not find any to make the call to her daughter, Enid, in Coral Gables. Dr. Santos-Buch, undaunted, looked around for help and found a well-dressed

45. Some six years later, Dr. Ellis was named Chairman of the Department of Pathology of the Cornell University Medical College and invited Charles to join him to continue his distinguished career in his alma mater.

American businessman to beg for them.

Enid answered and said, "Please don't worry, I'm on my way by car to pick you up. Find nice seats in a cool area. I should be there in an hour. We are so happy you are here. Much love, bye".

After a tearful emotional moment, a visibly disturbed Dr. Santos-Buch asked for a cool glass of water and silently found a corner seat in the apartment.[46]

Shortly after she found her steady voice, Herminia called me at my Emory University office. I wanted her to tell me the most important reason to abandon the homeland. She was, after all, the matriarch of an ancient Cuban family.

"There are many but the principal reason, Charles, is that they did not allow me to think."

Satisfied, nothing else crossed my mind.

THE END

---

46. He had not yet learned that he had contracted pulmonary tuberculosis. He was treated successfully in the facilities of the New York Hospital.

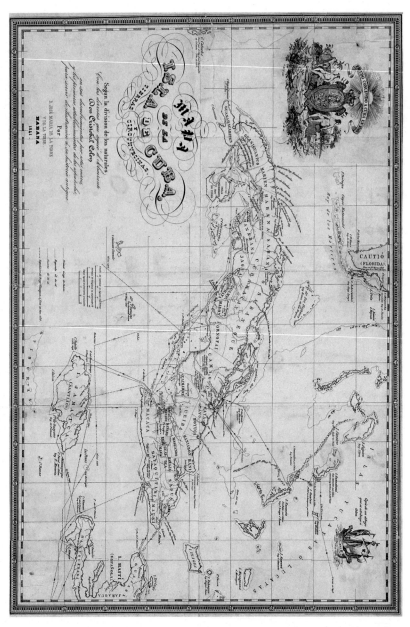

A 16th century rendition of the eastern lands of Cuba shows the relationship of de Céspedes' La Caridad de Macaca land grant with Jamaica, originally named "Santiago" on discovery by Cristobal Colon before the City of Manzanillo was built. "Jamaica" is derived from her original native American name. The map draws a direct cultural and commercial connection between the Encomienda and British Jamaica that was to last to the twentieth century. The captured de Céspedes women and their children were exiled to Kingston, Jamaica, by Spanish authorities near the end of the Ten Years' War of Independence (1868-1878). (Public Domain).

254

IMAGE LEGENDS

Preface

Page x. Coat of Arms of the Cossío and Céspedes Knights used during "La Reconquista" campaign to deliver Spain from Islamic occupation. (Family Heirloom)

Page xiii. Map of the territory of the de Céspedes "La Caridad de Macaca" land grant (Encomienda). From Coello, F. Atlas de España y sus posesiones de Ultramar. Madrid, 1853. The significant detail in the enlargement is that it shows Pueblo Viejo – the original 16th century site. Macaca, marked by arrow, is found just north of Pueblo Viejo near the coast. The rivers Yara, Vicana and Contramaestre are well traced. The old Indian caney of Yara is prominent in this map as are the cities of Bayamo and Manzanillo. The margins from near Manzanillo to the Turquino Mountain may be the probable borders of the original immense 16th century Encomienda (179,075 acre landgrant).

Page xv. Composite of photos of the Republic of Cuba paper money to honor the 19th century Criollo warriors, who, out-numbered 20 to 1, successfully faced Spain's Imperial Armed Forces, toe to toe, in the Ten Years War (1868-1878) and in the War of Independence (1895-1898). (Author's private collection).

A Differing View of Cuba's History

Part One

Page 8. Oil on canvas by Augusto García Menocal, 1930, titled, "I Don't Want To Go To Heaven." (From Cuba. Art and History from 1868 to Today. Prestel Publishing, New York, N.Y). In Yara, Hatuey, the captured Amerindian guerrilla leader, is shown shortly before execution by burning at the stake by Spanish Imperial Forces. Hatuey refused to accept a Roman Catholic priest's imploration to convert to Christianity on the grounds that he did not want to be with Spaniards in the Kingdom of Heaven. The 16th century "casullas" of the priests and the armor of the Spanish Captain are accurate. Captain de Céspedes, who successfully defended the city of San Salvador de Bayamo in 1512 against French corsairs, most assuredly used this characteristic armored uniform.

Page 11. Major General Carlos Manuel de Céspedes y del Castillo of the Cuban Liberation Army and President of the Republic of Cuba in Arms. (Family photo heirloom.) He was the family's patriarch. He was deposed by the Second Guaimaro Assembly, accused of abuse of power, exiled without adequate escorts, and killed in a firefight in his hacienda of San Lorenzo.

Page 12. Major General Pedro M. de Céspedes y del Castillo of the Cuban Liberation Army. (Family photo heirloom.) He was President Carlos Manuel de Céspedes' youngest brother and fellow insurgent and conspirator of the Ten Years War of 1868. He is my great-grandfather. He was captured in the expedition of the filibuster Virginius, and summarily executed by order of a Spanish Imperial Court Marshall in Santiago de Cuba, November 1873.

Image Legends

Page 17. The Battle Flag of de Céspedes (public domain). It was used in the fated battle of the Yara River, Oriente Province, October 1868.

Page 19. Sisa, Ana Tamayo y Tamayo's former African slave. (Family photo heirloom.) Ana was wife to Mayor General Pedro M. de Céspedes.

The eastern lands of Cuba are populated by Afro-Cubans whose descendants are from midwestern Africa. Their intelligence, frank and broad smiles, fortitude, zest for life, and good looks are legendary. In her last years of her life, Sisa, who lived over 100 years, was the close nanny of Charles and Adolfina Greig's children, including my mother, Herminia.

Page 21. Doña Adolfina Cossío y de Céspedes. Oil on Cuban mahogany wood. (Family heirloom.) Unsigned portrait by Kittill Bucher, an amateur and family friend. Santiago de Cuba, circa April 1942. The author restored it in June 1999.

Page 27. The Virginius from John Gilmary Shea, The Story of a Great Nation (New York: Gay Brothers & Company, 1886). Captain Fry of the side paddle vessel Virginius, which was registered and flying the American flag, surrendered his command in the high seas to the Spanish Frigate Toronado, November 1873, with four generals of the Army of the Republic of Cuba in Arms, their rebel soldiers, and his crew.

Page 39. "La Zafra" (public domain). The sugar cane harvest was the main economic thrust of Cuba for centuries and Afro-Cubans were the industry's unpaid indentured slaves until the Republic in Arms freed them by Proclamation, October 10, 1868. It was also a family business affair as shown in the image.

Page 45. Cuban insurgents attack a Spanish "fortín" in the early days of the War of Independence of 1895-1898. From a sketch by Georg Meisenbach (1841-1912). German copperplate and steel engraver of The Illustrated London News. This fortín was located near Vueltas, about eight kilometers west of Ciego de Ávila, Camaguey Province. The fortín was designed by the Spanish Imperial Corps of Engineers and was typically used in north to south "trochas" (a line of fortresses). Governor General Valeriano Weyler y Nicolau conducted a successful campaign against the Cuban Guerrilla Army by dividing the island with multiple strategic lines of fortines (Las Trochas). The insurgents in Vueltas used a sugar cane cart to approach the fortín and incurred multiple casualties.

Page 47. Photo of liberated survivors of 1896 Weyler "reconcentration camps" taken by American reporters when the camps were dismantled at the end of the 1897 campaign (public domain). More than 170,000 Cuban peasants interned in reconcentration camps died in less than a year during the successful Weyler campaign against the Cuban Liberation Army of 1895-1897. The savagery turned international opinion against the Spanish Empire, which was forced to fire General Weyler. His return to Spain was celebrated as one of its greatest heroes.

Image Legends

Page 48. Rear Admiral Alfred Thayer Mahan, retired, September 27, 1840 (public domain). He was a United States naval officer and historian, and is regarded as "the most important American strategist of the nineteenth century." His book, "The Influence of Sea Power Upon History (1660–1783)" won immediate recognition, especially in Europe, and with its successor, "The Influence of Sea Power Upon the French Revolution and Empire, 1793–1812, made him world-famous. Both books were written before the Spanish War of 1898. He had an enormous influence on the USA Department of War, President McKinley and Theodore Roosevelt. Roosevelt served as Assistant Secretary of the Navy under President William McKinley, but resigned from that post to lead the Rough Riders during the Spanish–American War. Returning a war hero, he was elected Governor of New York in 1898. The Department of War of 1898 planned a well-coordinated strategy based on Mahan's ideas that excluded attacking the Spanish Mainland but targeted the commercially valued Philippines as a base for new Asian markets. The strategically valued sea-lanes of the under-belly of the United States, Puerto Rico and Cuba, were also targeted. Admiral Mahan recommended the contractual contribution of active insurrectionists to allow the safe landing of the cavalry and foot soldiers. The five battleships that fought the Spanish Navy at the entrance of Santiago Bay were built with the mind of fighting in foreign seas, according to Rear Admiral Mahan's recommendations.

Page 50. The Battle of El Desmayo, Camaguey, October 8, 1896, by William Allen Rogers, 1899. Oil on canvas, (public domain). Rogers was celebrated for his accuracy and realism and many of his paintings were published in Harper's. It is an illustration of the characteristic lightning-fast charge of the cavalry of the Cuban Liberation Army in action during the blockade of Santiago de Cuba to prevent the reinforcement of trapped Spanish Imperial armed forces in the city. General Máximo Gómez planned and executed this key maneuver that allowed American expeditionary forces to land safely in Siboney and Daiquiri beaches in July of 1898. Captain Frederick Funston, an American eyewitness serving the command of General Máximo Gómez, wrote "At Desmayo, that little force of 479 Cubans rode against magazine-firing rifles firing seventy shots a minute, and breech-loading artillery and held their position in the face of that pitiless fire until fifty-two percent had tumbled from their horses killed or wounded."

A Differing View of Cuba's History

Page 51. *The destruction of Admiral Cervera's fleet outside of Santiago Harbor on July 3, 1898. (From a sketch of a correspondent of the Illustrated London News, July 1898.) Cervera's Spanish First Squadron was comprised of four fast cruisers and two destroyers; the American Atlantic Fleet deployed five slower battleships and one cruiser. It is the largest and deadliest surface naval battle of the Caribbean Sea.*

Page 52. *Generals William Ludlow and Calixto García before their assault on the fortress of El Viso, Caney, Oriente, July 1898 (public domain). Volcanic mountains in the background border the perimeter of El Viso. A native of Islip, Long Island, New York, and a graduate of West Point, William Ludlow was a veteran of the Civil War. In May 1898, he was named brigadier general of volunteers and commanded the First Brigade at El Caney in Henry Lawton's division in Cuba. As ranking overseas engineer, he was in charge of disembarking General Calixto García's forces at Aserraderos.*

Page 53. *Official photo of Spanish Expeditionary Forces hero of the battle of "El Viso and Village of El Caney," Major General Joaquín Vara de Rey (public domain). Spain honored General Joaquín Vara de Rey with the highest award for courage under fire posthumously. Mambises and American soldiers under the command of Generals Ludlow and García wiped out his command of 500 elite Spanish troopers in two to three hours.*

EXTMO. SR. D. JOAQUÍN VARA DE REY

Page 82. *Photo of the execution of an Afro-Cuban rebel by the Cuban Army in Oriente Province during the armed suppression of the Racial War of 1917 by Conservatives Forces (public domain). The savagery of this racial conflict resulted in a backlash that hurt the Conservative Party nationally and bolstered the Liberal Party to elect President Alfredo Zayas y Alfonso, a progressive aristocrat.*

In the decades following the last racial war the conservatives' political power faded and virtually all factions adopted a new brand of left of center autochthonous liberalism until the advent of Castro-Communism, which destroyed them.

Image Legends

Page 83. President Don Alfredo Zayas y Alfonso (1921-1925) (public domain). He was a civilian aristocrat who saw no combat in the wars of Cuban independence. The Liberal Party under his presidency evolved to a lasting Progressive Movement nationally.

Page 89. Brigadier General Gerardo Machado y Morales near the end of the War of Independence 1895-1898. (From Gerardo Machado y Morales, Ocho Años de Lucha, Editorial Cubana Luis J. Botifoll, Miami, Florida, 2006.) He sided with the Afro-Cuban insurgents fighting the Conservative Army forces of General Mario García Menocal in the last Racial War. His battle situation was unsustainable and he surrendered but was not strung up because an amnesty was immediately proclaimed. As a civilian later, he became a successful businessman and a member of the Liberal Party. Note the characteristic Mambi General's uniform, cavalry sabre with the bronze eagle head and other accouterments.

Page 90. Major General Mario García Menocal of the Cuban Liberation Army 1895-1898 (public domain). General Menocal, a Cornell University graduate, became the political leader of the Conservative Party, and later, president of the Republic from 1913 to 1921. His Conservative forces fought and forcibly suppressed two of the three Racial Wars.

Page 94. United States President Calvin Coolidge, second from left, and his wife, Grace, second from right, with the President of Cuba, General Gerardo Machado y Morales, right, and his wife, Elvira Machado, left, on the estate of President Machado in Habana on Jan. 19, 1928 (public domain). President Coolidge was a Republican who favored Adam Smith's small government conservative policies. He found a kindred spirit in Cuba's President Machado and became close friends.

261

A Differing View of Cuba's History

Page 103. Office building of the Habana newspaper is sacked (public domain). When United States President Franklin Delano Roosevelt's special envoy, Mr. Sumner Welles, deposed President Gerardo Machado together with progressive Cuban oppositionists, sporadic violent episodes happened in many Cuban cities and villages. In Habana, anti-American sentiments evolved in a senseless mob that sacked the offices of the Habana Herald, a subsidiary of the same New York City newspaper.

Page 104. A triumphant noncommissioned soldier celebrates the successful take over of the Cuban Armed Forces by the sergeant's Revolt, September 4, 1933, in the capital city of Habana (public domain). The successful Batista sergeant's revolution was largely motivated by the inequality between the "haves and the have-nots." It was widely supported by the Cuban underclass, particularly in Habana

Image Legends
Part Two

Page 111. *Fidel Castro speaks to an enthusiastic crowd (public domain). He learned very fast that winning the political war must be reinforced by victory of arms as General Claus von Clausewitz admonishes in his book "On War" (1832). The most famous thematic quote of General Clausewitz is "War is not an independent phenomenon, but the continuation of politics by different means." In this photo, populist Castro is addressing close to a million people in La Plaza de La Revolución of Habana, the capital of the island nation, early in 1959, before the Reign of Terror and the beginning of the massive exodus and exile of the Opposition.*

Page 117. *Los Cocos, Cuabitas, Oriente Province, 1923. (Family photo heirloom). Don Emilio Bacardi's home is in the foreground before his Mediterranean Mansion, Villa Elvira, was built to replace it. In the upper right hand in the distance on top of the hill is the main house of Chantilly, the future 1926 home of Dr. A. M. Santos-Buch and later, of his wife Herminia Greig Cossío.*

Page 120. *The giant roots of the Anacahuita on the Chantilly Property (family heirloom). The root system was complex and very large and used as a hideout for children's games. Amerindians and Criollos of Oriente Province named these giant primeval forest trees Anacahuita. In Habana, the university botany professors have classified another bush size species Anacahuita. This discrepancy has not been resolved to date.*

Page 128. *Carol's grandmother, Harriett Carter Farnsworth with her two children, Shirley and Edwin, in Atlanta.*

Page 139.
Carol, la hija de la Americana.

Page 150. Four Cuabitas friends. (Family photo heirloom.) They are Eduardo Cutillas, Santiago Pujals, me, Charles Santos-Buch, and Manuel Jorge Cutillas, Eduardo's older brother. The Cutillas brothers climbed the Bacardi Company's corporate ladder and Santiago Pujals received an MD degree from the Sorbonne and is a surgeon. I became a full-tenured, Cornell professor of the Medical College. Our close friendship lasted more than eight decades.

Page 187. Dr. George E. Murphy's research group included Cornell graduated interns and residents of the New York Hospital, including myself, and: Richard Minick, Wallace G. Campbell, Jr., and Carl Becker. (Family photo heirloom). All became well-known full Professors of Pathology of important American medical centers. Dr. Murphy was an advisor and personal friend of mine, and his influence had a great deal to do with me becoming an American citizen and with my early career development in the medical sciences.

Page 203. Dr. Angel M. Santos-Buch and Herminia Greig Cossío y de Céspedes (family photo heirloom). She was elected president of the Society of "Pro-Arte de Oriente" and for many years she was responsible for bringing world known concert artists to the Provincial Capital of Santiago de Cuba, such as Jascha Heifetz, Yehuda Menuhin, Arturo Rubinstein, the von Trapp family singers and many others. She and her husband, Dr. A. M. Santos-Buch, developed a close bond with Commander Frank Pais of the M26-7 Urban Guerrilla. Dr. Santos-Buch was a director and organizer of Resistencia Civica during Cuba's Insurrection.

Image Legends

Page 208. Vista Alegre's Sacred Heart School graduate Vilma Espin Gallois, armed and in uniform, shortly after the triumph of the Insurrection. Espin played major roles in the course of the victorious 1956-1959 insurrection. (public domain)

Page 214. Frank Pais, Commander of the Urban M26-7 (family heirloom). The photo was taken shortly before his death by ambush July 30, 1957. My mother's handwriting quotes Pais: "We must always act as if Life is just, as if Humanity is grateful, as if Men are good." Signed with his Nome de Guerre, Ariel.

Page 237. An execution by a Castro-Communist firing squad is prepared. (public domain). A frenzied period of fear ensued from the beginning of Fidel Castro's triumph in January 1959 that lasted nearly five years before it slowly faded over many other years. Pre-planned executions were organized to defeat an expected "Counter Revolution" by Batista army, police and active conservative civil remnants. With the cooperation of Communist Party members, the insurgents had created lists of possible suspects long before Batista's defeat. "Revolutionary Tribunals" ordered firing squad executions as fast as possible. The families were not allowed to retrieve the bodies nor they were told how or where or if they were buried. More than 5,500 Cubans were executed in the first 2 years of the Castro regime. By 2006, 9,240 Castro-Communist firing squad executions were documented by the New York Times. Andrew López, a UPI photographer, won the Pulitzer Prize for this photograph of the execution of José Cipriano Rodríguez, a corporal of Batista's army convicted of "two murders." He was executed the same day following a guilty verdict by a Revolutionary Tribunal. The fear created by the executions produced widespread disgust and dissidence among many Cubans but also curtailed further counter revolutionary conspiracies.

Page 238. Freed imprisoned M26-7 rebels occupy and guard the Morro Castle at the entrance of Santiago de Cuba early on, March 1959.

Page 250. Professors of the Department of Pathology of Cornell University Medical College (1968): Dr. Aaron Kellner, Director of the Blood Bank, The New York Hospital; Dr. Charles A. Santos-Buch, Dr. John G. Kidd, Retiring Chairman, and Dr. John Seybolt. Head of Dr. Papanicolaou's Cytology Laboratory and his student, and Dr. John T. Ellis, the newly appointed Professor and Chairman of the Department.

REFERENCES WITH COMMENTS

1. Álvarez, José. *Frank País: Architect of Cuba's Betrayed Revolution* (2009). Universal Publishers, Irvine, California. Excellent coverage of Vilma Espin's alledged role in his ambush and death.

2. Ballou, Maturin M. *History of Cuba (1854).* Boston: Phillips, Sampson and Company. New York: JC Derby. Philadelphia: Lippincot, Grambo & Company. The Ballou's "statistics" of Cuba of the mid-1800s based on official records of the prior five years.

3. Bondil, Nathalie. Editor. *Cuba. Art and History from 1868 to Today (2008).* Prestel Publishing, N.Y., N.Y. Excellent compilation of museum works of Cuba's artists, magazine illustrations and it also has essays on today's Castro-Communist ideals. Beautifully printed pieces and photos.

4. Caldwell Crosby, Molly. *The American Plague: The Untold Story of Yellow Fever, the Epidemic that Shaped Our History.* (2006). Berkley Hard Cover. California. The hair raising and exciting story of the use of normal humans in yellow fever studies in Cuba. Superb documentation.

5. Chester, Edmund. *A Sergeant Named Batista.* (1954). New York: Henry Holt and Company. His early years.

6. Clark, Juan M. *Castro's Revolution, Myth and Reality. Volumes 1 & 2.* Amazon Digital Services LLC – Kdp Print Us. Seattle, Washington. A scholarly "arbeiten." A must have for your library.

7. Cossío Esturo, Adolfina H. "Verdadera Fecha del Inicio de la Guerra de los Diez Años." Thesis. University of Habana. December 1938. Cossío Esturo also wrote an essay detailing the logistics of the Encomienda La Hacienda de Macaca I used in this narrative. It is the principal source of the history of the sixteenth century landgrant. (Family heirloom).

8. Cutillas, Manuel J. Editor. *Collection of Eye Witness Sketches,* illustrating the July, 1898, Battles of el Caney, el Viso and Loma de San Juan, and Kettle Hill in Santiago de Cuba. From the archives of Casa Bacardi of the Institute for Cuban and Cuban-American Studies of the University of Miami. These are sketches by eyewitnesses that give you a faithful understanding of the geographic layout of the targets and battles that governed the principal strategies followed by Cuban and American generals and their soldiers. It is a credible visual documentation.

9. Falcones, Ildefonso. *La Mano de Fátima* (2009). Knopf Doubleday, New York, N.Y. Historical novel detailing life under the Islamic occupation of Spain and the violence of the Reconquista. I had trouble with the "long words" but it is worthwhile in your library.

10. Gjelten, Tom. *Bacardi and the Long Fight for Cuba* (2008). Viking Press, New York, N.Y. The best narrative of the famous family. Truthful, significant and entertaining.

11. Gibbs, Jessica. *U.S. Policy Towards Cuba Since the Cold War.*

References

(2011). Routledge, Milton Park, Abington, Oxfon. Scholarly source and time-lines.

12. Gómez y Amador, Luis. *La Odisea del Almirante Cervera y Su Escuadra* (2001). Biblioteca Nueva, Madrid, Barcelona. Superb – not to be missed.

13. Johnson, Paul. *A History of the American Peoples* (1997). HarperCollins Publishers, Inc., New York, N.Y. Formidable history not to be missed by any one.

14. Machado y Morales, Gerardo. *Ocho Años de Lucha* (2006). Editorial Cubana Luis J. Botifoll, Miami, Florida. An important account of his fateful presidency.

15. McCallum, Jack. *Leonard Wood, Rough Rider, Surgeon, Architect of American Imperialism* (2005). New York University Press, New York, N.Y.

16. Morris, Edmund. *The Rise of Theodore Roosevelt* (1979). Coward, McCann & Geoghegan, Inc. New York, N.Y. It covers the battle of the Rough Riders with his sketches.

17. O'Toole, George J. A. *The Spanish War, an American Epic – 1898* (1984). W. W. Norton Company, New York, N.Y. Excellent researched account.

18. Pichardo, Hortensia, and Portuondo del Prado, Manuel. *Carlos Manuel de Céspedes* (1982). Editorial de Ciencias Sociales, Organizzacione internazionale italo-latino americana, Rome. A fascinating compilation of all written communications of the President

of the Republic of Cuba in Arms during the Ten Years War.

19. Portell-Vila, Herminio. *El Padre de la Patria de Céspedes* (1931). Libreria Anticuaria El Laberinto, Cordoba, España. I have a running feud with the famous historian but his book is informative.

20. Quirk, Robert E., *Fidel Castro* (1995). W. W. Norton, New York, N.Y. A Pulitzer Prize work.

21. Reynel Aguilera, Cesar. *El Soviet Caribeño: La otra historia de la Revolución Cubana* (2018). Penguin Random House Grupo Editorial, Buenos Aires, Argentina. The early Communist infitrations of Cuba is documented.

22. Roig, Pedro, *The Death of a Dream: A History of Cuba* (2014). Amazon, Seattle, Washington. Well-informed and detailed.

23. Santos-Buch, Charles J. "The Cuban Revolution: The Role of the Middle Class in Oriente Province (1956-1959)." Thesis, Harvard University, Cambridge, Mass., March 20, 1980. Excellent account based on personally taped interviews of many principals of the Cuban Revolution.

24. Schwartz, Zachary. *The Naval Career of William B. Cushing* (2012). A paper completed in partial fulfillment of the requirements for HH486A, The United States Naval Academy, Annapolis, Md.

25. Taber, Robert. *M-26. The Biography of a Revolution* (1961). Lyle Stuart Publisher, New York, N.Y. Taber reports his interviews of the M26-7 combatants and others. Truthful and exciting accounts. Excellent.

References

26. Thomas, Hugh. *The Pursuit of Freedom* (1971). Harper and Row Publishers, New York, N.Y. The first detailed account of Castro's Revolution that is still good information today.

APPENDIX

Charles A. Santos-Buch, M.D.
Abbreviated Curriculum Vitae

◊ Retired Professor of Pathology and Director of The Papanicolaou Cytology Laboratory, Cornell University Medical College, 1300 York Avenue. New York, NY 10021 (2019).

◊ Biochemistry Graduate of Harvard College under the supervision of Nobel Prize winner Professor George Wald, 1953, MD Graduate of the Cornell University Medical College with many Honors, 1957.

◊ Internship and Residency in the Department of Pathology under the tutelage of Professor John G. Kidd and Professor George N. Papanicolaou, The New York Hospital- Cornell Medical Center, 1957-1961.

◊ National Institutes of Health Research Fellow, Department of Pathology, Cornell University Medical College, 1959- 1961 under the tutelage of Professor George E. Murphy.

◊ Associate Professor of Pathology, Emory University Medical School, 1961-1968. Reorganized the teaching of pathology and neuropathology of a dysfunctional department.

◊ Associate Professor of Pathology, Cornell University Medical College, 1968-1976.

◊ Professor of Pathology with tenure, Cornell University Medical College, 1976-1997. Was the first Hispanic full professor with tenure of the Medical College.

◊ Associate Dean of Students, Cornell University Medical College, 1970-1974. With Dr. Jim Curtis, Associate Dean, organized and facilitated the admission of women and minorities into Medical College. Assisted with other associates curriculum reforms.

◊ Director of the Papanicolaou Cytology Laboratory, The New York Hospital, 1979-1997. Introduced Fine Needle Aspiration techniques and procedures. Managed billings and a four million dollar budget and payroll.

Honors

◊ Herman L. Jacobious Prize in Pathology, 1954.

◊ William M. Polk Research Award, 1957,

◊ John and Mary R. Markle Foundation Scholar of Academic Medicine, 1964,

◊ Alpha Omega Alpha Chapter, Cornell, 1973.

◊ Man of the Year Award by the editors of the *World Almanac* for contributions to the understanding of the autoimmune pathogenesis of Chagas Heart Disease, 1974.

Research Awards and Post Graduate Education Achievements

◊ National Institutes of Health Research Grants and other support sources: Several major research grants in nearly 30 years of academic service.

◊ Sponsored 25 Research Fellowships and PhD Candidates. All were awarded Honors.

◊ Publications: Authored nine chapters in several medical books and textbooks. Senior author of over 100 scientific papers in critically vetted and reviewed science journals, including the *New England Journal of Medicine, Nature, American Journal of Pathology, Laboratory Investigation, Journal of Immunology, Journal of Experimental Medicine, Archives of Neurology, American Journal of Tropical Medicine, Circulation, Molecular and Biochemical Parasitology, Clinical Immunology and Immunopathology, Journal of*

Origin of Duany

The surname Duany is derived from the Irish O'Duane, a family who came early on to Jamaica at the turn of the sixteenth to seventeenth centuries. They achieved prominence as architect/engineers of Spanish Empire military fortresses. The chief architect and engineer of the final expansion of the fortress in the entrance of Santiago Bay, El Morro, was designed and rebuilt in 1702 by O'Duane, which later became the phonetic Duany.

El Morro Castle, locally known as Castillo del Morro, is situated on a promontory at the entrance of the bay of the city of Santiago de Cuba on Cuba. Its full name is Castillo de San Pedro de la Roca del Morro. It is not to be confused with the El Morro Castle in Havana. An earlier fort at this location was built between 1590 and 1610. El Morro Castle was designed, in 1637, by the Italian military engineer Giovanni Battista Antonelli, who also built El Morro Castle and La Punta Castle in Havana, on behalf of the governor of the town, Pedro de la Roca de Borja. Its purpose would be to serve as a defense of the city against pirates.

Construction of the fort began in 1638. Works would continue intermittently for forty-two years. Antonelli had designed a fort adapted to its location; on a sixty-meter high promontory with steep sides. So, it was constructed on a series of terraces; there were four main levels and three large bulwarks to house the artillery. Some parts of the earlier fort were incorporated in the new one.

In 1662, while El Morro Castle was being built, a fleet of buccaneers under the English admiral Christopher Myngs, attacked and sacked the town of Santiago de Cuba.

They held it for two weeks during which the fort was partly destroyed and its artillery taken. After they departed the Spanish government restored the fort and garrisoned it with 300 men.

In 1675 El Morro Castle was damaged by an earthquake and subsequently restored. In 1678 and in 1680, the still unfinished El Morro Castle fought off two attacks from French pirates. In 1692 another earthquake damaged the fort. By 1700 the construction of the fort was finally complete.

Between 1738 and 1740 the fort was enlarged. Final changes to the fort were made after it had been damaged by earthquakes again in 1757 and 1766. By 1775 the threat of pirate attacks had diminished and parts of El Morro Castle were used as a political prison.

The fort regained its military use in 1898 when the United States' fleet attacked Santiago de Cuba during the Spanish-American War. At present El Morro Castle is a rather simple museum and can be visited for a small fee. A great fort on a beautiful location, really a "must see."

Gettysburg Address
Delivered by President Abraham Lincoln
November 19, 1863

"Fourscore and seven years ago our fathers brought forth on this continent, a new nation, conceived in Liberty, and dedicated to the proposition that all men are created equal.

"Now we are engaged in a great civil war, testing whether that nation, or any nation so conceived and so dedicated, can long endure. We are met on a great battlefield of that war. We have come to dedicate a portion of that field, as a final resting place for those who here gave their lives that that nation might live. It is altogether fitting and proper that we should do this.

"But, in a larger sense, we can not dedicate-we can not consecrate-we can not hallow-this ground. The brave men, living and dead, who struggled here, have consecrated it, far above our poor power to add or detract. The world will little note, nor long remember what we say here, but it can never forget what they did here. It is for us the living, rather, to be dedicated here to the unfinished work which they who fought here have thus far so nobly advanced. It is rather for us to be here dedicated to the great task remaining before us-that from these honored dead we take increased devotion to that cause for which they gave the last full measure of devotion-that we here highly resolve that these dead shall not have died in vain-that this nation, under God, shall have a new birth of freedom-and that government of the people, by the people, for the people shall not perish from the earth."

From Wikipedia

La Demajagua's

"Proclamation of Cuba's Independence"

of October 10, 1868, which started the Ten Years' War

"In rebelling against Spanish tyranny, we want the world to know the reasons for our action.

"Spain governs us with blood and iron; she imposes on us levies and taxes as she pleases; she has deprived us of political, civil, and religious freedoms; we are subjected to martial law in times of peace; without due process, and in defiance of Spanish law, we are arrested, exiled and even executed. We are prohibited free assembly, and if allowed to assemble, it is only under the watchful eyes of government agents and military officers; and if anyone clamors for a remedy to these abuses, or for any of the many other evils, Spain declares them a traitor.

Appendix

"Spain burdens us with rapacious bureaucrats who exploit our national treasure and consume the product of our noble labor. So that we may not know our rights, it maintains our people ignorant of those rights, and to ensure that the people are kept ignorant, she prevents the people from participating in responsible public administration.

"Without impending military danger, and without any reason or justification, Spain imposes on us an unnecessary and costly military presence, whose sole purpose is to terrorize and humiliate us. Spain's system of customs is so perverse that we have already perished from its misery and she exploits the fertility of our land while raising the price of its fruits. She imposes every imaginable obstacle to prevent the advancement of our Criollo population. Spain limits our free speech and the written word, and she prevents us from participating in the intellectual progress of other nations.

"Several times Spain has promised to improve our condition and she has deceived us time and time again. We are now left no other recourse than to bear arms against her tyranny, and by doing this, to save our honor, our lives, and our fortunes.

"Our aim is to enjoy the benefits of freedom, for whose use, God created man. We sincerely profess a policy of brotherhood, tolerance, and justice, and to consider all men equal, and to not exclude anyone from these benefits, not even Spaniards, if they choose to remain and live peacefully among us.

"Our aim is that the people participate in the creation of laws, and in the distribution and investment of the contributions.

"Our aim is to abolish slavery and to compensate those deserving compensation. We seek freedom of assembly, freedom of the press and the freedom to bring back honest governance; and to honor and practice the inalienable rights of men, which are the foundations of the independence and the greatness of a people.

"Our aim is to throw off the Spanish yoke, and to establish a free and independent nation. We appeal now to Almighty God, and to the faith and good will of civilized nations. Our aspirations are to attain our sovereignty and universal suffrage.

"If Spain recognizes our rights, it will have in Cuba an affectionate daughter; if she persists in subjugating us, we are resolved to die before remaining subject to her brutal domination. We have chosen a commander to whom will be given the mission of fighting this war. We have authorized a provisional administrator to collect contributions and to manage the needs of a new administration.

"When Cuba is free, it will have a constitutional government created in an enlightened manner."

Signed:

Carlos Manuel de Céspedes, Jaime M. Santiesteban, Bartolomé Masó, Juan Hall, Francisco J. Céspedes, Pedro de Céspedes, Manuel Calvar, Isaías Masó, Eduardo Suástegui, Miguel Suástegui, Rafael Tornés, Manuel Santiesteban, Manuel Socarrás, Agustín Valerino, Rafael Masó, Eligio Izaguirre

On The Execution of Pedro de Céspedes

"Ana de Céspedes del Castillo en Nov. 21, 1873 escribe a raíz del desastre del Virginius: "La patria está de duelo y llora la muerte de tantos hijos beneméritos. Mi pobre hermano Pedro selló con su sangre el juramento de volver a Cuba. Yo le había dicho que permaneciera en el extranjero, ocupado en servicio de la patria, conforme le permitieran sus males, y así podía atender también el cuidado de sus hijos. Su patriotismo lo arrastró y ha muerto en el campo del honor. Dichoso él que ha ceñido ese lauro inmortal! Su gloria inmarcesible me consuela de su muerte."

Quote contributed by Pedro G. de Céspedes
from his family heirloom.

Appendix

"Grant Us Brave and Enduring Hearts"
By Donald Tunnicliff Rice

"Major General Calixto Garcia Iñiguez was in his tent. He had one bullet left in his pistol. During the last few minutes he had killed or severely wounded five Spanish soldiers. Two of them were lying half in the tent, holding the flap open. More soldiers were running through the camp, firing their rifles. There was no chance of escape. Earlier in the day his good friend Felix Figueredo asked what he would do if captured by the Spanish. Garcia replied, "Nothing. I would not fall into their hands. My revolver has six bullets – five for the enemy and the last for me." This is the same vow he had made to his mother. He placed the barrel of the gun under his chin, aiming at his brain stem to ensure instant death. As he pulled the trigger a nearby explosion caused him to flinch. The gun fired into his head and the bullet came out between his eyes. Thinking he was dead, he passed out.

"When the battle was over, and all the Cuban insurgents who were still alive had been rounded up, the Spaniards began removing their own dead. It was then that a soldier found Garcia crumpled on the floor of his tent. He called Lieutenant Ariza, the daring young officer who had directed the raid. Carefully stepping over the bodies of the dead soldiers, Ariza entered the tent and looked at the hero of the battles of Santa Rita, Jiguani, Holguin, and many more towns and villages. He felt a moment of sadness and personal discomfort at seeing this esteemed soldier reduced to an ordinary corpse.

'I think he's breathing, sir,' the soldier said.

"Ariza felt Garcia's pulse and indicated with a nod that the soldier take his shoulders while he lifted his legs. Garcia was a large man – a head taller than most of his soldiers, which made him a conspicuous rallying point in military encounters. Ariza and the Spanish soldier, both of whom were slim men, struggled to place him on the cot. How the general could survive a bullet wound in the middle of his forehead and another under his chin, Ariza couldn't guess, but there he was. As he stared uncomprehendingly at Garcia's calm mustachioed face, he ordered the soldier to get the surgeon. "And have a detail carry these two boys away." Then he gathered up the maps and papers on the field desk. While he was doing this, Garcia opened his eyes. Instead of finding himself in heaven, he awoke in the dreary familiarity of his own tent and saw a Spanish officer rifling his desk. He yelled, but no sound came out. He tried again. Nothing. He somehow managed to clap his hands, startling Ariza.

'You're conscious!'

"Garcia pointed at his mouth and slowly shook his head to indicate that he could not speak. Then he made slight scribbling motions with his right hand on his left hand, signaling for paper and pencil. Ariza handed them to him and waited while Garcia laboriously wrote something on the paper and passed it back.

'I would like to have some soup.'

"He hadn't eaten for thirty hours and now when military matters were no longer of any concern he wanted to satisfy his hunger. Knowing nothing of this, Ariza thought the wounds to his head had left him demented. When Ariza didn't respond immediately, Garcia tried to get up, but hadn't the strength. He was a man used to having his orders obeyed and he waved his hands at Ariza, wanting him to fetch the soup. Then he signaled again for paper and pencil.

'I need a surgeon immediately.'

"As if in response to his request Captain Maximo Escalante entered the tent. He bent over Garcia to examine his wounds, realizing immediately that the hole in his forehead was an exit wound. Normally an exiting Mauser bullet fired from behind took most of the face with it. He turned Garcia's head to find where the bullet had entered. There was nothing there. Then he studied the wound under Garcia's chin. It became obvious to him what had happened. This was the entry wound, and the bullet had traveled up through Garcia's palette at a forward angle behind his nose, emerging between his eyes …"

(Journal of Caribbean Literatures Vol. 7, No. 2

(Spring 2013), pp. 187-191)

Appendix

Ignacio Agramonte

"Ignacio Agramonte era estudiante de derecho en la Universidad de La Habana cuando se pronunció sobre el Comunismo en 1862. Solo habían transcurrido 15 años desde la publicación del manifiesto comunista de Karl Marx and Friedrich Engels. Pero es que a las mentes claras lo absurdo siempre es evidente."

(From Professor Alberto Luzarraga, contributor.)

Translation: "Ignacio Agramonte was a law student of the University of Habana when he declared his opposition to Communism in 1862.

"It was only 15 years since the publication of Karl Marx and Friederich Engels' Communist Manifesto. But it is to those with mental clarity that the absurd is always evident."

"La centralización hace desaparecer ese individualismo, cuya conservación hemos sostenido como necesaria a la sociedad. De allí al comunismo no hay más que un paso: se comienza por declarar impotente al individuo y se concluye por justificar la intervención de la sociedad en su acción, destruyendo la libertad, sujetando sus pensamientos, sus más íntimas afecciones, sus necesidades, sus acciones todas....el gobierno que con una centralización absoluta destruya ese franco desarrollo de la acción individual, y detenga la sociedad en su desenvolvimiento progresivo, no se funda en la justicia y en a razón, sino tan sólo en la fuerza; ya el Estado que tal fundamento tenga, en un momento de energía anunciarse al mundo como estable e imperecedero, pero tarde o temprano, cuando los hombres, conociendo sus derechos violados, se propongan reivindicarlos, oirá el estruendo de cañon anunciarle que cesó su letal dominación."

Translation: "Centralization forcibly vanishes individualism whose conservation we have showed is necessary to our society. From that point on to communism there is just one step: it begins by declaring that the individual is impotent and concludes to justify the intervention of society, destroying liberty, restraining its thoughts, its most intimate affections, its necessities, all actions…. a government with absolute centralization destroys the transparent development of individual endeavors and will stop society's progressive development, because it is not founded on justice and reasoning but is enforced only by Force; once the State has this structure, and in a moment announces itself to the World as stable and infinite, whether late or early, Man will recognize the violation of his Rights and Man will restore them, and the thunder of cannons will announce the cessation of their lethal Rule."

Ignacio Agramonte, Thesis. Universidad de La Habana. 1862

Jose Marti's La Nación Article on Karl Marx (1883)

"Ved esta gran sala. Karl Marx ha muerto. Como se puso del lado de los débiles, merece honor. Pero no hace bien el que enseña remedio blando al daño. Espanta la tarea de echar a los hombres sobre los hombres. Indigna el forzoso abastamiento de unos hombres en provecho de otros. Mas se ha de hallar salida a la indignación, de modo que la bestia cese, sin que se desborde, y espante. Ved esta sala: la preside, rodeado de hojas verdes, el retrato de aquel reformador ardiente, reunido de hombres de diversos pueblos, y organizador incansable y pujante."

Translation: "Look at the immense meeting room. Karl Marx has died. As he was on the side of the weak, he merits this honor. But it is not good he who teaches a bland remedy for an injury. It is fearful to send men against other men. Indignity is to enforce the enrichment of a few men by exploiting others. Moreover there will be a solution to this indignity if the beast ceases to exist with limits and without terrifying others. Look at this meeting room, surrounded by green leaves, there is the photo of the fiery reformer, the unification of men from diverse nations and a tireless strong organizer."

"La Internacional fue su obra: vienen a honrarlo hombres de todas las naciones. La multitud, que es de bravos braceros, cuya vista enternece y conforta, enseña más músculos que alhajas, y más caras honradas que paños sedosos. El trabajo embellece. "

Translation: "'The International'" was his achievement: men from all nations come to honor him. The crowd is composed of brave workmen that tender love and comfort, display more muscles than jewels and honest faces than silky clothes. Work beautifies."

"Remoza ver a un labriego, a un herrador, o a un marinero. De manejar las fuerzas de la naturaleza, les viene ser hermosos como ellas."

Translation: "Rejuvenates to see a laborer, a blacksmith or a sailor. By managing natural forces they become beautiful like them."

"New York va siendo a modo de vorágine: cuanto en el mundo hierve, en ella cae. Acá sonríe al que huye; allá, le hacen huir."

Translation: "New York is like a vortex: when the world is boiling, she falls in it. Here, (Buenos Aires) smiles he who is fleeing; over there (New York) makes them flee."

"De esta bondad le ha venido a este pueblo esta fuerza. Karl Marx estudió los modos de asentar al mundo sobre nuevas bases, y despertó a los dormidos, y les enseñó el modo de echar a tierra los puntales rotos. Pero anduvo de prisa, y un tanto en la sombra, sin ver que no nacen viables, ni de seno de pueblo en la historia, ni de seno de mujer en el hogar, los hijos que no han tenido gestión natural y laboriosa."

Translation: "From this generosity, these people have acquired strength. Karl Marx studied the ways to restructure the world with new foundations and he has awakened and taught it how to overthrow broken pillars. But he was in hurry and somewhat in the shadows, unable to see that unviable pillars can come from people or from women with children who have not had a life of a laborer."

"Aquí están buenos amigos de Karl Marx, que no fue sólo movedor titánico de las cóleras de los trabajadores europeos, sino veedor profundo en la razón de las miserias humanas, y en los destinos de los hombres, y hombre comido del ansia de hacer bien. El veía en todo lo que en sí propio llevaba: rebeldía, camino a lo alto, lucha."

Translation: "Here are good friends of Karl Marx, who not only was a titanic mover of the anger of European workers but also a profound discoverer of the reasons of their misery, and of the destiny of men and men consumed by the wish to do good. He saw what I (Marti) possess: rebellion, a road to the heights, the fight."

"Aquí está un Lecovitch, hombre de diarios: vedlo cómo habla: llegan a él reflejos de aquel tierno y radioso. Bakunin: comienza a hablar en inglés; se vuelve a otros en alemán: "¡da! ¡da!" responden entusiasmados desde sus asientos sus compatriotas cuando les habla en ruso. Son los rusos el látigo de la reforma: mas no, ¡no son cimiento al mundo nuevo: ellos son la espuela, y vienen a punto, como la voz de la conciencia, que pudiera dormirse: pero el acero del acicate no sirve bien para martillo fundador."

Translation: "Here is a Lecovitch, man of the press: see how he speaks: he receives responses from that tender and radiant Bakunin. He starts to speak in English; he turns to others in German: "da" "da" enthusiastic responses from his compatriots when he speaks to them in Russian. The Russians are the whips of the reforms: But no, they are not the foundations of the new world; they are the spurs and they come on point, like the voice of your conscience, because the world may fall asleep: but the steel of the stimulus does not work well with the hammer of the foundations."

"Aquí está Swinton, anciano a quien las injusticias enardecen, y vio en Karl Marx tamaños de monte y luz de Sócrates. Aquí está el alemán John Most, voceador insistente y poco amable, y encendedor de hogueras, que no lleva en la mano diestra el bálsamo con que ha de curar las heridas que abra su mano siniestra."

Translation: "Here is Swinton, an elderly inflamed by injustices who saw in Karl Marx Mountains and the Light of Socrates. John Most, is an insistent voice and is somewhat uncouth, a starter of fires, lacking of comforting hands for wounds to open his left hand."

"Tanta gente ha ido a oírles hablar que rebosa en el salón, y da en la calle. Sociedades corales, cantan. Entre tanto hombre, hay muchas mujeres. Repiten en coro con aplauso frases de Karl Marx, que cuelgan en cartelones por los muros."

Translation: "So many people have come to hear them that they spill unto the street. Choral groups sing. Among so many men are many women; they repeat phrases of Karl Marx that they reproduce in cartons on the walls."

"Millot, un francés, dice una cosa bella: "la libertad ha caído en Francia muchas veces: pero se ha levantado más hermosa de cada caída".

Translation: "Millot, a Frenchman says a beautiful thing: "liberty has fallen in France many times: but it has risen more beautiful after each fall".

"John Most habla palabras fanáticas: 'Desde que leí en una prisión sajona los libros de Marx, he tomado la espada contra los vampiros humanos."

Translation: "John Most speaks words of a fanatic: 'Since my reading Marx's books in a Saxon prison, I have taken the sabre against the human vampires.'"

Dice un Magure: "Regocija ver juntos, ya sin odios, a tantos hombres de todos los pueblos. Todos los trabajadores de la tierra pertenecen ya a una sola nación, y no se querellan entre sí, sino todos juntos contra los que los oprimen. Regocija haber visto, cerca de lo que fue en París Bastilla ominosa, seis mil trabajadores reunidos de Francia y de Inglaterra.

Translation: "A Magure says: 'Elates to see enjoined, without hatred, so many men from all nations. All the workers of the world already belong to a single nation and they don't fight each other but against those who oppress them. Gladdens to have seen closely what was an ominous Bastille in Paris, six thousands united workers from France and England.'"

"Leen carta de Henry George, famoso economista nuevo, amigo de los que padecen, amado por el pueblo, y aquí y en Inglaterra famoso. Y entre salvas de aplausos tonantes, y frenéticos hurras, pónese en pie, en unánime movimiento, la ardiente asamblea, en tanto que leen desde la plataforma en alemán y en inglés dos hombres de frente ancha y mirada de hoja de Toledo, las resoluciones con que la Junta Magna acaba, en que Karl Marx es llamado el héroe más noble y el pensador más poderoso del mundo del trabajo."

Translation: "They read a letter from Henry George, a famous new economist, a friend of those who suffer. Loved by the people, and here and in England, famous. And amid resounding applause and frenetic hurrahs the public stands in a single movement while two men with broad foreheads and a sharp Toledo look (Toledo is famous for sharp steel sabers) read from the platform in German and English the complete resolutions passed by the directors of the Junta Magna in which Karl Marx is entitled the most Noble Hero and the most Powerful Thinker of the World of Laborers."

"Suenan músicas; resuenan coros, pero se nota que no son los de la paz."

Translation: "There is music, there are choruses, but we note that they are not of Peace."

José Martí. La Nación, Buenos Aires, 13 y 16 de mayo 1883.

Obras Completas, tomo 9, Editorial de Ciencias Sociales,

La Habana 1975, páginas 388-389

The Pentarchy of 1933

"It is also known as the Executive Commission of the Provisional Government of Cuba was a coalition that ruled Cuba from September 5 to September 10, 1933 after Gerardo Machado was deposed on August 12, 1933. Prior to the Pentarchy, General Alberto Herrera (August 12–13, 1933) and Carlos Manuel de Céspedes y Quesada (August 13 - September 5, 1933) served as President of Cuba.

The members of the Pentarchy were:

• Sergio Carbó y Morera (1891–1971), journalist

• Porfirio Franca y Álvarez de la Campa (1878–1950), attorney, banker and economist

• Ramón Grau San Martín (1887–1969), faculty member at the University of Havana School of Medicine

• José Miguel Irisarri y Gamio (1895–1968), an attorney

• Guillermo Portela y Möller (1886–1958), faculty member at the University of Havana School of Law.

"The first thing the Pentarchy did was to draft a proclamation which was written by Sergio Carbó and signed by eighteen civilians and one military man, Fulgencio Batista. That proclamation was published in every Cuban newspaper the following day. Carbó later promoted Batista from a sergeant to colonel without notifying the other four. Later they were ousted by the Student Directory and Ramón Grau was named president. Attempts to Overthrow the Pentarcchy. U.S. ambassador to Cuba at the time, Sumner Welles noted in a telegraph to the Secretary of State that on September 6, 1933 at night, Dr. Horacio Ferrer, Secretary of War in the Carlos Manuel de Céspedes y Quesada Cabinet, called to see him.

"He advised the ambassador that he was in contact with sergeants in control of the Fortress La Cabaña who advised Ferrer that they were deceived in participating in the mutiny and that they were prepared to make any reparation for their action. Ferrer's plan would be as follows, after taking some preliminary measures, Ferrer, accompanied with 80 loyal officers would proceed on September 8, 1933 to the Fortress La Cabaña with President Céspedes and several other members of his Cabinet and that on early morning September 9, 1933, Ferrer would proclaim the support of the Fortress to the legitimate Government of President Céspedes. Ferrer would then ask the ambassador whether "should this action be taken, and should Céspedes Government make such request the Government of the United States would be willing to land troops from the battleships now due to arrive at Cojimar immediately to the east of Cabaña Fortress, in order to assist the Céspedes Government in maintaining order.""

"Sumner Welles himself supported Ferrer and advised Washington of the following: "What I propose would be a strictly limited intervention of the following nature...entail the landing of a consider force at Havana and lesser forces in certain of the more important ports of the Republic.""

"The Franklin Delano Roosevelt administration was reluctant, however, to any form of direct military intervention as noted in the following telegram in response to Sumner Welles's telegram proposing the "limited intervention." The Secretary of State, Cordell Hull on September 7, 1933 at 8pm noted as follows to Sumner Welles, "Your 206 September 6, noon. We fully appreciate the various viewpoints set forth in your telegram. However, after mature consideration, the President has decided to send you the following message:

"We feel very strongly that any promise, implied or otherwise, relating to what the United States will do under any circumstances is impossible; that it would be regarded as a breach of neutrality, as favoring one faction out of many, as attempting to set up a government which would be regarded by the whole world, and especially throughout Latin America, as a creation and creature of the American government...strict neutrality is of the essence."

"In addition to Dr. Ferrer's attempt overthrow the new revolutionary government, there was also the Cuban Army on behalf of Batista seeking to make back-deals with Céspedes. As reported by Sumner Welles to the U.S. Secretary of State on September 9, 1933, " A commission of sergeants visited [former] President Carlos Manuel de Céspedes y Quesada this morning in his house to inform him that Colonel, former Sergeant, Fulgencio Batista was willing to support his restoration to the Presidency provided President Céspedes would confirm him in his position as Colonel and Chief of Staff of the Army and guarantee his safety and that of his associates in this mutiny. President Céspedes stated that he was unwilling to make any commitments whatever as to what would be done provided he was reinstated in power."

From Wikipedia

A Differing View of Cuba's History

On the Abrogation of Freedom of Speech
The Hour of Unanimity
Author: Luis Aguilar León
Published in Prensa Libre, Habana, Cuba,
on May 13, 1960

"Freedom of expression, if it is to be true, has to be extended to all and not be the prerogative or gift from anyone. Such is the case. This is not about defending the ideas of Diario de la Marina; it is about defending the right of Diario de la Marina to express its ideas. And the right of thousands of Cubans to read what they consider worth reading. For that full freedom of expression and choice people fought tenaciously in Cuba. And it was said that if a newspaper was persecuted because it favored one idea, in the end all ideas would be censured. And it was said that people yearned for a government where there was room for Hoy, the newspaper of the Communists, and Diario de la Marina, of conservative leanings. However, Diario de la Marina has disappeared as an expression of one type of thought. And the newspaper Hoy is freer and stronger than ever.

"Evidently, the regime has lost its desire for equilibrium.

"For those of us who crave that once and for all freedom of expression crystallizes in Cuba; for those who are convinced that in this our homeland unity and tolerance are essential to carry forward the most pure and fruitful ideals, the ideological disappearance of another newspaper has a sad and somber resonance. Because no matter how it is presented to us, the silencing of a way of public expression, or its unconditional capitulation to the government line does not mean anything other than the subjugation of a tenacious critical stance. There was the voice and there was the argument. And since the argument cannot be refuted, it became imperative to stifle the voice. Old is the method, well known are its results.

"What is arriving in Cuba, therefore, is the hour of unanimity: The solid and impenetrable totalitarian unanimity. The same slogan will be repeated by all media. There will be no dissenting voices, and no possibility of criticism or public rebuttals. Control of all means of expression provide persuasive work: fear will do the rest. Under the vociferous propaganda, silence will reign: the silence of those who can not speak and the silence of the accomplices that--even though they could — did not dare to speak.

"But, it is always yelled: The motherland is in danger! If it is, let us defend it by making it unassailable in theory and in practice. Let us wield weapons, but also rights. Let's begin by showing the world that here is a free people, truly free, where all ideas and all positions can coexist. Or is it that to defend the justice of our cause we must make common cause with the injustice of totalitarian methods? Would it not be much more beautiful and more dignified to offer the Americas an example of a people who are preparing to defend their freedom without compromising anyone's freedom, without offering even a shadow of a pretext to those who argue that we are falling here into the grip of a government by force?

"Unfortunately, this does not seem to be the chosen path. Faced with a healthy multiplicity of opinions, the preferred formula is one guide, one slogan, and total obedience. That is the way one arrives at the totalitarian unanimity. And then, not even those who have remained silent will find shelter in their silence. Because totalitarian unanimity is worse than censorship. Censorship forces us to shut our truth; unanimity forces us to repeat the lies of others. So we dissolve into a collective personality and monotonous chorus.

"And nothing is worse than that for those who have no vocation of obedient sheep.

Published in Prensa Libre, Havana, Cuba, on May13, 1960

A Differing View of Cuba's History
Pacto De Caracas, de Julio 1958

"Desde el golpe artero del 10 de marzo, que rompió el proceso democrático de la nación, el pueblo de Cuba se ha enfrentado con heroísmo y decisión a las fuerzas de la tiranía. Todas las formas de lucha se han utilizado en estos seis cruentos años y todos los sectores de la vida cubana se han opuesto con patriotismo a la dictadura de Fulgencio Batista. El pueblo de Cuba ha demostrado que su amor por la libertad es inquebrantable, derramando a raudales la sangre de sus mejores hijos, en su afán de ser libre."

Translation: "Since the treasonous coup of March 10 that interrupted the democratic process of our nation, the people of Cuba have confronted tyranny with heroism. All manner of counter attacks have been used these six years of oppression and all sectors of Cuban life have turned against the Dictatorship of Fulgencio Batista. The people of Cuba have shown their unwavering love of liberty shedding their blood of the best of its children in their efforts to be free."

"Desde los días lejanos de las manifestaciones estudiantiles, en que cayeron los primeros mártires de esta lucha, hasta recientes combates, como el de Santo Domingo en la Sierra Maestra, en que la tiranía sufrió la más aplastante de sus derrotas, al dejar en el campo de batalla un reguero de muertos, prisioneros y heridos y gran cantidad de armas y parque, mucha sangre se ha derramado y múltiples esfuerzos se han realizado en aras de la libertad de la patria esclavizada. Huelgas obreras, tres grandes conspiraciones militares, valientes protestas de todas las instituciones cívicas del país se han unido a heroicas acciones de Santiago, Matanzas, La Habana, Cienfuegos y Sagua la Grande. En las ciudades, el sabotaje, el atentado y múltiples formas de lucha revolucionaria han probado el espíritu indomable de una generación fiel a las estrofas inmortales del himno bayamés de que «morir por la patria es vivir.»"

Translation: "Since the yesterday years of student marches where the first martyrs of this struggle gave up their lives to the most recent battles on Holy Sunday in La Sierra Maestra where the tyrant's forces suffered the greatest of its defeats leaving the field of battle strewn with their dead, wounded and prisoners as well as a large quantity of arms and munitions, a lot of blood was shed on the onset of freedom of the enslaved fatherland. Labor strikes, three military conspiracies, courageous protests of all civic institutions have enjoined the insurrects of Santiago, Matanzas, la Habana, Cienfuegos and Sagua La Grande. In the cities sabotages, assassinations and other forms of revolutionary activities follow Bayamo's immortal hymn "to die for the fatherland is to live."

"El proceso insurreccional se ha extendido a todo el país. En las regiones montañosas de Cuba se han abierto nuevos frentes de batalla, y en las llanuras, guerrillas y columnas hostigan constantemente al enemigo. Actualmente, en la Sierra Maestra, miles y miles soldados, en la más grande ofensiva intentaba por Batista, se estrellan contra el coraje de los combatientes revolucionarios que defienden palmo a palmo, hasta la última gota de sangre, los territorios libres de Cuba. En la zona de Oriente, librando grandes combates fuerzas de la Columna numero seis Frank País dominan la tercera parte de la provincia. En las llanuras de Oriente, la columna número dos se bate desde Manzanillo hasta la región camagüeyana de Nuevitas. En las villas, el frente de los núcleos Auténticos y del 26 de Julio. En Cienfuegos y Yaguajay, guerrillas revolucionarias luchan y se mueven intensamente. Pequeñas guerrillas operan en Matanzas y en Pinar del Río. En cada rincón de Cuba, una lucha a muerte se libra entre la libertad y la tiranía, mientras en el extranjero numerosos exiliados y emigrados se esfuerzan por liberar a la patria oprimida."

Translation: "The Insurrectional process has extended in the entire territory of the nation. In the mountainous regions of Cuba there are new battlefronts and in the plains guerrillas and military columns constantly attack the enemy. Today, in la Sierra Maestra, thousands and thousands of Batista soldiers in the Sierra Maestra fighting against revolutionaries who defend their territory to the last drop of blood. In Oriente Column Number 6 "Frank Pais" dominates one third of the Province. In the plains of Oriente, Column Number 2 battles from the city of Manzanillo to the Camaguey port of Nuevitas. In the Province of Las Villas insurrects of the Partido Autentico and members of the M26-7 operate in the city of Cienfuegos and in Yaguajay. Smaller guerrillas also operate in Matanzas and Pinar del Rio. In each corner of Cuba there is a fight to death by freedom fighters against tyranny while abroad Cuban exiles are actively doing what they can to liberate the fatherland."

"Conscientes de que la coordinación de los esfuerzos humanos, de los recursos bélicos, de las fuerzas cívicas, de los sectores políticos y revolucionarios de todos los núcleos oposicionistas, civiles, militares, obreros, estudiantes, profesionales, económicos y populares, pueden derrocar a la Dictadura en un esfuerzo supremo, los firmantes de este documento unimos nuestro aporte, al adoptar un acuerdo en favor de un gran frente cívico revolucionario de lucha, de todos los sectores, para que codo con codo, aportando cada uno su patriotismo y sus esfuerzos, unidos arrojemos del poder a la Dictadura criminal de Fulgencio Batista y devolvamos a Cuba la paz ansiada y el encauzamiento democrático que conduzcan a nuestro pueblo al desarrollo de su libertad, de su riqueza y de su progreso. Todos estamos de acuerdo en la necesidad de unirnos, y el pueblo así lo demanda."

Translation: "Aware that the coordination of all human efforts include the military, labor, students, professionals, economists, and popular groups understand that they can overthrow the Dictatorship with a supreme effort, the signatures of this document are united in adopting a great Civic/Revolutionary Front of all sectors so that elbow to elbow we effect a great patriotic effort to defeat the criminal Dictatorship of Fulgencio Batista and return to Cuba peace and a democratic process to our beloved people to develop its Freedom, riches and progress. All of us are in accord to unify and this is what our people demand."

"Tres puntos son los pilares de esta unión de las fuerzas oposicionistas cubanas:

"Primero: Estrategia común de lucha para derrocar la tiranía mediante la insurrección armada, reforzando en un plazo mínimo todos los frentes de combate, armando a los miles de cubanos que están dispuestos a combatir por la libertad. Movilización popular de todas las fuerzas obreras, cívicas, profesionales, económicas, para culminar el esfuerzo cívico en una gran huelga general, y el bélico en una acción armada conjuntamente con todo el país. De este empeño común, Cuba surgirá libre y se evitará nueva y dolorosa efusión de sangre de las mejores reservas de la patria La victoria será posible siempre, pero más tardía, de no coordinarse las actividades de las fuerzas oposicionistas."

"Segundo: Conducir al país, a la caída del tirano mediante un breve gobierno provisional, a su normalidad, encauzándola por el procedimiento constitucional y democrático.

"Tercero: Programa mínimo de gobierno que garantice el castigo de los culpables, los derechos de los trabajadores, el orden, la paz, la libertad, el cumplimiento de los compromisos internacionales y el progreso económico, social e institucional del pueblo cubano."

Translation: "Three points are the pillars of this union of the Cuban Opposition:

"First: To develop a common strategy to overthrow the dictatorship by military means. Reinforcing all battlefields with thousands of armed Cubans who are ready to fight for their freedom as soon as possible will do this. Mobilizing labor organizations as well civic groups, professional and economic sectors, will carry out a great general strike. This will be coordinated with the military operations of the insurrection. This common effort will result in a free Cuba. Our victory will always happen but delayed in these activities are not coordinated.

A Differing View of Cuba's History

"Second: Following the overthrow of the tyrant the nation will be guided to its normality by a brief provisional government, which will follow a democratic constitutional process. Al pedirle al Gobierno de los Estados Unidos que cese toda ayuda bélica y de cualquier orden al dictador, reafirmamos nuestra postura de defensa de la soberanía nacional y la tradición civilista y republicana de Cuba.

"Third: A minimalist governmental program that guarantees the delivery of justice for the culpable protects the rights of workers, order, and peace. Freedom, honoring international treaties, economic, social and intuitional progress of the Cuban people."

Translation: When we petition the Government of the United States to cease all military and other aid to the Dictator, we reaffirm our defense of our sovereignty and of our civic and republican traditions."

A los militares decimos que ha llegado el instante de que nieguen su apoyo a la tiranía; que confiamos en ellos, que sabemos que hay hombres dignos en las fuerzas armadas y que si en el pasado centenares de oficiales, clases y soldados han pagado con la vida, la prisión, el destierro o el retiro su amor a la libertad y su oposición a la tiranía, muchos quedan en esa actitud. Esta no es una guerra contra los institutos armados de la República, sino contra Batista, único obstáculo a la paz, que desean, anhelan y necesitan todos los cubanos, civiles y militares. A los obreros, a los estudiantes, a los profesionales, a los comerciantes e industriales,

Translation: "To the military we say that the point to deny support to the dictatorship has been reached; they have our support and we know that there are honorable men in the Armed Forces and that if in the past hundreds of officers, noncommissioned soldiers and soldiers lost their lives, there were imprisonments, exiles, or have lost their love of Freedom and their Opposition to the dictatorship; many more remain with the correct attitude. This is not a war against the Armed Forces of the Republic. But it is against Batista, the only obstacle toward Peace, which is the wish of all Cubans, civil and military, our workers, students, professionals, merchants and industrialists."

"Como a los colonos, hacendados y campesinos, a los cubanos de todas las religiones, ideologías o razas, pedimos que se unan a este esfuerzo libertador, que derrocará a la infame tiranía que durante años ha regado con sangre el suelo de la patria, segando sus mejores reservas humanas, arruinando su economía, perturbando hasta sus cimientos todas las instituciones cubanas, al interrumpir el proceso democrático y constitucional del país, al que ha conducido a esta cruenta guerra civil que finalizará con el triunfo de la revolución por el esfuerzo unido de todos. Ha llegado la hora de que la inteligencia, el patriotismo, el valor y el civismo de sus hombres y mujeres salve a la patria oprimida con la decisión de todos los que sentimos muy en lo hondo el destino histórico nuestra nación, su derecho a ser libre y a constituir en la comunidad democrática, como forma esencial de la vida, el porvenir hermoso a que tiene derecho por su Historia y por las inmensas posibilidades que le dan sus riquezas naturales y la capacidad indudable de sus hijos. Exhortamos a todas las fuerzas revolucionarias, cívicas y políticas del país a que suscriban esta declaración de unidad, y posteriormente, tan pronto las circunstancias lo permitan, celebraremos una reunión de delegados de todos los sectores, sin exclusión alguna, para discutir y aprobar las bases de la Unidad."

Translation: "As well as farming tenants, landowners, and peasants, Cubans of all religious beliefs, ideologies, and races we ask you join us to overthrow the infamous dictatorship that has cost many lives, ruining our economy, perturbing the foundation of our culture, interrupted our constitutional and democratic process that has resulted in ruinous civil war and revolution. We have reached the hour when our intelligence, patriotism and courage of our men and women will save our oppressed fatherland. When circumstances permit we will have a meeting of all delegates of all sectors of our society without exclusion of no one to discuss and approve the basis of our Unity."

Fidel Castro, Movimiento 26 de Julio; Carlos Prío Socarrás, Organización Auténtica; E. Rodríguez Loeche, Directorio Revolucionario; David Salvador, Orlando Blanco, Pascasio Lineras, Lauro Blanco, José M. Aguilera, Ángel Cofiño, Unidad Obrera; Manuel A. de Varona, Partido Cubano Revolucionario (A); Lincoln Rodón, Partido Demócrata; José Puente y Omar Fernández, Federación de Estudiantes de la Universidad; capitán Gabino Rodríguez Villaverde, ex oficial del ejército; Justo Carrillo Hernández, Grupo Montecristi; Angel María Santos Buch, Movimiento de Resistencia Cívica, y doctor José Miró Cardona, coordinador secretario general.

Author's Abbreviated Translation

Territorio Libre de Cuba, Caracas, Venezuela (From Wikipedia)

La Coubre Explosion

"The French freighter La Coubre exploded in the harbor of Havana, Cuba, on 4 March 1960 while it was unloading 76 tons of munitions. Casualties may have been as high as 100, and many more were injured. Fidel Castro charged it was an act of sabotage on the part of the United States, which denied any involvement.

"Unloading explosive ordnance directly onto the dock in Havana was against port regulations. Ships with such cargoes were supposed to be moored in the center of the harbor and their high-risk cargo unloaded onto lighters. La Coubre, a 4,310-ton French vessel, was unloading her cargo of 76 tons of Belgian munitions she had transported from Antwerp to Havana when she exploded at 3:10 pm on 4 March 1960. Thirty minutes after the first explosion, while hundreds of people were involved in a rescue operation organized by the Cuban military, a second, more powerful explosion resulted in additional fatalities and injuries.

"At the time of the explosion, Che Guevara was in a meeting at the National Institute of Agrarian Reform (NIAR, INRA as originally named in Spanish) headquarters. He drove to the scene and spent the next few hours giving medical attention to the crew members, armed forces personnel, and dock workers who had been injured. The death toll was between 75 and 100; more than 200 people injured.

"Speaking the next day at a funeral for 27 dock workers killed by the explosions, Fidel Castro said that the United States was responsible for the explosion, "the work of those who do not wish us to receive arms for our defense", a charge U.S. Secretary of State Christian Herter denied on 7 March in a meeting with the Cuban chargé d'affaires in Washington followed by a formal note of protest delivered to Cuban Foreign Minister Raul Roa on 15 March.

"On 7 March, the *Miami Herald* reported other charges made by Jack Lee Evans, an American who had just returned from Habana where he had been working for and living with William Alexander Morgan, an American who had commanded rebel forces during the Cuban Revolution. He said he had boarded the La Coubre on 2 March with Morgan and others to transport machine guns and ammunition to the NIAR. He then learned of a plot by an anti-Communist dockworker to explode the ship, did not think Morgan was involved, and now feared for his life. Morgan denied ever being aboard the ship and said of Evans: "The kid has to be out of his mind to say a thing like that." Morgan was arrested seven months later, accused of supporting counter-revolutionaries, and executed in March 1961.

From Wikipedia

ACKNOWLEDGEMENTS

I am profoundly indebted to my mother, Herminia Greig Cossio y de Céspedes, and my sister, Enid Santos-Buch de Duany. Their passionate interest in our family's journey, their keen memory and our many forthright discussions have indelibly shaped this book. It is their collection of historical heirlooms that I have used in this narrative.

The input of my father, Dr. A. M. Santos-Buch, was extraordinary. Being a historical figure in Cuba, and a renowned doctor, my father influenced me in ways that continue to surprise me. Together with my mother Herminia, their courage and dedication to the commitment to the higher cause of Cuba's sovereignty and liberty was heroic. It is an unusual privilege to grow-up with their wisdom, triumphs and travails.

My wife, Carol Valle-Friend, at my side for more than sixty-three years of a peripatetic life, eased the rigors of an academic career and the consequences of a fearful revolution. She was my undaunted traveling companion in 1960 when we explored by car, horse, and foot the island nation during the early incipient Castro reforms. The trip included the mountains of the Sierra Maestra, Dos Rios, San Lorenzo, Cienaga of Zapata, Playa Larga, the Bay of Cochinos, Las Villas, Matanzas, El Escambray, and Pinar del Rio. That trip revealed to us the unadorned face of the Communist take-over of Cuba. Throughout the writing of this book, she was my living Spanish dictionary.

My three sons, Alan, Kevin, and Charlie, have been incredibly supportive and helpful in spurring me on through the years to continue writing down my stories. Their insightful questions have rekindled memories that have enriched this book. Kevin's assistance in digitizing images and organizing my files saved me countless hours as well.

Acknowledgements

My brother-in-law, Andres J. Duany, was a fount of information on the politics and management of the ancient Hato del Medio property and of his construction business in Santiago de Cuba. My lovely niece, Enid C. Duany, with her keen interest and intuitive intellect, supplied our family with her detailed findings of the Finlay-Greig ancestry when she explored Scotland. She is also the repository of valuable Cuban historic documents, which includes Pedro de Céspedes' hand-written will and testament.

My nephew, Andres M. Duany, contributed to the ancient history of the O'Duane military engineers and of his subsequent distinguished family.

I am grateful to Harvard College for showing me how to pursue the truth of biological conundrums utilizing the scientific method. The teachings of Professors Gurd, Wald, Fieser, Gray and Thorne are to this day etched firmly in my mind. Harvard, in those days, did not award many honor "A's" and that policy generated the intellectual pursuit to be the very best you could achieve. The Cornell University Medical College was incredible to us. Its faculty were accessible giants that helped my roommate, Wallace G. Campbell, Jr., and me in our successful research, as was the use of the apparatus shop that built a gizmo to measure blood pressure levels in living rabbits without trauma. Wally is my closest friend and partner in our academic journey. Professors Rogers, duVigneaud, Pitts, Riker, Swan, Murphy, Kidd, Vogel, Barr, Johnson, Wolf, Richter, Kellner, Ellis, and many others challenged us in every aspect of the practice of medicine. Professor John T. Ellis deserves special praise as my mentor at Cornell and Emory and when we returned to Cornell and the New York Hospital. The entire clinical faculty was dedicated to helping all of us, here and abroad.

When my participation in the Cuban Revolution became public knowledge after publication in New York's mainstream media, Cornell's administrative officers did not fire or discipline me. They appealed to reason and I responded in kind.

A Differing View of Cuba's History

Many contemporary Cuban intellectuals helped me. The contributions of Manuel Jorge Cutillas, Pedro G. de Céspedes, Alberto Luzarraga, Federico Justiniani, Yolanda del Castillo, Armando Cubelo, Jose Regalado, Luis Espino, Juan Portuondo, Enrique Lopez-Balboa, J. L. Madrigal, Caridad Maria Abascal, Rene Sagebien and Alberto Zayas-Bazan are significant.

The wealth of knowledge, in real time, from witnesses over the course of the Cuban Revolution, including Sergio Aguero, Antonio Valle-Friend and Agustin Pais, was crucial to the focused content of this narrative.

Special thanks are due to Antonio G. Valle Friend, my wife's brother, for his devotion and enthusiasm in supplying me with invaluable intelligence that covered the duration of the successful M26-7 Insurrection from 1956 to 1960. Commander Frank Pais Garcia recruited him shortly after the November 30, 1956, assaults in Santiago de Cuba. He was under the commands of Frank Pais, Jorge Sotus and Carlos Iglesias Fonseca (Nicaragua) and was a member of the Action/Sabotage group of the M26-7. Under orders from Haydee Santamaria, he coordinated the press interview of Fidel Castro in the Sierra Maestra headquarters by *Chicago Sun Times* reporter Ray Brennan, author of *Castro, Cuba and Justice*, published in 1959. As a first lieutenant combatant and a member of the General Staff (Estado Mayor) of Commander Raul Castro, he was assigned to audit the Second Front "Frank Pais." After Batista's fall he kept his rank but he joined a counter-revolutionary cell of the Movimiento de Recuperacion Revolucionaria (MRR) when he was secretly recruited by Commander Rogelio Gonzalez Corso, one of its founders. Corso was later arrested and executed by a firing squad. He was under constant surveillance by a beautiful Castro-Communist assigned to watch him and following the Bahia de Cochinos debacle he was hunted by Castro Communist operatives but was able to escape to the U.S. Naval Base in Guantanamo. Tony's eye-witness accounts of key events that devolved in the 1956-60 M26-7 Insurrection, greatly

Acknowledgements

his book.

ica de Moya, a life-long friend, critically edited portions of
uscript and made lucid corrections and suggestions that I have
ntly employed. I am deeply indebted to her for this incredibly
ortant task.

Finally, TriMark Press Publisher Barry Chesler was very support-
e of this book project and he lent his expertise when ever necessary.
His Publishing Director Lorie Greenspan was remarkably helpful in
putting the book together and made sure my prose was easy to read.
Her suggestions were excellent and I followed her recommendations
to the letter. It was a pleasure to closely work with her. I am very
grateful to have had them by my side.

Charles A. Santos-Buch, MD

April 25, 2019, Key Biscayne, Florida, USA